Marketing Your Invention

Second Edition

Thomas E. Mosley, Jr.

Upstart
Publishing Company
Specializing in Small Business Publishing
a division of Dearborn Publishing Group, Inc.

This publication is designed to provide accurate and authoritative information in regard to the subject matter covered. It is sold with the understanding that the publisher is not engaged in rendering legal, accounting, or other professional service. If legal advice or other expert assistance is required, the services of a competent professional person should be sought.

Managing Editor: Jack Kiburz
Interior Design: Lucy Jenkins
Cover Design: S. Laird Jenkins Corporation
Typesetting: Elizabeth Pitts

©1992, 1997 by Dearborn Financial Publishing, Inc.®

Published by Upstart Publishing Company,
a division of Dearborn Financial Publishing, Inc.®

Printed in the United States of America

97 98 99 10 9 8 7 6 5 4 3 2 1

Library of Congress Cataloging-in-Publication Data

Mosley, Thomas E.
    Marketing your invention / Thomas E. Mosley, Jr. — [2nd ed.]
       p.   cm.
    Includes bibliographical references and index.
    ISBN 0-57410-072-6 (paper)
    1. Inventions—Marketing.   I. Title.
T339.M915   1997
609'.068'8—dc21   97-2315
                                                                          CIP

Dearborn Financial Publishing books are available at special quantity discounts to use as premiums and sales promotions, or for use in corporate training programs. For more information, please call the Special Sales Manager at 800-621-9621, ext. 4384, or write to Dearborn Financial Publishing, Inc., 155 N. Wacker Drive, Chicago, IL 60606-1719.

Dedicated to the apples of my eye:

Monica R. Mosley
Valerie H. Mosley
Meredith M. Mosley
Thomas E. Mosley III

Trademarks

Business Dateline® is a registered trademark of Data Courier, Inc.

Cambridge Classics™ is a trademark of Mervyns, Inc.

Coca-Cola® is a registered trademark of The Coca-Cola Company.

Crayola® is a registered trademark of Binney & Smith, Inc.

DataTimes® is a registered trademark of DataTimes Corporation.

Dialog® is a registered service mark of Dialog Information Services, Inc.

Dun & Bradstreet® is a registered trademark of Dun & Bradstreet, Inc.

Hula Hoop® is a registered trademark of Wham-O Manufacturing Company.

Kellogg's® is a registered trademark of Kellogg Company.

Kodak® is a registered trademark of Eastman Kodak Company.

Lexis® and Nexis® are registered service marks of Mead Data Central, Inc.

Lux® is a registered trademark of Conopco, Inc.

Macintosh® is a registered trademark of Apple Computer, Inc.

Monopoly® is a registered trademark of Tonka Corporation.

NewsNet® is a registered service mark of NewsNet, Inc.

Pente® is a registered trademark of Tonka Corporation.

Scotchgard® and Post-It Notes® are registered trademarks of Minnesota Mining
and Manufacturing Company.

Seldane® is a registered trademark of Merrell Dow Pharmaceuticals, Inc.

Slinky® is a registered trademark of James Industries, Inc.

Teflon® is a registered trademark of E.I. Du Pont de Nemours and Company.

Thomas Register Online® is a registered service mark of Thomas Publishing
Company.

Tie Traveler™ is a trademark of Jetwind Products, Inc.

Trade & Industry ASAP™ is a trademark of Information Access Company, Inc.

Trademarkscan® is a registered trademark of Thomson & Thomson.

Velcro® is a registered trademark of Velcro Industries.

Workmate® is a registered trademark of The Black and Decker Manufacturing
Company.

FOREWORD

The title of this book does not do it justice. Tom Mosley has provided much more than a "how to" discussion on marketing. While he makes the fundamental points of inventing to meet a need and the overwhelming importance of marketing, his treatment of the commercialization process in general and the dos and don'ts of specific activities greatly expands the scope suggested by the title.

Mr. Mosley provides a wealth of information on governmental and other programs that can be utilized by the inventor. His lucid text and generous use of anecdotes make the book easy to read. It reflects an excellent understanding of what it takes to move an invention to market, as well as his hands-on experience with many individual cases under an active state government program of inventor assistance. Thorough reading by the inventor will greatly help to answer the question usually posed after invention: What now?

On a broader note, Mr. Mosley should be commended on the very practical perspective he provides on a subject of great national interest. With the continuing furor about industrial policy, critical technologies, competitiveness, and the need for effective technology transfer by our universities and federal laboratories, we need to be reminded that the core issue is still new product development and sales. The Oklahoma Department of Commerce program Mr. Mosley represented focused activity at the "grass roots," linking a client inventor with a client manufacturer. This book reflects initial program experience, delineating basic strategies, many tactics, and the innumerable constraints involved, relative to operation of the technology development and commercialization process. It should be read and assimilated not only by inventors (technology sources), but also by staff of other state programs wishing to increase manufacturing in their respective states.

George P. Lewett, Director
Office of Technology Evaluation and Assessment
Technology Services
National Institute of Standards and Technology
United States Department of Commerce

ACKNOWLEDGMENTS

The author gratefully acknowledges the contributions of many people—manufacturers, engineers, professional marketers, economic development staff, finance professionals, new product trailblazers, and of course, inventors—for making this book a reality. For being the best boss I ever had thanks goes to Donald Byers. We interviewed many an inventor together and stayed at the office late at night brainstorming ways to move their projects forward. He also taught me the purpose of an employee. For being a great partner at the Oklahoma Department of Commerce, Pam Speraw deserves a medal. We experienced the "glory of the grind" to discover solutions to commercialization problems we never would have found separately. My former secretary, Rana Brown from Snyder, Oklahoma, played a more vital role than she will ever know. To Harry Tipps, investment banker par excellence, goes thanks for teaching me to critically analyze deals from an investor's perspective. Jerry Dunlap and Charles "Skip" Codding of the law firm of Dunlap, Codding, Peterson and Lee in Oklahoma City, brought us up to speed in record time concerning intellectual property law. They freely served as our mentors, and continue to teach me how much I do not know about the subject. Also deep appreciation is expressed to Wes Spradley, my former pastor at Grace Bible Church in Del City, Oklahoma, who told me to write a book only if I had something significant to say. I am thankful to Marla Mosley for her proofreading and constructive criticism of the first edition; the publisher said it was one of the cleanest manuscripts they had ever seen. Finally, to my former partner, Jim Harris, without whom there would be an empty void in some sections of this book.

I would also like to thank Sir Alexander Flemming, the inventor of penicillin. Without it I am certain I would have died very young.

The inventor or inventors of Seldane also deserve recognition for eliminating the effects of my allergy to freshly cut grass. Thanks to Mr. Silverman, the Oklahoma inventor of the shopping cart, for making it easier to shop. And where would I be without baseball, Monopoly, chess, tennis, the telephone, television, the cassette deck, or my Macintosh computer? Hats off to inventors everywhere—past, present, and future—without you this world would be absolutely miserable!

No part of this work should be considered to be, or substituted for, legal advice. New product development would not be possible were it not for the work of patent attorneys and agents. It is written from the marketing perspective of a new product developer.

Further, it should not be assumed that I am dogmatic in my conclusions. We are all in the process of learning. The following principles are general truths seen in light of the big picture. Most general truths have exceptions. They are intended to guide our thinking but not dictate the details of our commercialization efforts as though we were programmed robots. Remember every project is different—just like people. I welcome comments or case studies that might be included in future editions of this work and that hopefully will result in more commercialized inventions.

CONTENTS

INTRODUCTION

The United States is an inventive nation, with over five million patents granted since the Constitution was signed in 1787. As a result of James Madison's proposal, Article I, Section 8 of the Constitution grants to Congress the power "to promote the Progress of Science and useful Arts, by securing for limited Times to Authors and Inventors the exclusive Right to their respective Writings and Discoveries." The first U.S. patent was granted to Samuel Hopkins of Pittsford, Vermont, on July 31, 1790. It was signed by both President George Washington and Secretary of State Thomas Jefferson and was economically significant in that it increased the nation's export trade of our first industrial chemical—potash.

The United States is also an entrepreneurial nation, with angels, venture capitalists, manufacturers, and marketers willing to invest both time and money in new ideas. These attributes are critically important now as we are in the midst of a new product explosion unparalleled in history. The pace of change is so dramatic and the economic stakes are so high, both companies and governments are focusing attention on new product development.

In the midst of this boom, independent inventors, business, and government must work together as partners. Business decisions must not only be made, they must be made rapidly. Accurate information and its intelligent use is absolutely critical to successful commercialization. While some federal government policies have catalyzed new product development, others have allowed countries like Japan to reap the rewards of American ingenuity. As our federal government is rethinking the importance of technological leadership in the private sector, individual states also have begun to recognize the economic importance of new products. Many small business development centers (SBDCs) throughout the country are trying to focus on technology-based businesses. It is significant for the future that almost every small manufacturer in the country is within 50 miles of one of these centers.

In 1987, the Oklahoma legislature adopted the Inventors' Assistance Act. This Act provided for a seven-year state income tax abatement on earned royalties from patented or patent-pending products or processes. It also provided for a professional staff of new product developers to serve as catalysts in commercializing new products. A separate bill, passed in 1991, regulates "invention development companies" that extract huge up-front fees from inventors on a "best efforts" basis.

This book, prepared from my vantage point as a new product developer while at the Oklahoma Department of Commerce and currently as the president of ONPC, Inc. (New Products Coalition, Tulsa, OK), was written to provide inventors with the information they need to market new product ideas and inventions, describe them correctly to the most appropriate resources, avoid many of the pitfalls, and thereby increase their chances of success. Based on hundreds of invention evaluations and counseling sessions with inventors, negotiations with investors and licensees, and over 80 completed licensing agreements and joint ventures, this book attempts to fill a vacuum in the literature of new product development by offering straight talk to independent inventors on what to expect in attempting to commercialize their product ideas.

For the most part, I assume the reader is familiar with the basics of patenting and prototype development. If not, he or she should search for the closest inventor organization and join up. These groups have tons of experience. Most members have received patents or are working on one. The inventive spirit driving these organizations combined with knowledgeable commercialization techniques may someday result in 5 or 10 percent of all patented items making money for inventors, instead of today's mere 1 or 2 percent.

New products are often described as the lifeblood of manufacturers. They are a vital part of company expansion, diversification, and competitiveness. New products also are the lifeblood of our economy. Some reasons for this are the constantly changing market conditions that create new economic environments; shrinking product life spans; and new technologies that advance our quality of life or increase profit margins.

Recent studies have identified new product development as the key growth strategy for the 90s. Hewlett-Packard derives over 50 percent of its sales from products developed within the past three years. Recently, it was reported that 25 percent of 3M's sales are from products new to the market during the previous five years. Johnson & Johnson has reported similar figures. A study by the Conference Board revealed that, by an eight-to-one ratio, CEOs believed their firms would be much more dependent on new products in the years ahead. Results of a 1985 Coopers & Lybrand survey published in the May/June 1990 issue of *Business Horizons,* reported that most companies are counting heavily on new product development for growth and profitability.

In Oklahoma, 85 percent of all manufacturers have fewer than 50 employees. Most lack the resources for research and development or even to hire staff to find new products developed outside the firm. Most are stuck in a "job shop" mentality and do not own their proprietary products. Other states look about the same and have similar problems. Although U.S. companies recently spent $68.8 billion on research and development, these expenditures were made primarily by very large firms—firms that account for a small percentage of total employment.

Of Oklahoma's 4,000 manufacturers, over 500 expressed an interest in producing new products, according to a 1989 survey conducted while the author worked with the Inventors' Assistance Program. Most of these manufacturers neither conducted formal product development activities nor had a staff dedicated to finding new products. The IAP served many of these manufacturers by introducing them to new products and, in a sense, became their new product and business-development arm. The principles of commercialization presented in this book were learned through trial and error. They worked successfully in Oklahoma as a government program and are continuing to work even better in the private sector through the New Products Coalition.

There are very few sources for seed capital venture funds anywhere in the country. But by helping structure licensing agreements and other strategic alliances, we plug inventors into the most readily available seed capital source for launching new products—the working capital and asset base of successful small businesses striving to expand and grow through new products. Leveraging these assets has proven to be critically important to launching inventors' new products and also to the country's economic development strategy.

ONE

Invention Marketing Today

"It takes two kinds of men to develop a mining country: the men who find the mines and the men who develop them, and they are rarely the same person. The prospector, the discoverer, is not often equipped in money and the business ability to open up and develop a mine. Many of them sold their claim off for what seemed nothing. And yet it was to them a great deal. And if they'd persisted in operating their mines they might have lost everything."

—Louis L'Amour

Developing new products and bringing them to market may be today's gold rush. A gold prospector started with an idea of the best location. He then developed a plan to get there. He had to have picks and shovels, some engineering expertise, maybe a mule or two, food, and clothing. Finally, he had to have the courage to face and over-come the danger of claim jumpers, outlaws, hostile Indians, wild animals, and natural disasters.

Today the struggle to find, develop, and market new products may not be as dangerous, but it is certainly difficult, expensive, and laden with hazards. From fraudulent invention development companies and intellectual property expenses to Rube Goldberg prototypes and convoluted marketing schemes, the path to commercialization is at best annoying and at worst disastrous for the person attempting to launch a new product.

For a typical new product to be launched, it must go through many developmental phases. If failure occurs at any point along this process, the idea may be lost to the marketplace forever.

Soon after a concept is firmly established in the mind of the inventor, its uniqueness should be validated and a working prototype constructed. If it works and still proves to be unique, a preliminary determination of market acceptability should be conducted. A decision must then be made to seek a patent, copyright, or trademark, or to treat the product or process as a trade secret. Intellectual property work and government filing fees are expensive, usually costing from five to ten thousand dollars or more for an issued patent. Yet a product with true potential deserves the best possible professional assistance from a patent attorney or patent agent. The more extensive the patent coverage proves to be, the higher its value to a licensee. Gaining the most effective protection is no job for an amateur.

If the new product has come this far, a decision must now be made to either venture or license. Second only to the barrier of gaining intellectual property protection, this is where most new product concepts fail. Venturing involves building a company or finding a joint venture partner. It means writing a business plan, gathering a management team, locating a funding source and convincing that source to invest (like the prospector seeking a "grub stake"). Yet most inventors, as well as most people in general, simply do not possess the entrepreneurial skills necessary to overcome the obstacles faced in venturing.

Therefore the only other option is to license the intellectual property to someone already in business who has the cash flow and proven experience necessary to manufacture and market the item. It is here that history's lesson should be learned again. It takes two kinds of people to develop a product: the ones who create them and the ones who develop them, and they are rarely the same person. If the creator of the new product persists in developing it, he may lose everything.

There is much more work to accomplish and money to be spent after a product is in the patent-pending stage. A company looking for new products understands this only too well. It has the ability and experience to evaluate, refine, manufacture, and market the product. Once a potential market is confirmed, the company can conduct further market research; direct a focus group; create a production plan; write a marketing plan; establish the packaging; attend a trade show; advertise; order and pay for raw materials; hire and pay the production, sales, and support employees; cultivate the distribution channels; ship the product; and collect the receivables. It is far more likely for an existing company to qualify for expansion capital, if needed, than for an inventor/entrepreneur to attract start-up funds.

Creativity works both ways. It is without a doubt an essential ingredient in discovering a new product, but it is also a key element in developing it to the point of launch and beyond. Because both forms of creative prowess are essential for successful new product launches, and because most profitable companies possess proven ability to do all post-discovery development, the most logical way to accomplish new product commercialization is through the mechanism of licensing intellectual property to existing companies. This is called technology transfer.

The most logical way to accomplish new product commercialization is through the mechanism of licensing intellectual property to existing companies. This is called technology transfer.

There seems to be a mystical aura surrounding the meaning of *technology transfer*. The term "technology transfer" is commonly used in several ways. Government laboratories describe the mere transfer of research reports or documentation as technology transfer. If this is true, librarians practice it every day. Other governmental entities occasionally send an employee with a technical background into the private sector for a sabbatical and describe this as technology transfer. If this is true, then employment services providing engineers to industry could legitimately describe their activity as technology transfer.

But the best government definition seems to refer to patented products or processes invented by employees of the government then transferred to the private sector through licensing. From what I have seen during the past four years, the commercial efficacy of government or university technologies does not seem to be any better or worse than those of independent inventors. The federal government makes it very difficult to license inventions from its bureaucracy, while the universities appear to be interested primarily in up-front licensing fees to complete the research and development. Yet in our capitalistic society the validity of a new product lies in how it sells in the marketplace and is utilized by the consumer. What is the best kind of invention? The one that is used. A technology cannot be purchased and enjoyed by the public if it is only gathering dust in a government file or university lab.

What is the best kind of invention? The one that is used. A technology cannot be purchased and enjoyed by the public if it is only gathering dust in a government file or university lab.

I once attended a conference on technology extension and technology modernization. Over and over again technology transfer was mentioned as the mechanism in achieving the modernization of our manufacturers. Afterward the president of a manufacturing firm and I were discussing his business. He mentioned that he licenses to other companies the use of both his equipment and process for making cement. I commented on how that was a great example of technology transfer. He looked at me for a moment and said, "Do you mean we have been doing technology transfer for 20 years and didn't know it was called technology transfer?" We had been talking about it for two days, and he unfortunately had not made the connection.

We do not seem to have our minds around the meaning of technology transfer. According to Webster's Ninth, the word *technology* means applied science; a scientific method of achieving a practical purpose; and the totality of the means employed to provide objects necessary for human sustenance and comfort. So true technology is applied and used, or at least is capable of being used, in a practical sense by humans for their sustenance and comfort. I wonder which technology Webster would say is the best technology—the mousetrap we purchase at the hardware store and put to immediate use or the ingenious electronic circuitry that speeds computers tenfold and cannot be commercialized.

Technology transfer is simply the transfer of intellectual property rights (patents, copyrights, trademarks, and trade secrets) through a licensing agreement or outright purchase to another entity for the ultimate purpose of commercialization. It can be from the government to the private sector, from a university to a small marketing firm, from an independent inventor to a Fortune 100 company, or from an independent inventor to a small manufacturer with only five employees. Further, technology transfer may involve a cure for cancer or AIDS, the next generation of lasers, a new board game, or even a fishing lure.

Discovering a new product idea is only the first step in the commercialization process—and the most simple. Transferring the technology then getting it in the marketplace is the tough part.

Discovering a new product idea is only the first step in the commercialization process—and the most simple. Transferring the technology then getting it in the marketplace is the tough part.

The role of the inventor is thought to be one of inventing. While this is generally true, it is not the only role independent inventors must accept to commercialize their products. When someone is introduced to an inventor, he rarely thinks of all the trials and tribulations the inventor has gone through to get his item into the retail store or into the hands of industry. If a conversation ensues, the inventor might be asked how he thought of his idea or whether he has a patent.

While there is nothing wrong with these questions, it demonstrates a shallow understanding of what inventing is all about. It is okay for the public not to know much about inventing. The problem with the public's ignorance of inventing begins when it carries over to those who would be inventors.

As a ten-year-old catcher on Traub Elementary School's baseball team I was trying to learn how to throw to second base in time to catch the little base thieves. All my throws highly arced and arrived several seconds after the base runner. No matter how hard I tried to throw the ball on a straight line, it refused to fly without arcing. Watching the Yankees on television, I thought I could get a clue to solving my problem. Yogi Berra had no such problem. His pegs were a clothesline to the second baseman's ankles. I did not understand why I could not do that. Then one day I went to a high school game and watched an 18-year-old Johnny Bench. He did not have my problem either. As a matter of fact, the pitcher had to duck to keep from being decapitated. Both Yogi and Johnny made it look simple. I never was able to throw to second base without an arc. But I could hit, so in high school they moved me to the outfield.

The point is that prospective inventors or those with a new patent are looking in from the outside. It looks simple. They may see the results of years of hard work combined with an abundance of natural ability, but they have not seen how tough it is to commercialize an invention.

To get more inventions manufactured and marketed, inventors must be willing to see themselves as more than just inventors. They should expand their perceived responsibility of merely being the creator of a new product or process. At the same time it is necessary for them to recognize their limitations and be willing to "play the outfield" for the good of the project.

A successful inventor is like the conductor of an orchestra. He knows only a little about each instrument and yet somehow organizes the playing of a symphony. He is a salesperson, marketing researcher, technical researcher, public relations officer, talent scout, evaluator, and negotiator. These roles should, at first, be willingly accepted and then gradually given to those who are specialists. As a matter of fact, this book can be said to be all about inventors learning when to hand off.

A successful inventor is like the conductor of an orchestra. He knows only a little about each instrument and yet somehow organizes the playing of a symphony.

TWO

Where New Products Come From

"Ideas are flashes of genius in the darkness of thought."
—Thomas Edison

"Now why didn't I think of that?" is a question frequently asked when we first see a new device. One answer might be that while we are all creative, it is in different ways. We have different combinations of experiences, backgrounds, emotions, thought patterns, and dreams for the future. These different characteristics combine in diverse ways to form unique ideas. If the idea is a product or a process, it may be patentable and thereby protected by the Constitution of the United States.

Inc. magazine senior writer Tom Richman wrote "A company's future depends on how well it sustains a flow of ideas." Fortune 500 companies get new product ideas from R&D researchers; its customers, sales force, field service personnel, and engineers; brainstorming sessions, focus groups; and even idea contests. In comparison, *Inc.* 500 CEOs feel most product ideas "just came to them." Indeed, results of a 1991 survey asking where they got their product ideas concluded that 46 percent of the CEOs "just saw a market niche," 20 percent came from a formal R&D or product development process, 17 percent came from customers, 3 percent by acquiring another company, and 32 percent from some other source. (The total is greater than 100 percent due to multiple answers.)

Sometimes product ideas are accidental. The Slinky, Kellogg's Corn Flakes, Coca-Cola, Scotchgard, Post-It Notes, and Teflon were all discovered while trying to accomplish something different.

Independent inventors receive about 20 percent of the 90,000 to 100,000 patents issued each year. The best product ideas seem to come from those who have experienced a problem in their own field of work and labored to find a solution. A painter may think of a way to store nails, nuts, and bolts on a ladder. A chemist develops an improved biodegradable cleaner. A teacher creates a board game that makes it exciting for her students to learn geography. A hair stylist designs a device that cuts one-third off the normal time it takes to give her client a permanent.

While painters, chemists, teachers, and hairstylists may all be experts in their respective trades or professions, they usually have no background in manufacturing or marketing new devices. They might seek tooling quotes from manufacturers or price materials from suppliers; visit their bank for a loan; or sign up with an invention development company. These activities usually prove to be futile, but they are at least trying to move their project toward commercialization.

I was asked to speak at the first meeting of a new inventors' organization in Enid, Oklahoma. In attendance were approximately 25 inventors from Enid and the surrounding area. To get things started I asked, "Why do inventors invent?" Each answered in his or her turn. The unanimous response went something like this: "I enjoy making life easier for other people," or "I invent for the betterment of mankind," or "I really like solving problems." Frankly, I was stunned. No one said, "I invent for money." I pressed the point. While they all agreed that money was the grease that made inventing possible, the primary reason for inventing was not for the bucks. Maybe that is why I am not an inventor. If I were, I would be doing it for the money. Nevertheless I am glad we have those who invent regardless of the reason. They have made our lives easier, more productive, and longer lasting. This was a real eye-opener for me. On one hand we have creative people dedicated to "bringing new ideas to life," but who lack the business skills to do it. On the other hand we have creative businesspeople with excess manufacturing capacity, who lack the ability to develop ideas. Somewhere there should be a deal.

Protecting an Idea

I once received an inquiry from the *Tulsa World* newspaper regarding a reader's question. He said he had an idea and wanted to know how to protect it. The following was my response:

> *First let me begin with a caveat. The Inventors' Assistance Program is not in the business of providing detailed intellectual property advice. We rely on patent professionals authorized by the U.S. Patent Office and who represent our IAP clients. Having said that, since our mission is to commercialize new products, our knowledge of patent protection is from that perspective—and only as laymen.*
>
> *There are three documents the new product innovator might wish to keep in mind in protecting his idea: the U.S. Patent Office's disclosure document, the inventor's logbook and a confidentiality agreement.*
>
> *A disclosure document form and instructions can be ordered from the Commissioner of Patents, U.S. Patent and Trademark Office, Washington, DC 20231, 703-557-3158. This form basically establishes the Patent Office as a witness to the date of conception of the idea. It does not provide patent protection. The commonly practiced method of mailing to oneself a certified letter has been ruled invalid by the courts.*
>
> *"A logbook is recommended by many patent attorneys as an even better way to establish the date of conception. This is a bound notebook with the pages numbered and sewn in place. Plastic or wire binding is unacceptable. At intermittent stages of development, the pages are dated and witnessed. This does not provide patent protection either.*
>
> *Since it is important to receive as much marketing analysis as possible prior to applying for a patent, a confidentiality agreement may be used in some situations. While these are standard legal documents available at most local libraries, it may be wise to ask an attorney to draw one up. Keep in mind, however, that not everyone is willing to risk litigation in order to see a new idea. Many repu-*

table firms as a matter of policy will not sign such an agreement. This is usually because they do not wish to jeopardize their own research and development activities that may be similar in nature.

Once the patent application is filed with the patent office, it is considered patent pending. At this stage it is okay for the innovator to begin licensing, joint venture, manufacturing, or marketing negotiations and treat the patent pending as a trade secret. He should not reveal his patent-pending number, but he should be prepared to verify that it has been filed. Potential business partners will also expect to examine the full text of the document. The participants in the deal will recognize that when and if a patent is granted it will carry full rights according to U.S. patent law. Foreign patent coverage may also be applied for during the first year the patent is pending.

We have discovered from our invention commercialization efforts that two of the first things a potential licensee wishes to know about a new product are "Who did the patent work?" and "How broad is the coverage?" If the inventor has filed the patent himself or in conjunction with others not approved by the patent office, then it is extremely difficult to keep the potential licensee's interest in the project. In other words, it lessens the value of the patent in most cases. This is why we recommend that patent attorneys and/or agents always be retained. The chances of licensing the resulting intellectual property are much greater.

In conclusion, while there are various ways to protect ideas and trade secrets, none is absolutely certain. Even issued patents can be overturned in federal court. There is simply no certain protection until a patent has been challenged and rights won in court. With this in mind, remember that experienced marketing advice should be sought early in the project's life. And while it is good to take reasonable precautions to protect your idea, try not to fall over the edge of the precipice of paranoia. Whenever in doubt, consult a patent attorney in whom you have confidence.

The patent office's disclosure document program does not constitute protection. It establishes the patent office as a witness toward proving in court the date of your idea's conception.

Because this was written several years ago there have been some changes in the patent laws. Some of it centers on the provisional patent application, or PPA. Through the GATT patent laws, the United States now has this special category of patent applications.

Many other countries have had similar laws for years. There seems to be a lot of controversy about provisional patent applications within the ranks of patent attorneys, so expect to get conflicting opinions. Some claim it is only good for low and medium technologies, yet some patent firms specializing in biotechnologies use it exclusively. One attorney has suggested the real reason that the PPA is criticized is because it is far less difficult to file; patent attorneys therefore cannot charge as much for a PPA as they used to charge for filing a regular patent application.

All we know at the New Products Coalition is that once a PPA is filed, it is patent pending for one year, and during that year it is theoretically more safe to allow the market to speak regarding the efficacy of the potential product or process. If it looks like the market will accept the new product during the one-year window, the inventor can convert the application to a regular utility application. It seems to be a very efficient way around this problem.

Once a PPA is filed, it is patent pending for one year, and during that year it is theoretically more safe to allow the market to speak regarding the efficacy of the potential product or process. If it looks like the market will accept the new product during the one-year window, the inventor can convert the application to a regular utility application.

Keep in mind, however, that an investor or a potential licensee may want to wait until the regular patent application is filed or the first office action has taken place before investing or licensing. The first office action may take as long as four to eight months after filing, but your financial partner may feel more comfortable at that point that claims will be granted sufficiently broad in scope for an investment to be made.

Can an Idea Be Sold?

Many believe they can sell an idea without a patent or patent-pending status to a company and that somehow they can make money from the transaction. One day a woman came in to see me with an idea for a bathroom accessory. She had only enough money for a crude prototype and no money for a professional patent search, no money to file a patent, and, of course, no money to make better prototypes. She asked me to help sell her idea to one of the large bathroom tissue manufacturing companies. I tried to explain that while it was possible for any business transaction to occur, not all proposed business transactions are probable. If it is true that only 1 or 2 percent of all patents make money for an inventor, what are the possibilities of a mere idea with no proprietary position?

Let's say I agreed with the inventor, and that we should try to sell her idea (as is) to a large company. We would send out letters generally describing what the idea might do for the company, but not being too specific. Several months later, if there were any response at all, we would receive a letter or brochure stating the company's policy on receiving ideas from outside the firm. It would thank us for our interest, send an "unsolicited suggestions agreement," and invite us to submit the idea under the two following conditions:

1. It is understood by the submitter that the Company does not wish to receive any ideas in confidence and no confidential relationship or obligation of secrecy will be established between the submitter and the Company with respect to the submitted suggestion and materials.
2. The submitter by this agreement does not grant any rights to the Company under existing or future patents. The submitter agrees to rely for protection and as the basis for compensation solely upon patent rights that the submitter may obtain.

The company is saying it will not enter into a secrecy agreement with an inventor. Unless the idea is protected by patent rights, the company may very well elect to exploit the idea and pay the submitter nothing. It has happened before and will happen again. That's business.

Companies have the responsibility to make profits for their shareholders. The shareholders have invested their hard-earned money into the company and expect a good return. Entering into a secrecy agreement with anyone wanting to give it an idea would open the company up to litigation problems and possibly contaminate its own research and development projects.

Secrecy agreements almost always contain noncompete clauses. If the company had been working for years on the cure for cancer and an inventor submitted an alternative cure for cancer under a secrecy agreement, then the company might wind up being contractually bound not to take their product to the market when it was perfected. If they stayed in that business, the company would have to take the inventor's cure, even if they rejected it as inferior. That is an overly simplistic illustration of the problem, but it serves well enough to basically explain why companies are not eager to enter into secrecy agreements. Their position is totally understandable, justifiable, and desirable.

Companies do not "have it in" for inventors, but they have their own interests to protect. If they do not choose to accept ideas with a secrecy agreement in place to protect the inventor, so be it. Some large companies even have staff members whose only job is discouraging ideas from the outside. This is the epitome of the "not invented here" syndrome. Understanding this about companies, what are the chances of selling them a mere idea with no proprietary position? Who would want to waste their own time to submit one?

It is extremely difficult to license an idea with no proprietary position. If your product or process cannot get to the patent pending stage, it is usually best to forget about it.

It is extremely difficult to license an idea with no proprietary position. If your product or process cannot get to the patent pending stage, it is usually best to forget about it.

There are other ways to sell an idea that have worked, but not often. They involve a lot of big "ifs." Let's take another look at the same scenario. An inventor has an idea for a bathroom accessory. She has only enough money for a crude prototype and no money for a professional patent search, no money to file a patent, and no money for further development of prototypes. She begins to look for ways to commercialize it. *If* she could find a person with money, *if* this person were interested in investing in new ideas, *if* this person would sign a confidentiality agreement, *if* this person liked the idea and thought it capable of intellectual property protection, *if* this person had excess cash or other clear assets when she contacted him, *if* this person were willing to invest it in this deal, . . . and *if* the investor and inventor liked each other, *then* maybe a deal could be constructed. In exchange for paying for the patent work, further

R&D and prototyping, the investor might ask for 50 to 60 percent of the patent rights. He may also want his company, or one he puts together, to be the exclusive licensee. And this could be great for the investor, who is now moving the idea toward ultimate commercialization. For the inventor, 40 percent of the patent rights is better than 100 percent of nothing.

So here are the answers to the two common inventor questions: Is it possible for an idea be sold? Yes. Is it likely? No. The farther along an idea is in its development, including intellectual property protection, the better the chances are of turning it into a profitable innovation.

The farther along an idea is in its development, including intellectual property protection, the better the chances are of turning it into a profitable innovation.

THREE

How to Know
When to Proceed

"When you come to a fork in the road—take it."
—Yogi Berra

Knowing when or if one should proceed can be tricky. One can never know for sure. It is a matter of faith that is grounded in logic—not blind faith. It depends on how much money and time one is willing and able to risk.

Birth of an Idea

Over a year ago, Pauline, a cosmetologist, had an idea for a new product in the beauty business. It was such a strong idea she could not sleep at night just thinking about it. She could envision how it would look, what color it would be, and how it would save her a lot of time and, therefore, money. She tried to forget it, but it kept coming back. She wished she had one to use in her business. She knew that if others could see her using it, they would want one too. She wondered how in the world she could get one to every stylist in the country. She wondered how much money she could make. She fell in love with the idea. It came from her own creativity. It was her baby. She did not realize it at the time, but she had just completed the first and easiest step in the invention process—thinking of the idea.

Market Research

Pauline knew she had never seen anything like her product idea in her 20 years as a cosmetologist. During that time, salespeople would call on her shop at least five times a week selling all kinds of equipment and chemicals to the beauty professionals and their clients. Given her professional experience, Pauline was probably right. In all likelihood nothing else like it was on the market.

Most good new product ideas seem to come from those who have experience in the very industry in which their invention will be sold. What if Pauline had not been a professional? What if she had come up with the idea while getting a perm? What if she did not have the experience of talking with salespeople five times a week for 20 years? This is where most inventors make their first mistake. They assume that because they have been a consumer all their life and have never seen a product, it must not exist. If they have never done market research, they do not know where to begin. Combining the problem of not knowing how to conduct market research with the realization of having no protection, they skip this step and go on to the next one. Skipping this step really becomes justifiable to them when they suppose the odds are highly against someone else coming up with the very same idea.

Market research is critical at this point for three reasons:

1. Everything else that follows costs money.
2. The inventor may have invented that which has already been invented but was never developed and sold.
3. The inventor may very easily have invented that which is or has been on the market.

In short, as much market research as possible should go into the project prior to building a prototype or filing for a patent.

In short, as much market research as possible should go into the project prior to building a prototype or filing for a patent.

A visit to the public or academic library can yield a wealth of information. It does not take a professional market researcher to dig it out. A good librarian can quickly help determine who the key players are in an industry, who makes similar products, and maybe the size of the potential market. The librarian does not have to know the details of the idea, but it would be helpful to explain that you are conducting market research on a general subject for the purpose of determining a product's uniqueness.

A possible side benefit of the library research is the possibility that one's thinking on the characteristics of the product idea may be refined and improved upon from the study of the market. Another benefit is that gathering information will help you present your invention in the best possible light when approaching an investor or licensee.

If the idea is not unique or does not constitute a significant improvement in some area, the chances of making money are even worse than the chances of making money with something that carries a proprietary position. This is discussed later in greater detail. Nevertheless, there can never be enough market research, and the sooner one gets started the better.

Establishing a Date of Conception

Pauline had heard about patents. She felt that if anything ever deserved a patent it was this—her baby. So she called the U.S. Patent and Trademark Office and asked for information on getting a patent. Among the forms and booklets she received two weeks later (What took them so long? Don't they realize how important this is?) was a disclosure document. It was simple enough to fill out. Just sketch a diagram of the new product, describe it, and send it back to the patent office with $10. Should she do it? Should she risk revealing her idea to even the patent office? What if someone in the patent office stole her idea? Could she afford the $10 dollars? She realized she had to trust someone to witness her date of conception. She also looked at her checkbook. No problem there. So she sent her check attached to her disclosure document to the patent office for two years of safekeeping.

She had never heard of an inventor's logbook being an even better way to establish a date of conception. Nevertheless Pauline had made a logical decision utilizing the information and resources she had in her possession. What more could anyone ask?

Building the Prototype

Pauline now had an idea, confirmed its uniqueness as well as she could, and filed a disclosure document with the patent office. What should she do next? Should she proceed? She knew the idea would work, but could not prove it without building a working prototype. She gathered her thoughts by making a list of everything she would need to build a prototype. She carefully figured her projected costs. She needed to find assistance in making the plastic pieces, so she located through a friend someone who had experience in making plastic parts. She got a quote from him for his time. She estimated that it would cost her approximately $500 and about 80 hours of her time. What would her family think of her spending that much money on her idea? Would they be happy with cooking their own food or eating TV dinners for several weeks?

For Pauline, the decision was easy. Her family was 100 percent behind her. The money could be saved over several months without seriously hurting the family budget. She decided to go for it. A couple of months later she completed her prototype. It worked even better than she thought it would.

I wish it were always so easy to decide to go to the next step. What if her family thought she was a bit eccentric? What if they really did not want her to succeed in anything, much less in getting an invention marketed? What if they strenuously objected to her spending $500 out of the family's cookie jar? What if the complexity of her idea required a $15,000 investment and ten months to build the working prototype? These questions cannot be answered easily, especially without knowing the particular aspects of each individual's situation.

Nevertheless, the general questions one must ask before making an investment in prototype development are: Is it really worth it? Is it worth the sacrifice in terms of my time and especially my family's time? What effect will it have on them? Can I (or we) afford to lose every dime spent on this and never question whether it was the right risk to take? If you and your family cannot answer these kinds of questions with a whole-hearted yes, then maybe it is best to wait until you can. Remember: The chances of recouping your investment are much less than those of breaking even in Las Vegas.

More Research

Once the prototype has been built, more market research is needed. Legitimate independent evaluations can help expedite commercialization at this point (for more on this, see Chapter 4). A technical evaluation, for instance, can suggest improvements and add credibility to the product if it is not apparent that the prototype works as suggested. An inventor should take the previously gathered information and make sure the product is unique in some way. An approximate cost of manufacturing should be calculated, along with the ultimate retail price. Why? The inventor has probably made some refinements in his thinking and some changes or improvements in the working prototype. An engineering prototype might be needed to optimize the design or perform tests on reliability, accuracy, speed, durability. Generally this is only required in the more advanced and complex technologies.

It might be very helpful to participate in the Preliminary Innovation Evaluation System (PIES) at this point (for more information on PIES, see Chapter 4). The product will, of course, score low on intellectual property protection (unless it has already been patented), but the primary purpose of the evaluation is to help make the inventor aware of problems that may have been overlooked. If done for the right reasons, PIES can be extremely helpful in assisting inventors in research. By participating, the inventor is preparing for the next step possible—having a professional patent search performed—and needs as much help as possible to decide whether to proceed. If a significant amount of additional money is required, one should ask again: Is it worth it?

Patent Search

Before completing the prototype stage, it might be good to do a preliminary patent search at one of the patent depository libraries. This will not be as good as one performed by a professional patent searcher, but it can be used in your market research to determine possible competitive activity. In addition, you may discover that you have to design around a feature of another patent. It would be better to know it before your prototype is finished than after.

Patent searches generally cost between $400 and $1,000. (The patent search is described in greater detail later in Chapter 4.) If a significant amount of additional money is required you should ask again: Is it worth it? Can I (or we) afford to lose every dime spent on this and never question whether it was the right risk to take?

Patent Filing

Although Pauline filed a disclosure document with the patent office, she knew it did not constitute having protection. She knew that in order to keep others from manufacturing and selling her "baby," she had to have a patent. A disclosure document just did not cut it, contrary to the rumors she had heard.

Patent filing fees and attorney fees cost anywhere from $3,000 to $10,000 for even the most simple concepts—more if it is exceedingly complex. Fees are even higher if one is going to file foreign patents. There is no guarantee that a patent will be granted, or if it is, that it will look the same as when it was originally filed. It will probably take 18 months or so if all goes well. Part of the patent attorney's job is to debate with the patent examiner and obtain the greatest possible scope of coverage. Just getting a patent really is not the greatest goal to strive for anyway. Getting a patent that is broad enough in scope to help capture and keep a significant niche in the marketplace is the real goal.

Patents are marketing tools. Marketing tools are not necessarily patents.

Patents are marketing tools. Marketing tools are not necessarily patents. Many inventors have a warped perspective about this. They view winning a patent as the ultimate experience when it really is only secondary. If the item does not sell, it's not worth much. A patented product does very little good unless others are able to experience its benefits. In other words, it has to get into the marketplace for people to buy and use. A patent can facilitate that process. Winning a patent is a function of marketing. It provides the future marketing effort with a product that cannot be manufactured or sold without the permission of the patent owner or his licensee.

For the independent inventor, deciding to proceed with the patenting step is an important one. This is undoubtedly where most good product ideas are killed. If one works for a large company and does nothing except explore new formulas or designs, it can be a simple matter to file and win patents. The company pays for the patent fees, attorney fees, prototype development, state-of-the-art equipment, market research staff, etc. The company inventor also has the advantage of working with his engineering or scientific peers daily to stimulate his creativity and keep him on track. When you contrast this with the independent inventor who has hardly any resource support and where money is precious, it is nothing short of a miracle that 20 percent of all patents are granted to independents.

For the inventor still wanting to proceed, this is where all the market research will once more come in very handy. Proper analysis of the research, combined with input from a patent attorney on the potential scope of the inventor's intellectual property should suffice to answer the questions: Is it worth it? Can I (or we) afford to lose every dime spent on this and never question whether it was the right risk to take?

The Greatest Catch-22

"I can't show my invention until it is protected, but I can't get it protected, because I don't have the money necessary to get a patent."

This is always a tough problem. The solution is relative. If the inventor is wealthy or has some capital socked away, it is no problem. Most of us, however, really have to struggle for extra money. If the project is going to move forward, we have to get creative.

To illustrate, I'll share the story of a man who called me several years ago. He was a medical technician and had an idea that would save hospitals thousands of dollars. He said it was a simple solution to a long-standing problem. Every patient would need one whenever they had a very common test performed. My client said he would have to raise about $4,000 for a mold and a small run of samples. These units would be sold for approximately $2 each and carry a substantial margin.

He had seen a patent attorney and hired him to perform a patent search. It looked pretty clean, and the decision was made to file a patent application. The attorney needed $1,000 to work up the patent and wanted $4,000 more in about a month to file it with the patent office.

He had seen an advertisement on television from an invention development company and it was calling every other day wanting him to send them $6,000 to represent him before manufacturers. He said he had $1,000 in savings and excellent credit and thought he could get a loan from the bank, but he called the Inventors' Assistance Program to see if it had some grant money or low-interest loans.

What advice would you give?

- Get a $5,000 loan and send the money to the invention developer.
- Get a $4,000 loan and pay the attorney.
- Give the attorney $1,000 and in 30 days get a loan for $4,000.
- Get a loan to make the mold and samples.
- Get a loan and do all of the above.
- Buy a book on free government money and apply for grants.
- Give up.

This is what I advised the inventor: First, call the patent attorney and ask how long he had to file his patent after the invention was made public. The answer should be one year. Then ask what constitutes making it public. There will be several general ways: an article in a periodical, actually selling the item, offering to sell the item (even without it actually being ready to sell), etc. Then, while making sure there was no public disclosure, get a loan to make the mold and samples.

It seemed to me that while the inventor had access to some funds through the bank, he did not need much more than $5,000 or $6,000 to get his invention test marketed. If he could get the parts made and sold quickly—or even given away to get them used and experienced by the marketplace—he would have a much better chance of finding the money to go into full production either through venturing or licensing. Once convinced the market wanted the product, he could then file his patent using the profits from sales. Caution: This strategy should be attempted only after a full understanding of the risks and a knowledge of all the options as explained by patent counsel.

How does this relate to the Catch-22? It is one way to defeat it. The inventor was on the verge of becoming a Catch-22 victim and giving up. There may now be another way with the advent of the provisional patent application. My partner, Jim Harris, did most of the work in thinking through the following example. Remember, I am not offering intellectual property advice and that competent intellectual properties counsel should be included in your decision-making process. Remember, an ideal answer for every project does not exist, but the following example may provide a cost-effective option for some.

T. A. Edison, Jr., an independent inventor, developed an idea for a new widget. Almost all his savings went toward developing a working prototype. He knew the market would love it, so he decided to license it. He wanted anyone thinking of stealing his idea to be discouraged from actually doing so. He decided he needed to go to the patent-pending stage. He visited a patent attorney who informed him that, based on the degree of difficulty in his case, his total patent costs might be anywhere from $7,000 to $10,000.

Having limited funds, he called us. Jim advised him to check with a Washington, D.C., firm that could do a patent search for as little as $200. As a result, Edison found nothing close to his widget's features, and now had significant reasons to believe his patent might prove to be very broad in scope.

Then he purchased and read David Pressman's 5th edition of *Patent It Yourself* for $40, and decided to file a provisional patent application. The filing fee was $75. He learned from Pressman some of the most common mistakes inventors make when they file themselves, such as not making the PPA abstract as broad as possible to cover any conceivable claim.

So, he wrote the application as best as he could and just to make sure, decided to have a patent attorney review his abstract for him. (He did not want to risk doing *all* the patent work himself.) With a little detective work, he found a local attorney who agreed to do it for $100. (Had he not been able to find a local attorney, Harris could have referred him to several who have agreed to review PPA abstracts for between $100 and $200.)

Once the PPA was filed, Edison had a year to get feedback from the marketplace while claiming patent-pending status. Although intellectual property is not protected in the ultimate sense until litigated and won in court, patent-pending status can discourage potential competitors from replicating an inventor's concept. These competitors do not know how broad the claims might be and are often concerned about finding themselves infringing once the patent is granted.

Should interest in the project be forthcoming from a potential licensing or joint venture partner, Edison understood his royalties might be less or his project could be put on the company's back burner until he filed his regular patent application. This is because companies are understandably interested in a product's scope of protection. In other words, how easy will the claims be to design around? This cannot be determined until at least after the first or second office action when the attorney argues with the patent examiner for the broadest possible scope. It is an attorney's job to make it easy for someone to infringe on you. Then that attorney can prosecute the infringement. The patent examiner's goal seems to be to grant only narrow claims, so more patents can be filed, and therefore, more fees can be earned for the patent office.

Edison started with his idea. Now he has taken it to patent-pending status. Although licensing is less likely to occur with a PPA than it is after the first office action on a regular utility application, at least he can claim that the patent is pending while checking the market's response to his project.

This stage of development has now cost less than $450. It is an important stage. The extreme difficulties involved in obtaining a commercialization review of a potential product or process with no proprietary position are often insurmountable. Many potentially great products go by the wayside each year because the specter of spending thousands of dollars in patenting fees and attorney time is just too great for the average inventor to overcome.

This scenario is a possible solution to the problem of allowing the market to speak when not having a war chest of funds to spend on the patenting process. It may not be perfect for all projects, yet it provides the independent inventor with the ability to allow the market to help in making the decision of whether or not to proceed with the project.

Finding Investors

There is another possibility—OPM—other people's money. Sometimes early-stage development money is raised from family and friends. The problem with this is that if the invention never makes enough money to pay them back with a healthy return, the inventor has alienated those closest to him. The inventor should not ask for more than the family member or friend can comfortably afford to lose, because the odds are it will be lost.

If money has to be raised, it is probably best to approach someone successful in business with extra capital. It should be one who is experienced and able to assess the risk. The closer to the industry in which the invention will be sold, the better. This way the inventor has a knowledgeable partner who can provide valuable advice—an arrangement he would probably not have with family or friends as his investors.

This can be accomplished through several structures. The inventor can incorporate and sell shares; form a general or limited partnership; or simply assign a percentage of his intellectual property rights to his investors.

It is critical that these deals be structured correctly and understood thoroughly by both parties. When there are no profits to be distributed, there are few problems. When money begins to flow, memories become short and tempers can flair. It should always be in writing. No "handshake" deals should be allowed. Should the investor want to suggest a structure with which he is comfortable, the inventor should let him do so, unless he has good and valid reasons otherwise. A good corporate attorney can be invaluable in structuring a win/win deal.

Confidentiality Agreements

The proper use of confidentiality agreements or secrecy agreements can sometimes be helpful prior to patent-pending status. If the project requires technical assistance in developing a prototype or an investor to provide funds for the patent filing or prototype development, one should consult a patent attorney for assistance in drawing up a good agreement. There are many examples of generic forms that may be used if there are no funds to pay an attorney. One is provided in Appendix A for your consideration and use should you so desire.

Most investors are reluctant to open themselves up to litigation by signing a secrecy agreement, so do not be surprised if this happens. This often becomes another dilemma. How can you show this idea to a potential investor to invest in gaining protection, if he will not sign a secrecy agreement? There is no easy answer. You have to decide either to trust him or not to trust him. Every situation is different, and no one can give you a magic list of ways to determine if it is okay to reveal your idea to him. You have to use your own common sense and maybe enhance it a little by talking it over with a trusted and respected confidant. Could this person be trusted to look after your children? With a key to your house? Has he looked at confidential ideas or business plans before without revealing them to others or stealing the idea? What is his standing among his peers in the community?

Venture or License

Once the protyping is finished and the patent is pending, you are ready to do all the things necessary to commercialize your idea. It is not unusual for you to have spent $10,000 to 30,000 by this time. The decision must now be made to venture or license. Venturing is building a company around your product and, hopefully, your future intellectual property. Licensing is allowing someone else the right to manufacture and/or market the product while paying the inventor a royalty. Selling a patent outright is considered a venture for the purposes of this work.

The business of inventing is very, very risky. It is risky because many inventors have lost all their money, their family, their friends, and their self-respect while chasing their dream. It can become an addiction more powerful than cocaine. It can cause nervous breakdowns and hysteria. If one can think with his or her head and not with emotions, vast amounts of money can be saved, psychological disturbances squelched, and more new products successfully launched.

If one can think with his or her head and not with emotions, vast amounts of money can be saved, psychological disturbances squelched, and more new products successfully launched.

FOUR

The Myth of
Objective Evaluations

"Mr. Bell, after careful consideration of your invention, while it is a very interesting novelty, we have come to the conclusion that it has no commercial possibilities."

—J.P. Morgan

At some point, an inventor will be told that he should have his invention objectively evaluated by a third party. Through this evaluation, the inventor most often hopes to get a glimpse of the future success of the product or idea. He reasons that a good score will strengthen the business plan or increase the invention's value in some way. If these are your expectations, a better use of your money might be in visiting a palm reader. If it were possible to receive a truly objective evaluation by those knowledgeable in all areas of the invention's field, then these evaluations would indeed be extremely helpful. But is it possible to be truly objective—or merely independent? If it were conceivable to be truly objective, would it be possible for the evaluator to also be knowledgeable in all areas of the invention's characteristics that make up its future success or failure?

Think it through with me. What would a service like that really be worth? Look at the time and money inventors would save if someone could predict the success or failure of inventions. No more money wasted on patenting fees or attorney fees; purchasing raw materials; building prototypes; or conducting market research, hiring employees, packaging, advertising, or inventory. Let's say someone hung out his shingle as "Expert Predictor of New Product Success—100 Percent Guaranteed." We check him out and sure enough, he's right every time. What would he charge to evaluate our invention? Probably more than any independent inventor could afford. He would be so busy working for the big boys he would not be able to spend time with us. Even retail buyers cannot predict success to any great degree. That job depends entirely on one's ability to buy products the store's customers will purchase. Next time you talk to buyers, ask how they feel about their ability to predict a product's success. Ask them what percentage of the time they are right about a never-seen-before product. I bet they say about half the time. Of course, they are usually specialists in buying certain kinds of products, for example, sporting goods, automotive supplies, or lawn and garden tools. They also have the luxury of only deciding on products ready to be sold, that is, those that have the manufacturing and distribution problems ironed out and the packaging designed, completed, and ready to sell. If they have been around awhile, you know they are good. Should their "sell throughs" fall below a certain percentage, they are out of a job in a New York minute. Pressure like that tends to make one pretty good at picking products. It also tends to make one pretty conservative in choosing new lines. But if the buyer is right half the time on brand new products, his job is pretty secure.

Nevertheless the buyer's decisions are not objective. They are subjective, based on his own unique background and prejudices, and on current market conditions. Maybe his store has had a good year, has set aside more budget for new products, and has told the buyers to take more chances, but only during the Christmas buying season and only if they can mark the item up 110 percent. The buyer then sees 20 new items. Ten are dismissed out of hand because he does not feel the store's customers will pay the manufacturer's suggested retail price. Five are cut because he does not like the packaging. Of the remaining five, two cannot pay the store's slotting fee and one just does not seem to fit the store's image. Of the last two he feels either might do well, but he remembers one of them is similar to a product that did not do too well about three years before. Out of 20 he chooses one. And not because he deliberately chose the one out of the 20, but because he found reasons to eliminate 19.

Professional buyers whose very jobs depend on correct buying decisions make subjective buying decisions. Invention evaluators whose jobs do not depend on correct conclusions also make subjective, not objective, judgments. Unless accurately predicting the future 100 percent of the time is one of their attributes, they are in no position to claim they can help the inventor predict the success of his idea. It would be far easier to predict the failure of an item, because 98 percent to 99 percent never make money for the independent inventor.

In short, all evaluations are subjective. No one can predict product success. There simply are too many variables.

Now that we see that evaluations are inherently subjective, let's look at several kinds of invention evaluations common in the new product development world. There is the patentability evaluation, technical evaluation, and the marketability evaluation. There is also the "friends and relatives" evaluation and the "dialing for dollars" evaluation. Let's deal with the last two first.

The "Friends and Relatives" Evaluation

Several years ago, a man came into our office, closed the door (so no one could overhear), and said he had the greatest invention of all time. We were curious about how he arrived at that conclusion, so we asked him, "How do you know it is the greatest invention of all time? We've seen some pretty good ones." He said although he had invented many items, his wife never liked any of them. But this one she really liked, so it must be great. We told him that was wonderful and asked if we could see it. He had left it boxed up in his car, so he had to go get it. When he returned a short time later, he took it out and demonstrated it to us. Well, he had invented the ashtray! That's right—the ashtray. The kind with the push-down lid that pops up after the cigarette is pushed through. The man was devastated when we retrieved our office supply catalog and turned to a picture of his invention. He could not believe it. The only invention his wife ever liked, and it had already been invented.

Friends and relatives of an inventor generally cannot be relied upon to give an honest evaluation, but not because they are untrustworthy. If they think it is the dumbest idea of all time, they do not want to risk hurting the inventor's feelings or somehow making him angry. In our ashtray example, it is not hard to imagine a scenario where the wife was simply trying to encourage her husband. After all, that's what spouses are supposed to do. On the other hand, some spouses do not want their mates to succeed—in anything. It might make them independent. In either case, the evaluation was purely subjective, and in all likelihood resting on many other factors than the merits of the "invention."

It should go without saying that most friends and relatives are not even qualified to give a meaningful evaluation. How many are technical or marketing experts in the field of the invention? Although not impossible, it is highly unusual to find a friend or relative with the kind of expertise necessary for a good product evaluation. And even if the inventor had a qualified friend or relative, his view should not be trusted. Am I advocating an inventor never sharing his ideas or prototypes with friends and relatives? Absolutely not. In addition to providing encouragement and support, they are usually the best ones to witness the pages of the logbook.

So trust friends and relatives for what they do best—providing encouragement and support. Never trust a friend or relative's opinion about the future success of the invention.

So trust friends and relatives for what they do best—providing encouragement and support. Never trust a friend or relative's opinion about the future success of the invention. Thank him for his views, good or bad, but do not make decisions based solely on his stated feelings. The inventor might be wise to put himself in the other person's shoes. He should ask himself what he would say if his friend or relative came to ask his opinion of their invention. In short, never spend time or money on continued development based solely on the evaluation of a friend or relative.

The "Dialing for Dollars" Evaluation

For several years now I have been backpacking and hiking as often as possible. I have learned (and relearned from my Boy Scout days) much about nature. During the late spring and summer I have discovered the importance of using insect repellent to keep little blood-sucking insects like ticks, chiggers, and mosquitoes from having their way with me. I also stay completely away from anything that even looks like poison ivy or poison oak. Having two weeks worth of itching and swollen skin is definitely not fun.

But there are other dangers along the way. In Oklahoma there are several kinds of poisonous snakes: the rattlesnake, copperhead, and water moccasin. Although my nine-year-old son, Thomas, likes to take the lead in his role as pathfinder, I like to lead when the snakes are active. I have seen only three snakes while hiking (just one was poisonous), and none were lying in wait in the middle of the trail. It seems that if snakes are anywhere close to trails used by people, they like to hide just to the side so as to catch unsuspecting rodents and such.

The "dialing for dollars" evaluation was created by human snakes hiding in the brush waiting for would-be inventors to come along the path of commercialization. At the Department of Commerce we must have talked to over a hundred folks with ideas and inventions who had done business with the so-called invention development companies and never made any money. Although a list of these companies could be generated, they periodically change their names. The best way to recognize them is through their modus operandi.

We see slick advertisements on television, in the classified columns of magazines, in the newspaper, or in brochures: "Have you got an invention? Do you have a million-dollar idea? Send us your idea or call for free information." We get the nice four-color packet and read the wonderful stories about what might happen if only the inventor's idea were in the right hands. For about $500 they will give the inventor an "objective evaluation" and "market research."

They will usually throw in for "free" the filing of a disclosure document with the patent office and lead many inventors to believe they are somehow protected just as if they had already filed a patent. The disclosure document program costs only ten dollars and was specifically designed to be easy for the inventor to do himself. It establishes the patent office as a witness to the date of conception. Most attorneys recommend keeping a logbook as the best way to establish the date of conception.

Some even offer to get a patent for their client. They, of course, do not bother to explain the difference between design patents and utility patents, and how in most cases design patents will be worth next to nothing as far as obtaining a broad scope of patent protection. Guess what the inventor gets: A design patent.

So, if the inventor sends in his $500 or so for his "objective" evaluation, he receives a nice glowing report along with an analysis of a huge potential market. This highly positive evaluation combined with mostly boilerplate pages that could apply to almost any product serve as a 20- to 30-page sales pitch for continuing to the next step. This is not an objective evaluation. If these companies were any good at evaluating ideas, surely a large number of licensing agreements would be the result because ideas and inventions always receive glowing evaluations. The company has gotten paid for providing nothing of value to the inventor and wants more.

Then comes the big pitch: For fees ranging from $4,000 to $10,000 (actually whatever the market will bear), the invention developer will represent the inventor's idea or intellectual property on a "best-efforts" basis to manufacturers around the country. One inventor from Oklahoma said the only thing she ever received were stacks of copies of inquiry letters allegedly sent to manufacturers. After two years of this the invention development company wanted another five grand for two more years! She told them she had not paid off the second mortgage on her home from the first time around.

What's even worse is that while her idea was supposed to be circulating for over two years before manufacturers, she had no patent protection or patent pending. Only a disclosure document had been filed by the invention developer. She thought she had protection, yet she may have lost any potential patent rights she might have won. An inventor has only one year to file once the invention has been made public. To what degree was her idea revealed? No one but the invention developer knows for sure.

These people really hammer the inventor. They are well trained in telephone sales techniques, and they are tenacious if they smell money. Many of the salespeople may even actually believe they are doing something worthwhile. The fact is that not once in four years with the Inventors' Assistance Program did I or any other staff member hear of a successful licensing agreement or any other kind of strategic alliance that resulted from doing business with an invention development company. We only heard complaints of being ripped off. It is estimated that only 1 or 2 percent of all granted patents ever makes more money for the inventor than he spent to get his patent. Invention developers know this, too. That is why they want their money up front and on a best-efforts basis.

In 1991 I sent for information from an invention development company. I then received a letter saying they had not received my reply. It said, "There is a good possibility that your idea may have commercial potential, and a response now could lead to establishing your prior right to the idea." Do you see the sales pitch? Without knowing what my idea was, the company was trying to encourage me to work with them, because I might make a lot of money and, at the same time, keep the rights to my idea.

An invention developer's definition of success is not the same as the inventor's definition. An invention development company's primary measure of success is sales revenue from services rendered. An inventor's definition of success is a licensing agreement with a company that can generate significant royalties back to him or an outright purchase of his patent. There is a big difference in the two definitions! Because it is easier to find, qualify, and get inventors to send them $5,000 than it is to find, qualify, and get licensing agreements for these inventions, invention developers simply take the path of least resistance to increase their revenues and profits.

The past several years have seen hundreds of thousands of dollars flow from independent Oklahoma inventors to out-of-state invention development companies. The Inventors' Assistance Program supported Representative Tim Pope's legislation regulating these "invention development companies" by requiring thorough track-record disclosures in their contracts and posting a bond prior to doing business in Oklahoma. The effect of this legislation should work to free up capital to be used for more worthy aspects of new product development, such as patent fees, prototype costs, packaging, etc. At least eight other states have similar legislation: California, Texas, Illinois, Ohio, Kansas, North Carolina, South Dakota, and Minnesota. Any patent attorney in your state should be able to tell you whether such laws govern invention development companies in your state.

Some of the contracts drafted by these firms were very sly. The terms of payment offered the inventor his choice of two methods. The first called for the inventor pay a flat fee —let's say $5,000. The other would offer a "bargain" to the inventor of say $3,000. If the lower-priced method was selected, however, the invention development company insisted upon receiving 40 percent of whatever the inventor received from the idea or invention. From this the inventor might conclude the company would work harder if it had a vested interest in the invention. He also could save a couple thousand dollars.

It never occurred to the Oklahoma inventors with whom I spoke that the invention development company might not care whether it received an ongoing percentage—that it might have been enough to receive the up-front, nonrefundable cash and move on to the next "client." They did not see these two program choices as a way for the invention development company to close more business. At least it never occurred to them until weeks and months passed while nothing tangible happened to move their projects forward.

One invention development company provided an inventor with a list of companies it claimed to have contacted on her behalf. Her questions were, "How do I know these companies were contacted? How do I know what was sent to them?" The answer is, no one ever knows. To make matters worse, it was readily apparent that the vast majority of companies allegedly contacted were not prime candidates to license or even manufacture her invention. Why did they send her prosthetic bra idea to a company selling to the automotive aftermarket?

Invention development companies (also referred to as invention promotion companies) are very good at drafting contracts. They have spent huge sums of money for attorneys to write and modify contracts requiring them to do hardly anything except produce a brochure and give it to "industry contacts." To those unfamiliar with invention marketing practices, these contracts are replete with semantic ambiguities. There have been so many complaints with state attorneys general, consumer fraud units, and the Federal Trade Commission that invention development companies have learned to be very precise about what they say on paper.

To illustrate, following are a few excerpts from an invention development company's contract with an Oklahoma inventor who had taken out a second mortgage on her home in 1987 and sent the proceeds to the company.

In exchange for $3,495, the company agreed "to submit to industry one of the Client's ideas/inventions/products and prepare a brochure. The brochure will include 'a graphic or other illustration' and a description of the product."

According to the contract, the term *industry* "includes manufacturers, marketers, distributors, dealers, retailers, sales/manufacturers representatives or agents with whom we make contact and/or who contact us through our business associations, advertising, and attendance at Trade Shows, Seminars and Conventions." This sounds great. The company says it is going to send a brochure to all these people—from manufacturers to retailers—and even take it to trade shows! Or does it?

Later in the contract we read, "Client agrees that the number and selection of manufacturers and marketers contacted are to be at the discretion of the Company." It is now conceivable that a representative of the company can take the brochure with him to lunch, show it to the guy who just made his pizza, and be in full compliance with the contract. The company selected the type of manufacturer (a pizza manufacturer) and the number (one).

The next sentence of the contract states, "Nothing in this Agreement shall be construed as a representation, inducement, promise or guarantee that Company will obtain any results, sales or licensing agreements for Client." Oh, really? What kind of success can we expect from showing an automotive aftermarket item to the pizza man?

The next sentence tells us "the Company agrees only to use its best efforts to package and present the Client's idea, invention or product in the form of a brochure to manufacturers and marketers for the purpose of reviewing interest which may be expressed." Who knows the meaning of the term "best efforts"? *Black's Law Dictionary* defines *best* to mean of the highest quality; of the greatest usefulness for the purpose intended. For example, where one covenants to use his "best endeavors," there is no breach if he is prevented by causes wholly beyond his control and without any default on his part. So, does it mean a mailing to 5,000 manufacturers? 500? 50? 5? Does walking next door for a pizza constitute "best efforts"? The company does not even offer to report to their client what the pizza man thought of the idea—if anything. In fact, the company merely says the pizza man *may* express an interest. It would undoubtedly require a judge to decide what "best efforts" means, and this requires litigation.

The next section of the agreement is classic semantic ambiguity: "Client understands and agrees that Company does not develop, manufacture, market or promote ideas, inventions or products nor does Company represent inventors. Company is solely engaged in the business of assisting and aiding inventors in submitting inventions, products or ideas to industry and reviewing any interest which may be expressed." Most reasonable people would interpret the acts of creating a product brochure and then submitting the brochure to industry as a function of marketing or promotion. And most would assume that whoever did this on behalf of the inventor would, in fact, be representing the inventor. So, because this invention development company says it both does and does not market an inventor's idea, invention, or product makes this a great contradiction. Inventors have been led to believe primarily through telephone sales pitches that the company will make them wealthy.

Inventors believe they are hiring the company to aggressively market and promote their idea, invention, or product, yet there it is in black and white. The company *does* and *does not* market and promote the idea. Further, the company does and does not represent the inventor. Is that clear? Beware of any verbal agreements that are not included in the contract. One of the last clauses in the agreement states, ". . . any verbal statements not specifically incorporated into this written agreement are abandoned, void and of no force and effect; and this written Agreement is the entire and only Agreement between the parties."

What about the brochure? Doesn't the client have the ability to approve or disapprove of the art, text, and color? Call a graphic designer sometime. Before he or she begins to design a brochure you will be asked if you have a concept in mind. The artist will then use his skills and experience to add enhancements to your concept. But he will not vary too far from your idea, because he knows if you do not like it he won't get paid.

Does the invention development company afford its clients the same consideration? Let's see. The contract states, "Company will submit drafts of descriptive material to Client for approval and/or revision suggestions prior to printing." To the unwary this sounds as though the company must first gain its client's okay before printing the brochure. However, closer scrutiny reveals that the company really only has to *ask* for its client's approval or suggested changes. The company can accept or reject the inventor's ideas for changes. For example, if the company wanted to superimpose a cheese pizza over the drawing of the invention to impress the pizza man next door, the inventor could object until he or she turned blue, and the company would be under no contractual obligation to change it.

Well, what if the inventor wanted to fire the company at this point? That would be fine with the company. It already has its money in the bank. Undoubtedly, the company will claim to have given its "best efforts" to submit the idea to industry.

Still another troublesome clause reads, "If the new idea or invention is unpatented, Company will register it for two (2) years with the U.S. Patent Office under the Disclosure Document Program." First of all, the Disclosure Document Program establishes the patent office as a witness regarding the date of conception of the product idea. It costs $10 but provides no protection. Most attorneys recognize that a logbook and witnesses are best at establishing a date of conception. Even patent attorneys can establish a date for you without using the patent office.

Second, according to one patent attorney in Oklahoma City a good case could be made that this inventor inadvertently gave up any future patent rights. If her idea was put in a brochure and actually sent out to industry as the invention development company promised, her idea could have been made public. She only had one year from that date to file for a patent.

Finally, the contract binds the client exclusively to the company for two years: ". . . Client agrees that Company shall have the exclusive right to submit the new idea, invention or product, which is the subject of this Agreement, for the sole purpose of reviewing interest . . ." In others words, even the inventor cannot submit his or her own idea to any other company unless permission is granted. Nor can he or she seek help from an inventors' organization or any other group that might have a "reviewing interest" in the idea.

There are many more reasons to approach invention development companies with great caution. I have discussed these which were lifted from an actual contract, that you might be wary and think twice before sending your hard-earned money to an invention development firm. Rarely should an inventor send hundreds or thousands of dollars to anyone without knowing that firm's reputation.

Regarding the question of how many clients have made more money from their idea than was paid to the invention development company, the company will usually say zero. This should be enough not to do business with them. They will try to explain that their sole function is to present ideas to industry, and that they have contracted with another company to sell the ideas or do the licensing. Treat this with a grain of salt. In my opinion, even if there is another company it is just for show. Invention development companies are not interested in licensing products. They are interested in only one thing: getting your money.

Invention development companies are not interested in licensing products. They are interested in only one thing: getting your money.

I once asked an invention development company's attorney how many employees worked for his client's company. (He had been sent from Pittsburgh to threaten us with a lawsuit if we did not quit saying bad things about his client's firm.) "About 200 nationwide," he answered. I asked him how many licensing agreements they had closed in the past five years. He said, "None." I informed him that with only two staff people and a secretary we had closed (completed) over 50 licensing agreements and joint ventures on behalf of inventors in four years at the Department of Commerce. I asked him how 200 employees with a multimillion dollar budget over five years could not close even *one* licensing agreement. He just shrugged his shoulders. Of course, the answer should be obvious. They do not want to close licensing agreements. It is not part of their strategic plan.

If you would like more information from the perspective of a former invention development company executive, contact Robert G. Lougher, President, Inventors Awareness Group, Inc., 1533 East Mountain Road, Westfield, MA 01085-1458. His phone number is 413-568-5561. Bob was hired to be the marketing manager of an invention development company and resigned upon discovering how the company really operated. He estimates his organization has now saved many thousands of people from being victimized by these companies.

The Federal Trade Commission (FTC) also has information. Write the Federal Trade Commission, Public Reference Branch, Room 130, 6th Street and Pennsylvania Avenue, NW, Washington, DC 20580, or call 202-326-2222. In February of 1996, it issued a press release stating the Invention Submission Corporation of Pittsburgh, Pennsylvania, had agreed to pay $1.2 million in consumer redress to settle FTC charges it misrepresented invention promotion services. Ask for a copy of the consent decree, news releases, and FTC's brochure #F030382.

Finally, more information can be obtained from Senator Joe Lieberman's office by calling 202-224-4041. Senator Lieberman recently held hearings on invention development companies. He plans to introduce legislation to crack down on phony invention marketing companies.

I hope this information has been helpful. Millions of this country's product development dollars have been diverted into the pockets of fraudulent promoters. Consequently, these new product ideas have died prematurely from a lack of capital that otherwise might have been used to successfully commercialize them.

Here are a few final thoughts: To a potential licensee the perceived value of work subcontracted to a patent attorney by an invention developer is almost zero. Why? One reason is that these patent attorneys are not local. They are usually located in Washington, D.C. It is difficult to establish a relationship with them. I am not saying that if an inventor's patent attorney is in another state it is a deal killer, but it makes it easier to license an invention if the patent work is done by a locally respected attorney, someone who has been around awhile and is known in the community.

Second, a potential licensee or joint venture partner understands the subjective nature of a patent search. It is an art, not a science. A $500 patent search prior to filing a patent is nothing compared to a $20,000 patent search conducted during litigation. Those expensive searches are the only ones that could be described as coming close to being objective. Therefore, realizing that all patent searches performed prior to filing a patent are subjective, the licensee may prefer one from an attorney working directly for the inventor. Having a skillful and knowledgeable professional working on gaining the broadest possible claims increases the value of the potential intellectual property. This relationship between the inventor and his patent attorney may also minimize the necessity for the licensee to hire his own attorney to help evaluate the likely worth of the patent.

Having a skillful and knowledgeable professional working on gaining the broadest possible claims increases the value of the potential intellectual property.

Third, when an invention developer subcontracts work to a patent attorney on behalf of an inventor, who is the patent attorney's client? The one who pays him. A potential licensee is looking for credibility. Anything that causes him to be skeptical makes it more difficult to reach an agreement. An inventor is better off hiring his own patent attorney or agent.

An inventor should never give thousands of dollars of up-front money to an invention development company on a "best-efforts" basis. If they are worth their salt, they should be willing to make their profits from a percentage of the royalties they are able to get for their inventor.

Note: This does not necessarily apply to all business consultants an inventor may need to launch his product. Many reputable patent attorneys, marketing consultants, researchers, investment bankers, etc., require an up-front payment as part of their retainer. Future payments are then made according to a negotiated schedule based on the amount of service performed.

I realize this may be confusing. It seems there are certain things for which up-front fees are customary and some things for which they are not. As a general rule if you plan to *license* your patent by using an intermediary (broker), then he or she should expect to earn the bulk of his or her profits from a percentage of whatever is received by the inventor. However, if you are going to *venture* your project (more about that in Chapter 9), then expect to pay for services rendered as you go. This may involve up-front fees, or maybe a combination of up-front fees to cover the consultant's expenses plus a percentage of the profits.

Regarding the obtaining of references from firms with which you are thinking of doing business, it is interesting that the Inventors' Awareness Group does not recommend relying on better business bureaus (BBBs) to determine legitimacy. Its July 1996 newsletter points out that BBBs are paid membership organizations, and this may influence a local bureau's willingness to report complaints. The story is told of sending one such bureau two to three pounds of complaints received against an invention development company, and how it continued to tell inventors there were no complaints.

This view is also held by Clayton Williamson of Kansas. Clayton has been a distinguished inventor advocate for years. He is cofounder and president of the Kansas Association of Inventors in Great Bend, Kansas. He has helped inventors recover over $700,000 from these so-called invention development companies.

The Patentability Evaluation

Those with new product ideas and who are new to the world of patents often perceive a patent search to be an objective method of determining the patentability of an invention. While the patent search conducted prior to filing a patent might be the most well known, there are many other reasons for a search. There are also a number of different kinds of patent searches. I have performed patent searches for investment bankers as part of due diligence investigations before taking companies public. I have searched the patent databases as an element of preemployment background investigations. And I've also searched the patents in order to establish product uniqueness while preparing to locate potential licensees for an inventor. But I have never conducted a patent search for the purpose of advising an inventor on whether to file a patent. Why? Because it takes a skilled patent professional with years of search and interpretation experience to authoritatively give advice of that nature.

If the only purpose is to verify that a person has a patent, a simple author search in the claims files of the Dialog database is usually all it takes. Anyone knowing how to search Dialog—an information broker, librarian, or marketing professional—can do this kind of patent search. If one is gathering competitive intelligence and trying to verify uniqueness, it requires more expertise and can get so difficult that a patent attorney or agent has to be retained. These usually require esoteric class and subclass searches combined with key words, phrases, and synonyms. So depending on the subject and one's reason for a patent search, the degree of complexity can quickly overtake a novice patent searcher.

Other factors go into a good search. One of the top considerations is budget. Professional patent searchers cannot spend more on the search than they earn and stay in business very long. With over five million patents, each with an estimated average of five claims, one must be able to sort through over 25 million claims. That is just for the United States, not any foreign patents! The cost of wading through all that information is significant. In the midst of infringement cases before the courts, attorneys have stated it is not uncommon to spend $20,000 or more just on the patent search. The quality of patent searches, then, increases with the amount of money one has available. And why not? The old adage, "You get what you pay for," applies to patent searches just as it does to buying a home, furniture, or a car; choosing an attorney or a doctor; or eating out.

(Because we have touched on the subject of infringement, it might be interesting to note that in 1991 the American Intellectual Property Law Association's Committee on Economics of Legal Practice placed the median cost of defending a charge of patent infringement at $503,000 in New York and $400,000 in Los Angeles. Patent "protection" means the patent owner or licensee can litigate against an alleged infringer—if he can fund the costs of the suit or find an attorney willing to take the case on a contingency basis.)

Finally, there is the skill of the searcher. Most of us would find the patent reference tools to be confusing, complex, and frustrating. It's a foreign world. If we find ourselves accused of a crime, would we defend ourselves? If we needed brain surgery, would we operate on ourselves? So it is in patentability searches. I ask these questions because we all know that in these professions there are the good, the bad, and the excellent. But even the worst professional patent searcher is going to be much better than one who has never done it. Also, there are searchers skilled in specific areas like electronics, chemicals, plants, or mechanical devices. An electronics specialist is probably not too good on chemical searches. As in other professions, there are specialists in the specific areas of intellectual property. A patent search performed to determine whether or not to file a patent is subjective. It is an art, not a science. Get the help of a professional.

All this variety leads to the conclusion that patentability evaluations (patent searches and their interpretation) are in no way objective. A patentability evaluation is subjective and depends primarily on the skill of the searcher, the interpretation of the results, and the money that can be spent to conduct a patent search. Patent attorneys are the first to characterize patent searches as extremely subjective. However, good patent attorneys know the good patent searchers and retain them for their searches. They have learned through trial and error. If an attorney files a patent on the basis of a search and the examiner cites critical patents the searcher did not find, chances are that searcher will not be used again. Patent attorneys who make their living practicing patent law generally know what they are doing.

There are those who advise inventors to patent their products themselves, but those who conduct their own searches and file their own patents based on their searches to save a few dollars are treading on dangerous ground. Gaining the maximum possible scope is critical for successful commercialization: the broader the scope, the higher the number of products that may infringe. Patenting is a marketing maneuver. It is designed by the Constitution to provide you with the exclusive rights. In other words, it is designed to limit competition. Without assistance from an attorney or agent authorized by the patent office and experienced in the field, one risks wasting valuable time and money that could be spent on more productive matters such as market research, prototype development, or licensee location. If the inventor really believes he has a winner, he should not try to short-circuit the system regarding intellectual property. It will backfire as soon as the potential licensee or investor asks, "Who did the patent work?" Get the biggest bang for your buck. Hire a professional.

How do you find the best? Ask those in the community who might know. You just have to dig it out. A good place to start might be the Yellow Pages or the chamber of commerce. But most patent attorneys and agents who are publicly practicing are going to be in the Yellow Pages, and just because someone is a member of the Chamber does not mean he is good. The U.S. Patent Office publishes the *Roster of Attorneys and Agents Registered to Practice before the U.S. Patent Office.* The *Annual Martindale-Hubbell Law Directory* also lists patent attorneys. Clark Boardman also publishes a *Directory of Intellectual Property Lawyers and Patent Agents.* From the patent attorneys' own responses, the directory maps out the labyrinth of subspecializations. Check with your library or order it by calling 1-800-221-9428.

Another good source might be with your own local inventors' organization. Because most members of inventors' clubs have received a patent or are working on obtaining one, they are usually familiar with the good attorneys and agents and the not so good, the expensive, and the not so expensive. Another suggestion is to contact the companies in your area that might do a lot of patent work. Ask for their staff patent attorneys or the vice president over intellectual property. They might be willing to refer you to a good attorney.

If an inventors' organization or company of this type cannot be located, contact the closest Patent and Trademark Depository Library (PTDL). There are at least 70 of these libraries across the country. A local reference librarian can find the phone number of the closest one. Ask the depository librarian for a list of local independent inventors to contact for advice in finding a good attorney or agent. If all else fails, call or write the U.S. Patent Office. It might also be able to provide a list of patent authors in a specific area for a small fee.

You can get a free consultation with a patent attorney in your area through the American Intellectual Property Law Association's Inventor Consultation Service. The application form is included in their booklet, *How to Protect and Benefit from Your Ideas.* The cost of the booklet is $9.95. The address is AIPLA, 2001 Jefferson Davis Highway, Suite 203, Arlington, VA 22202.

The Technical Evaluation

Above all else, a technical invention needs technical credibility. Establishing this credibility should be the primary goal of the technical evaluation. Most patented items do not need a technical evaluation; it is usually apparent whether or not a product works. In those cases where there is doubt, a prospective licensee or investor will never get serious unless he can first be assured that the invention performs as represented by the inventor. We have seen various computer chips, pumps, heaters, meters, dryers, solar-powered devices, microwave units, laser-beam modules, soil-moisture detectors, secret chemical formulas, automotive braking systems, recycling machines, and so on.

The best way to get an independent technical evaluation is to hire a consultant or consulting firm that specializes in your invention's industry; contract with a technical school, college, or university; request assistance from a state or federal agency; or have the potential licensee or investor perform the evaluation. All of these ways have been used successfully, but it is better that the prospective licensee or investor make the final evaluation. It may very well be that the invention needs some type of optimization prior to the launch. The more market-ready an invention is, the higher its value.

Should the invention need improving at someone else's suggestion, it could be that he or she will need to be listed as a coauthor if the improvement is incorporated into the intellectual property. If this is not done and the patent is challenged in court someday, it could lose its validity. Check with your patent attorney or agent if you plan to have or have had help in design or prototype development. A confidentiality agreement might also be wise at this point.

So important is it to obtain credibility, it may be well worth giving up a piece of the intellectual property to the evaluator. This, of course, must be considered very carefully, and only if it is impossible to get a competent evaluation by paying a fee or in some other way. It may work out that having evaluated the invention and having a vested financial interest in its success, the evaluator becomes a key player in locating the proper funding source for commercialization.

The best technical evaluation program is probably the Energy-Related Inventions Program (ERIP) implemented by the National Institute of Standards and Technology (NIST) and the U.S. Department of Energy (DOE). NIST performs the technical evaluations while DOE awards grants and provides commercialization assistance. Since 1974, NIST has processed over 32,000 evaluation requests. Of the two-stage evaluation process, about half are accepted in the first stage. Ten percent of those go on to the second stage and more intense evaluation. About 30 percent of these have received recommendations for grants. Each grant averages about $85,000. Whether or not a grant is received, a recommendation for one certainly establishes credibility. Unfortunately, due to recent funding cuts, the average turnaround time from receipt to recommendation or rejection is now 40 weeks. Inventors retain patent rights to their inventions, and these rights are not compromised by the evaluation. Submission does not constitute a public disclosure, so the evaluation can be used to help determine whether or not to file for patent protection. All evaluators are required by federal law to sign a confidentiality agreement and a non-conflict of interest form.

An invention submitted for consideration must consist of any new concept, device, product, material, or industrial process that will, when used, save energy, make more efficient use of energy, or increase energy supplies from nonnuclear sources. When an invention is submitted, both the first and second stages look at three general criteria: technical feasibility, commercial feasibility, and societal benefits. The evaluation is performed by a NIST staff engineer with input from a network of over 400 paid consultants.

In assessing technical feasibility, the NIST staff evaluator examines the technical soundness of the proposed new product or technology. He verifies the basic scientific and technological principles involved and determines whether projected performance is likely to be achieved. He estimates developmental, design, and production requirements and determines whether projected problems or difficulties can be overcome without compromising projected technical performance, economics, or potential benefits. A limited patent search is conducted. In assessing commercial feasibility the evaluator focuses principally on determining whether the proposed

technology has intrinsic characteristics or advantages over competing technologies or products, and that there is a definable market or
market niche. Projected performance, manufacturing difficulty, and
operating costs are the key factors for comparison with existing or
potential competitors.

Determination of the societal benefits are varied. If economic
impact is the issue, benefits will be judged in such areas as job creation, taxable income, and productivity. Considerable attention will
be given also, however, to potential benefits that are of particular
interest to the mission of the Department of Energy.

Should the invention make it to the second stage, a formal report
from one of the technical consultants will be forthcoming. The report
will include the following eight items:

1. A description of the invention and its intended use, high-
   lighting unusual features
2. A review of pertinent technology, with comments
3. A comparison of the invention with the state of the art,
   including description of known alternatives
4. A description of possible applications of the invention
5. A description of the process visualized for preparing the new
   technology for the marketplace, including discussion of
   anticipated difficulties
6. A discussion of the invention's commercial value and probability of success
7. A discussion of the invention's energy-saving potential
8. A recommendation of whether the invention should receive
   program support

Without belaboring the point, each of the above eight subjects requires subjective opinions. Not one can be characterized as objective.
However, one must really do one's homework to authoritatively dis-
agree with these technical experts' independent analyses. I have
found the NIST evaluations to be the most helpful of all evaluations
in the commercialization process. If our elected representatives are
really serious about developing and commercializing America's technology in America, this is one program that should be expanded and
strengthened. For more information, contact the National Institute of
Standards and Technology, Office of Technology Innovation, Building 820 North, Room 264, Gaithersburg, MD 20899, 301-975-5500.

The Marketability Evaluation

The marketability or commercial feasibility evaluation is what most people have in mind when they advise inventors to get an objective evaluation. For a fee of about $150, this evaluation system attempts to look at the 30 to 40 most important characteristics of a new product. It ranks each aspect with a score from 0 to 100. The zero means "it will definitely not be successful," and the 100 means "it will definitely be successful."

Almost all of these evaluation systems are based on Dr. Gerald Udell's Preliminary Innovation Evaluation System (PIES). Having received a grant from the National Science Foundation and developed and tested the system with more than 5,000 evaluations at the University of Oregon beginning in 1974, Dr. Udell is the de facto father of invention evaluations performed on behalf of inventors. "On behalf of inventors" is the operative phrase. Udell would not claim that invention evaluations did not exist prior to 1974. The job was then, as it is today, the primary domain of companies seeking new products to launch.

In a recent review of evaluation systems Udell reported that most provide little or no feedback, are scored by those without appropriate backgrounds, have inadequate follow-up, and bestow inflated evaluation scores. If this is the case, they are meaningless.

In one instance, an inventor received a very high score on his evaluation. In his mind, success was almost a sure thing. In the section that dealt with the existing competitive environment the evaluation said "existing competition appears to be very low." When we took the prototype to a potential sales organization, we also showed the organization's president a copy of the terrific evaluation. He looked at the prototype, then the evaluation, and said, "We're not interested." When I asked why, he explained that there were at least three existing direct competitors and maybe two other indirect competitors (products that are not quite the same, yet accomplish the same purpose). He said if the evaluation missed this point, he had absolutely no confidence in what it had to say about pricing, promotion, potential sales, or any of the other 35 criteria. So here is an example of the evaluation being worse than meaningless—it killed the deal.

The argument might be made that the deal was dead anyway with or without the evaluation. This may be true, but one very popular method companies and investors use to decide whether to license new products or begin new ventures is to try to think of a reason not to do it. Once they see what is in their opinion a "deal killer" aspect to the project, they trash it and go on to the next one. Once they trash it in their mind, it is very difficult to overcome the objection. The poorly done evaluation was all this company president needed to trash the deal.

Having said all that, I believe the PIES evaluation format is a good one. All the most critical aspects of launching an invention are evaluated. It can be helpful in the same way that writing a business plan can be helpful to an entrepreneur. If used correctly with input from those knowledgeable in an invention's own industry, it forces an inventor to think about aspects of his invention that he may have overlooked—not seeing the forest for the trees.

One inventor I worked with brought to the Inventors' Assistance Program an electronic invention for emergency vehicles. Because I have a background in two-way communications equipment, I was able to immediately recognize the potential usefulness of this invention. I was also able to recognize some of the potential problems. Number one on the list of problems was obtaining FCC frequency authorization. While the inventor assured me the device would work even though the prototype had not been developed, I told him it was worthless without FCC authorization. I seemed to remember the FCC must authorize use of all new products and had to test the unit before it could be sold. I also remembered that the FCC might agree in principle to a new concept prior to completion of a final unit. Therefore an innovator could continue to pursue his idea with the understanding that it could be licensed once completed. In my opinion the invention required this type of research before anything else was done, or it might end up being done in vain. I advised contacting an attorney specializing in FCC matters for help.

This inventor had recently been through an intense commercialization workshop, yet none of the faculty of teachers and evaluators had pointed out to him that if the FCC would not license his invention's use, everything else he did on the project was for nothing. Although he received a lot of great advice at the workshop, none had a specific background in radio frequency communications and the FCC, so no one was able to address this watershed issue.

The point is that just because an organization hangs out its shingle as an invention evaluation service, it does not mean it has an evaluation staff that can immediately identify benefits and problems relating directly to your invention's industry. Do not take it for granted that an evaluator or team of evaluators has special knowledge or insight in your field. It would not be out of place to ask for résumés of the evaluators before agreeing to an evaluation.

This might make the difference between spending hundreds of hours and thousands of dollars on frivolous activities or really putting that time and capital to good use. Also keep in mind that even a PIES evaluation is subjective. The best an evaluation can be is independent and knowledgeable, yet it is still subjective when predicting market success. The PIES evaluation may rate your invention highly on safety issues, the environment, investment costs, pricing, competition, etc., but it cannot predict success. Its success likelihood rating (SLR) should, if it is any good at all at forecasting, rank 98 to 99 percent of all the inventions it sees as "definitely will not be successful," because only 1 or 2 percent ever make it to the marketplace.

What is success anyway? To many it is in having one's idea appear at Wal-Mart. Some think it would be in selling $30,000 worth of their product or in making a million dollars. To others success lies in increasing humanity's quality of life. The word *success* is defined in the PIES evaluation as the evaluator's summary judgment of the likelihood that the inventor will be able to successfully market and/or license the invention. But what does that really mean? I can think of many examples of products that have been launched or licensed that have failed to bring any profits to the inventor.

Most inventors who have their idea evaluated with a PIES type of evaluation system seem to look to the evaluation to confirm success. If future success is confirmed, they believe it will be easier to raise capital to build a company around the idea and make a fortune. I wish this perception were true. But it is not, never has been, and never will be. Please do not fall into this mindset.

Most evaluations do little for the actual commercialization process unless they are performed by those who have the power to commercialize. Other kinds of evaluations can actually be detrimental.

Most evaluations do little for the actual commercialization process unless they are performed by those who have the power to commercialize. Other kinds of evaluations can actually be detrimental.

If one understands the strengths, limitations, and motivations of those evaluating the invention, good things come from it. It can help one think through the invention's strengths and weaknesses. It can point to areas where more work needs to be done. It can give you practice in positioning it to those who have not yet seen it. Finally, it can be a helpful marketing tool to determine whether you should proceed, go on to another idea, stick with your job or go find one. Above all, whatever the evaluation's score, do not take it personally. It is just an opinion.

The following are three of the more well-known and reputable organizations offering marketability evaluations. If you have your invention evaluated, it might be wise, if you have the funds, to have two or three done for comparison purposes. You may pick up some insight one of the others missed.

Wisconsin Innovation Service Center
University of Wisconsin, Whitewater
402 McCutchan
Whitewater, WI 53190
414-472-1365

Washington State University
Innovation Assessment Center
2001 Sixth Avenue, Suite 2608
Seattle, WA 98121
206-464-5450

WIN Innovation Center
College of Business Administration
Southwest Missouri State University
901 South National Avenue
Springfield, MO 65804
417-836-5667 or 417-836-5680

The small business administration's Small Business Development Center (SBDC) program is an excellent source for locating other evaluation centers that may be in your area as well as providing assistance with market research and its analysis. With numerous offices in each state, SBDCs usually can be found in the telephone book under U.S. Government—Small Business Administration—Business Development. The SBA's answer desk can also be called for information at 1-800-827-5722.

Most SBDC staff are either themselves experienced in business or have become experienced in dealing with business-related problems through counseling with hundreds of small business owners and beginning entrepreneurs. They can be a tremendous resource for interpreting the PIES evaluation and helping one think through the next step toward commercialization.

Summing Up

One can objectively describe a mountain—the type of foliage, animals, rock formations, and people who live on it. If one begins to surmise how that mountain will be different next year or the year after or how many visitors will see it, he begins to form subjective opinions. One starts thinking of the future. Who would have thought 30 years ago that Mount St. Helens would be so radically changed today?

The same is true with inventions. While an evaluator can objectively look at some aspects of an inventor's prototype, for example, its color, shape, or moving parts, most additional evaluation criteria are subjective. Evaluators can in no way be good indicators of potential success. There are simply too many unknowns that will occur along the commercialization path.

Indeed, the dean of invention evaluations, Gerald Udell, wrote the following in his article, "Invention Evaluation Services: A Review of the State of the Art," published in the *Journal of Product Innovation Management* (Vol. 6, 1989):

> *It is not the function of evaluation to identify ideas or inventions which will become innovations. Rather, the purpose of evaluation is to identify those ideas or inventions with serious technical or commercial flaws. In order to be beneficial, evaluation should occur well before sufficient data are available to prove either technical or commercial success. Thus, projecting success in either case can be extremely unreliable.*

FIVE

Invention Positioning

"If a man can write a better book, preach a better sermon, or make a better mousetrap than his neighbor, though he builds his house in the woods, the world will make a beaten path to his door."

—Attributed to Ralph Waldo Emerson

Whoever coined this sentence must have been smoking something funny. It is not true now, and it wasn't true then. They must not have known the story of Eli Whitney's cotton gin. The market was so ripe for it that some farmers put in a 1792 crop, hoping by harvest time someone would have worked out a way to remove the seeds. He could not have been in a better economic time or place for a path to be made to his door. He invented the gin in 1793, but the only beaten path the world made was to produce over 300 infringing replicants within a year. Court battles ensued over and over. Whitney said he never received more from his patent than he spent in litigation.

Nevertheless, the cotton gin revolutionized the textile industry, and the American economy obtained a vital shot in the arm.

Cyrus McCormick, inventor of the reaper, received his patent on June 21, 1834. He died in 1882, a multimillionaire. He and Emerson died in the same year, 1882. They were contemporaries. In his excellent history, *American Made: Men Who Shaped the American Economy*, Harold Livesay states, "McCormick faced a market made up of thousands of independent farmers. Tough customers in every sense of the term, they refused to buy reapers the way McCormick bought gold mines, sight unseen. They demanded demonstrations, especially ones where manufacturers pitted their products against one another. Success at such competitions demanded the presence of an expert at the reap-off to adjust the machines to local conditions and to make running repairs." Salesmen had to be hired and trained to teach the farmers how to use the reaper. Even the mules and horses had to be retrained for the job. Licensed manufacturers were slow and made too many mistakes. So in order to commercialize his patent, McCormick invented the first sales and service marketing organization of its kind and built his own manufacturing plants. The marketing network was the forerunner of the way we buy cars and large computers today. With his reaper the vast plains of the western frontier were made available for production and made certain a plentiful supply of grains. Did McCormick believe the world had beaten a path to his door? On the contrary, he seems to have beaten a path to the world's door.

Another contemporary during Emerson's time was Thomas Edison. His first invention was a device to be used by legislative bodies to immediately record votes—the automatic vote recorder. Edison undoubtedly thought this was a great idea. It would move the proceedings along much faster, save the government money, and enable more work to be accomplished. Their reaction? "Young man, if there is any invention on earth that we don't want down here, it is this." They did not beat a path to Edison's door, but from that experience Edison resolved never to invent something without an immediate market. This is a lesson that should sink down into the ears of every independent inventor if he is expecting to make money from his idea. (Most state legislatures and Congress today have exonerated Edison's idea by employing modern automatic voting systems.)

The concept of the world beating a path to the door of one who invents a better product is simply ludicrous. It is commonly referred to in marketing circles as the great mousetrap fallacy. How this quote has received so much play, we will never know for sure, but it has been a great disservice to those who accept it. If you do, even a little, here is an assignment: Visit a patent depository library and locate the *Patent Gazette*. Pick ten or 20 inventions on which patents were issued from five to ten years ago that you feel should have become winners. Track down the inventor and ask if the world has beaten a path to his door. Or better, ask if he has made money or lost money on his idea. You will be lucky to find even one who has made more than he spent for his patent.

The point to all this is that the mousetrap quote is wrong, wrong, wrong. As a matter of fact, I do not believe Emerson spoke it or wrote it. Everyone assumes he did. Check any college marketing textbook, and it will give credit to Emerson, then point out how and why it is incorrect. Check any newspaper or magazine article discussing building better mousetraps and Emerson is always given credit for the quote.

If we look more deeply, however, into the available evidence and think deeply about the lack of logic in the statement, it is actually very difficult to conclude Emerson was the culprit behind the quote.

First, let's look at Bartlett's *Familiar Quotations*. Emerson is recognized as writing in his journal the following: "I trust a good deal to common fame, as we all must. If a man has good corn, or wood, or boards, or pigs, to sell, or can make better chairs or knives, crucibles or church organs, than anybody else, you will find a broad hard-beaten road to his house, though it be in the woods," and is dated February 1855. Alas! There is also a footnote. At the bottom of the page the great mousetrap fallacy appears with the explanation: *Attributed to* Emerson (*in a lecture*) by Sarah S.B. Yule and Mary S. Keene, *Borrowings* [1889].

Notice the journal entry contains nothing about a sermon, book, or a mousetrap. In comparing the above text of 57 words with the mousetrap fallacy, Yule and Keene were successful in matching only ten words! Apparently some 34 years after Emerson penned the "common fame" pericope in his journal and seven years after his death, two women on the lecture circuit tried to quote him and actually paraphrased him very badly.

It gets worse. Emerson was a pretty sharp man. Why would anyone living in the mid-1800s beat a path to the home of an author who wrote a better book or a minister who preached a better sermon? Did those writers have printing presses in their homes? Did preachers preach from their porches? It seems much more likely that books were sold at stores and sermons delivered from church pulpits—not homes.

The thought never crossed Emerson's mind of the world beating a path to the door of an inventor who developed a better product.

What he did write about was how a person in a home-based business with higher quality products than anybody else also had a hard-beaten road to his house, which was created from the traffic of those customers who heard about those high-quality products through the grapevine (common fame). It is true today, just as it was then: Word-of-mouth advertising is the best advertising—especially for a home-based business.

The next time you see it in print or hear the great mousetrap fallacy spoken, please do your best to clear Emerson's besmirched name. A hundred years is too long for anyone to be misquoted.

Myths run strong in the hearts of Americans. I will never forget the time I was in New England for a sales training school. On the weekend I visited Lexington and Concord where the Revolutionary War began. Having memorized *The Midnight Ride of Paul Revere* in high school, I was shocked to read the story on a historical marker just outside of Lexington. It seems that Revere barely made it out of town with several of his friends when the Redcoats stopped them. His friends escaped through the woods but Revere, just an average horseman, was captured and sent back to Lexington. I couldn't believe it. I wondered how many other things I had been taught were not true. It felt like the time I learned the truth about Santa Claus.

The myth of Emerson writing about building a better mousetrap and having the world beat a path to its inventor's door should be exposed just like the myths of Paul Revere's ride and Santa. Only then will inventors begin to understand how difficult it is to market anything—much less a new invention.

If an invention is to be moved toward commercialization, it has to be marketed correctly. Its features have to be described and its benefits communicated in an appropriate manner to those who can help make it happen. In other words, positioning has to occur.

If an invention is to be moved toward commercialization, it has to be marketed correctly. Its features have to be described and its benefits communicated in an appropriate manner to those who can help make it happen. In other words, positioning has to occur.

If the patent is pending, there should be little reluctance to position the idea to anyone who has a need to know about it. It is up to the patent attorney or agent to duke it out with the patent office, and whatever protection is received will be governed by patent law.

While I am thinking about it, another commonly held misconception is that you have to wait until a patent is granted before it can be commercialized. Nothing could be farther from the truth. That is why so many products we purchase have the words "patent pending" printed on them. While it is not required to put "patent pending" on an item, it is advisable. It makes potential competitors think twice about duplicating the product or maybe even competing indirectly, because they will not know precisely what claims will be granted. Once the patent is granted they may find themselves infringing on one or more claims. All it takes is to exactly replicate even one claim in its entirety.

Also be sure the patent has actually been filed with the patent office before putting "patent pending" on the item. It is a federal misdemeanor to assert patent-pending status when it has not actually been filed.

I remember working on a computer chip project several years ago. The owners were trying to raise a significant amount of money to commercialize it. One of the points of their prospectus was in how the patent on the chip was pending. To their way of thinking, patent-pending status was in getting it ready to file only after the money was raised. Fortunately, no money was ever raised. This false statement could have been grounds for significant litigation.

In addition to being a marketing strategy, patent-pending status also can be considered a trade secret if appropriate care is taken to keep it secret. When one first presents his product concept to an investor or potential licensee there is no real need to disclose all the paperwork on the filing. Proof of filing is sufficient. This can be done with the receipt from the patent office. If he asks for more information, give him the patent filing, less the claims and the patent-pending number. An investor, licensee, or future partner should generally only be interested in the claims sometime just prior to closing on the deal or while visiting with your attorney about the scope of the patent. It should never be necessary to reveal your patent-pending number to anyone without your attorney's approval. For more advice about what you can and cannot do to protect your intellectual property during the patent-pending stage, consult your attorney.

What is positioning? Positioning is a form of communication. It is not what is done to the product, it is what is done to the mind of the listener. It is positioning the product in the mind of the prospective investor, licensee, product champion, or joint venture partner. It is communicating what you want the listener to think about your idea or product. This might sound somewhat manipulative at first, but it is only good, practical selling. What someone thinks about your invention from the outset is critical. Large Fortune 100 companies spend hundreds of thousands of dollars each year training their marketing and sales personnel, and this is the very foundation of their education. If someone cannot "get his mind around" your invention quickly and easily, he will quickly and easily lose interest. He says to himself, "If it's this tough for me to understand, no one else will either."

In the early stages of the Inventors' Assistance Program we needed to see what kind of inventions we had in the state. We interviewed hundreds of inventors concerning their inventions and ideas during the first year. A common description went something like this: "I am the inventor of the greatest pump in the world. My pump does what no other pump will do. I got a patent on it in 1982. It has 24 claims. Every company needs one, and if I just get five percent of the market, everyone in it with me will get rich. I have already spent tens of thousands of dollars on it, then I ran out of money. But I know that if I had another $20,000, I would make it—big."

That is not the way to position an invention. There is no substance to what has been said. If that is the way he presents his invention to a funding source or prospective licensee, what might be going on in the prospect's mind while the inventor is rambling? Let's see.

Inventor: I am the inventor of the greatest pump in the world.
Listener: Good grief, another pompous inventor.
Inventor: My pump does what no other pump will do.
Listener: If that's true, it might have a niche. Prove it.
Inventor: I got a patent on it in 1982.
Listener: Big deal. You and five million others. Hmm . . . 17 minus 10. There's only seven more years on this one. If this is so great, why hasn't it gotten done in ten years?
Inventor: It has 24 claims.
Listener: So what? How broad is the coverage? If it is as broad as I would like, surely in ten years there's an infringer somewhere. What would a good patent attorney say? Am I going to have to pay an attorney to review it?
Inventor: Every company needs one, and if I just get 5 percent of the market, everyone in it with me will get rich.

Listener: I am already rich! Why do I need to put up with this amateur telling me every company needs one? That can't be true. My companies do not need one and never will. This guy doesn't even begin to realize how difficult it is to get a five percent market share of anything, much less a crowded pump market. It is a great goal to shoot for, but how will a 5 percent share be achieved?

Inventor: I have already spent tens of thousands of dollars on it, then I ran out of money.

Listener: What did he spend it on? A new car? Does he have other investors who will muddy the waters?

Inventor: But I know that if I had another $20,000, it would make it big.

Listener: I'm not giving this guy diddly. He'd just blow it. No business background.

If positioning is implanting into the mind of the listener precisely what one wants him to think about the invention, this inventor really messed up. He has disregarded his listener's needs in favor of presenting his own need to launch his product. With a "rah-rah" sales pitch he has completely turned off one who might have helped him commercialize his product. I can just imagine the body language of the listener. His arms are folded across his chest, his legs are crossed, he is leaning back in his chair, and his eyes are somewhat glazed.

What is the best way to get the attention of those who could help? First we have to make sure they would really like to commercialize a product. Just being financially able does not guarantee that.

What is the best way to get the attention of those who could help? First we have to make sure they would really like to commercialize a product. Just being financially able does not guarantee that. This seems almost too simple to mention, yet it is critical. We saw people with money almost every day through our work at the Department of Commerce. Many have made it from oil or cattle. Guess what deals these folks want to see? That's right, oil or cattle deals. Those are the kinds of investment opportunities they know best. They understand the risks and the potential payoffs. Others have made their money through advertising, real estate, new cars, or publishing. Only the most stout-hearted of these can ever be expected to take on a totally different product. Diversifying into virgin territory is just not the normal thing to do. It is not normal, but it is possible. When these folks are approached it has to be with the utmost sensitivity to their needs and comfort levels.

The best potential source is one who has experience making money in the industry into which the invention fits.

Second, the best potential source is one who has experience making money in the industry into which the invention fits. The president of a manufacturing company or marketing firm or someone who has already licensed or brokered a similar product are excellent candidates. But even having experience does not guarantee interest. Two years ago, we surveyed almost 4,000 manufacturers in Oklahoma and found only 500 who were looking for new products to make. That's only 12.5 percent! We were incredulous. How could a company not want to grow? When we looked into it, we found that the 87.5 percent of those not interested in new products had good reasons, albeit possibly invalid ones. Some did not want to grow their businesses because they did not want to increase the degree of difficulty in running them. They were already making a good living. Some did not want to expand into new markets because they were too busy expanding into the ones they already had begun to develop. With some the timing was not right; a key employee had departed or they had cash flow problems. Some did not think a state agency could possibly help them find new products.

So there can be many varied reasons why people are not willing to get into the new product business. Only after making sure of a source's financial ability, experience, and interest should he or she be approached with the possibility of launching a new product.

We once found a company we thought was perfect. The president was definitely interested in new products, had experience, and had the capital through his parent company to pull it off. We licensed our most promising invention to him. Within four weeks, his business shut down and he moved away. What happened? We still do not know the whole story, but we later discovered he had lost a major contract. He had neglected to tell us he was having this kind of trouble, and in spite of our having done thorough due diligence, there was no way we could have known. *Due diligence* is a term borrowed from securities law. Whenever an investment bank is about to take a firm public, it must perform with an effort of due diligence to make sure that what the company is saying about itself is true. Perform your due diligence and keep a wary eye open for those hurting in some imperceptible way. They may be thinking a new product will get them out of a bind.

Returning to the subject of positioning, after you have qualified a prospective investor, licensee, or business partner and have assurance no one's time will be wasted, a presentation is in order. Whether an inventor presents it himself or is represented by someone else, the inventor himself must get his mind around what it is about his invention that will make it sell. It is not the fact that it is different from anything else in its 24 or 124 claims. It is not in the fact that "everyone needs one." Why will people buy it? This is what an investor or licensee is initially asking. The best way to begin is with a feature and benefit analysis. We have often used this method in our work commercializing new products with great success. Try one first on the claims of your patent. Then add to it by analyzing your prototype. A feature is the structure, form, or appearance of the product. A benefit is an advantage or its usefulness. Features may or may not have a benefit, but we are trying to identify all the benefits we can by first identifying the features.

Begin by drawing a line down the center of a piece of paper, dividing it into two columns. On the left column, write the word *features;* on the right column, write *benefits.*

Let's use for an example the abstract and other text from the patent of William Gray. His invention is the Single Track Roller Skate. Mr. Gray's patent number is 4,418,929 and was granted December 6, 1983. It states in patentese:

> *A roller skate comprising a platform formed from two aligned plate segments extending downwardly and aligned together to form a channel in an undercarriage support member; the said undercarriage support member having two slots for mounting a pair of roller wheels, front parts of the said platform having attached thereto a sliding adjustable plate, the said adjustable plate having attached thereto a first foot strap useful as a front foot support stabilizer; an adjustable rear bracket mounted on the rear of the said platform having a base and an upper section and a second*

*foot strap on the said rear bracket useful for attaining ankle support
structure, a pair of pivot bolts for attaching a leg support device for
aiding in the support of the ankle; a pair of bumper stopping cush-
ions located singularly on a bracket on each end of the said undercarriage for fast stopping.*

Whew! Glad we're not sending that to a funding source.

The main object of this invention is to provide the public with a
set of single track roller skates that will let the skater maneuver more
freely and stop quickly and more easily by using adjustable back
braking.

Another object of this invention is to disclose an improved ankle
support attached to the skate, which is positioned and anchored to a
heel support bracket behind the pivot point of the rear roller wheel
so as to give better balance and control to the skater.

Another object of this invention is to mount the roller wheels in
an undercarriage for rigid strength in all directions and to better balance the skater for skate maneuvering on the skating surface.

Still another object of this invention is to provide stopping means
on the undercarriage of the skate to prevent the skater from falling
backward.

Features	*Benefits*
Single track roller skate	Maneuvers more freely
Adjustable back braking	Prevents skater from falling backward
Improved ankle support	Allows for more balance, control, and safety to the skater
Roller wheels mounted in an undercarriage	Better balance to skater; stronger skate; more maneuverability
Foot strap	Provides ankle support
Rear bracket	Attains ankle support structure
Pivot bolts	Allows attachment of a leg
Pair of bumper stopping cushions	Enables fast stopping

If we add to this list by observing the prototype, we might find
some additional features and benefits as to its color or shape. But just
with what we have identified above, we now have a way to quickly
and easily explain the invention. It is a skate that allows the skater to
maneuver freely while providing improved ankle support. It is also
safer, because it allows for enhanced balance and control, and faster
stopping.

The next step is to conduct a feature/benefit analysis on the competition—meaning all the other skates on the market and/or patented skates not on the market. From these exercises you will be able to learn the invention's strengths and weaknesses compared to what is already selling and what might be sold in the future. This is precisely what will be uppermost in an investor's or licensee's mind. Although this might admittedly be a tough assignment, there is nothing better that can prepare you for a meeting with a key player in your commercialization efforts.

Once you have listed the significant features of your invention and how they translate into benefits, one more thing remains to be done—gather testimonials.

Once you have listed the significant features of your invention and how they translate into benefits, one more thing remains to be done—gather testimonials. This technique goes back 200 years, yet is as applicable today as it was then. The world might not have experienced the cotton gin had it not been for testimonials from independent parties. While Whitney was working through the patent process in existence in 1793, the secretary of state, Thomas Jefferson, wanted a cotton gin for his plantation at Monticello.

Whitney wrote to his father, "A number of the first men in America [say] that my machine is the most perfect & most valuable invention that has ever appeared in this country." Those testimonials opened many doors for Whitney, and testimonial letters and surveys can open a lot of doors for inventors and their inventions today. Without them the project is virtually doomed. These written testimonies should come from potential customers and industry experts. If a survey is used, a form in Appendix B might help gather comments from the targeted group. Ten to 20 should do it. Their purpose is to give credibility to the product.

When we are in the process of deciding which projects to work on, testimonials get our attention. We allow the market to speak. When a couple of professional painters brought us their ladder accessory invention to make it easier for painters to paint, their background spoke highly of the invention's potential worth. It generated a stream of interest. When we saw the testimonials from hardware store managers, reporting how the inventor-made units sold, the stream turned into a river. The same can be said of one of our hospital products. Nurses who were representative of the rest of the market provided us with positive opinions. We therefore saw the potential market and went to work on licensing it.

There are inventions that do not pass this test. Testimonials can be negative or point out specific flaws or competitive factors not previously considered. We first discovered the value of this process with a bicycle cover. The inventor had a design patent and a prototype. He assured us that no competition existed, and, furthermore, it could be made inexpensively enough that every bicycle owner would want one. He had done no research prior to, during, or after expending funds for patenting and prototyping. He said he did not know how to do it. We went to the computer and quickly located one of the largest bicycle and bicycle accessory distributors in the nation. My colleague Pam Speraw called them up and talked with one of the salespeople. He informed her that there were many bicycle covers on the market and that he bought primarily from four different sources. He gave us pricing, information on the different materials, and offered to send us samples. Knowing our inventor's cost of manufacturing, we realized he was fighting an uphill battle. After spending about $50 on computer research and $15 on a phone call, we knew this was not going to make it. It is too bad the inventor did not do this before spending $4,000 on his patent and prototypes. Making the collection of testimonials a high priority early in the development process has indisputable advantages.

SIX

Inventor Positioning

"The vitality of thought is in adventure. Ideas won't keep. Something must be done about them. When the idea is new, its custodians have fervor, live for it, and, if need be, die for it."
—Alfred North Whitehead

If you saw the movie *Gremlins*, you observed the typical stereotype of an inventor. The inventor and father of the hero had his workshop where all kinds of gadgets were developed. The scriptwriters had him inventing the Bathroom Buddy, a multifunctioned travel accessory that had a toothbrush and toothpaste built into the unit. It was an obvious Rube Goldberg device. It was overengineered and did not work; nevertheless, the inventor was hopeful that the day would come when he would sell millions, oblivious to the fact that it was not perfected and the only market was in his own mind. Throughout the movie were scenes of his other inventions, beta tested by his family, and they never worked either.

Like it or not, this is the image most people have of inventors. I know a plastics manufacturer who has seen quite a few inventors over the years. Most have wanted him to invest in their deal. He told me that now when he sees someone walking up to his door who looks like an inventor, he heads out the back way! Da Vinci, Edison, Einstein, Marconi, Whitney, Land, and all the great inventors who have done so many wonderful things for this world cannot seem to overcome the stereotype.

So why fight it? Read a good biography of Thomas Edison. Then ask yourself, "Am I really like Edison?" If not, maybe it would be wise not to consider yourself an inventor, even if you have a patent. After all, one should expect a real inventor to earn a living from inventing. If you do not receive royalty checks or income from your invention, why refer to yourself as an inventor? It buys nothing. You are just one of over five million people listed as the author of a United States utility patent.

Ideas are not born in a vacuum. Most good independent inventions come from ordinary working people solving problems in their daily routines. So tell it like it is. You are a commercial painter with a better idea for painters. You also just happen to have a patent on the idea. Nothing can be stronger than that. This gives your product instant credibility because as a professional painter you are familiar with items that are available to professional painters.

Avoid pulling rank. Whatever you do, don't tell anyone outside your church that God gave you the idea for the invention. As an ordained minister, I can assure you that God is in control of and shapes everything in the universe, including your invention. Most people, and most Christians, simply do not believe that God speaks to us today in the same manner in which He spoke to Adam, Abraham, or Moses. Saying or implying that He blessed you with special revelation implies that you have a special relationship with the Almighty that others do not. This leads to instantaneous credibility loss. A prospective funding source or licensee may tell you that if God really speaks to you, He also should be willing to hand you the money to launch your product.

Avoid pulling rank. Whatever you do, don't tell anyone outside your church that God gave you the idea for the invention.

At the commerce department, we saw more than a few "inventions from God." Only one to my knowledge ever made any money for the inventor. In this case, a doctor and my former boss, Don

Byers, raised over $1.5 million in a public offering to market a new treatment for psoriasis. While God was given His due credit in the business plan the offering document did not claim the invention was from God.

Those investing had the doctor's excellent credentials and test results to guide them in their decision-making process. The authorship of another invention from God is actually being disputed by an engineering professor who says he gave the invention to his student, who has always claimed God gave him the idea in a vision. But if anyone knows of a successful invention from God, please write to me. I would be very interested in this case study both from a professional and theological perspective.

Then there were some letters from folks who seemed to be playing with less than a full deck. One such letter began, "As we know, this is the day in time for our mechanical engineers, inventors, etc., to leave the third dimension in time and space, leap into the fourth dimension with science and physics all the way. Yes, so with Taoism, to hold on to the fourth dimension."

Another inventor wrote the following in a letter describing his idea:

> *Without being intimate of invention, the accompanying single-sheet excerption from our half-finished business plan is as explicit in defining the conceptualized status quo as we care to submit just now. Patentability is in how the buildings deal with atmospherics and mycological materials; structure is coincidental; the need is statistical; aesthetics are deliberate—trademark is practically assured. A coordinate goal of the pristine stages is to capture as much data as possible on magnetic film by a professional type can-corder [sic], to be used in training and promotional documentaries for advancing enviableness of our buildings toward worldwide predominance in domiciliary.*

These examples are given not to make fun, but to drive home the point that inventors and entrepreneurs must be very careful about what they say and write. While long sentences and unusual wording are meant to impress, they easily can have the opposite effect. There are other things that cause immediate red flags to go up in the minds of investors, licensees, bankers, and economic developers. The following are examples of possible "deal-killer statements." Because they are heard so often, they tend to turn off the very people who might be in a position to help.

"There is no competition." There is always competition. If an invention solves a problem, it is likely that people are already solving it in some way. Maybe they are not using the ideal solution, but it nevertheless represents competition. There are two kinds of competition: direct and indirect. Direct competition occurs when two products are offered that do the same thing in about the same way. All the various dishwashers, clothes dryers, and televisions compete directly with one another. Each also has indirect competition. People still wash dishes in their sinks. Clothes are still dried on clothes lines. And television has radio, books, movie theaters, zoos, operas, etc., that draw away viewers.

Even toilet paper had a problem with indirect competition. It took over 20 years to be accepted, because people did not want to pay for plain paper when they already had newspapers and catalogs that also doubled as reading material. Indirect competition, then, is anything that draws money away from your invention.

"If we just get five percent of the market, we'll all be rich." Getting a measurable share of any market is tough work. There has to be a plan to get it. This statement, without thinking through how to get that 5 percent share, is impotent to those immune to emotional zeal.

"My invention will generate hundreds of jobs. Don't you want to help the state's economy?" Economic developers make it their business to help their state's economy. That's what they live for. By bringing that into question, you suggest that people who do not like your invention really do not want what is best for their state. There is no faster way to demonstrate to an economic developer you are a real fruitcake.

"I am a good friend of the governor." So what? The governor cannot make the market fall in love with your product. If he can, maybe you should talk to him about licensing your invention.

"Texas will do my deal. I just thought I'd give Oklahoma a crack at it." Then go see them. I'd like for Texas to get a few deals, too. I have friends and relatives down there you might be able to put to work. But I need to work with those who need help and want to stay here.

Another thing to keep in mind is that investors and licensees don't have to do business with the inventor. To them, a single project is not a life-or-death situation. They are not worrying about putting beans on the table. They see deals all the time. I have worked with far too many inventors who think that because of the "greatness" of their invention, companies would be compelled to do business with them. One was so pretentious he thought one of three major battery companies should not only give him a huge running royalty and up-front money, but also market the item precisely in the manner he dictated. Knowing this project would be wasted effort due to the inventor's attitude, none of the staff would work on his project. There is no place for arrogance in the commercialization process. If the people involved in that process do not like the inventor, his chances of success are virtually nonexistent.

An *Inc.* magazine article about dealing with banks drives this point home. The banker interviewed said, "If they were unpleasant, abrupt, or just downright nasty, I was predisposed not to like them. If you're known to be 'difficult,' you're going to be dumped on the meanest SOB in the bank or someone too green to know better if your loan officer leaves."

In July 1991 I was trying to follow up on an electronic invention I had given to a prospective licensee. I thought it was a perfect match because the licensee had years of experience in the business. He had been the president of a large electronics firm, had launched several new products on his own, had contacts galore, and was looking for more new products. The invention was an improvement over the competition and would be priced significantly lower. I had presented the idea in February over breakfast. It looked like a sure deal. As time went by I knew he was busy, so I did not press him. In June I began trying to reestablish contact for a go or no-go decision. By July when he had not returned my calls, I mentioned it to my partner, Pam Speraw. I was mystified and concerned that he would not get in touch with me. She said, "He didn't like you. His wife told me." What a blow to my ego! How could someone not like me? I liked him. I thought he was a really sharp guy. Then I thought of several others who did not particularly care for me either. Then I thought of the people that do like me as a friend and business associate. Pam said, "Forget it, Tom. You can't please everybody all the time." So my advice to an inventor is essentially the same. Try to be liked personally, if for no other reason than because it will help get your deal done. But if the chemistry is not there, forget it. Do not let it dash your enthusiasm. Keep pursuing your project, but in another direction. Business runs on the strength of relationships to a far greater degree than many would like to admit.

Try to be liked personally, if for no other reason than because it will help get your deal done. But if the chemistry is not there, forget it. Do not let it dash your enthusiasm. Keep pursuing your project, but in another direction.

One successful strategy in positioning yourself is to get out of the way—find someone else to be your product champion in your commercialization efforts. In general, companies do not like to talk to or negotiate with inventors. Also, because your product champion is not the inventor, he is not immediately dismissed as "just another inventor." The potential for emotionalism is taken away, and in the funding source's mind the idea already has at least one independent party who recognizes its potential value.

I hope this strategy is not dismissed out of hand, because we have seen it work over and over. Before a product can have any hope of commercialization, it has to be seen by those who have the financial resources to make it happen. A licensee or investor is much more likely to take a serious look at an invention if it is presented to him by someone he knows or trusts. An attorney, accountant, insurance agent, salesperson, government employee, or someone other than yourself will stand a much better chance of getting a hearing if the inventor stays out of the picture until asked to be introduced by the funding source.

You might think that no one else can explain your product like you can. Well, that may be true, but be patient. If a funding source invites the inventor into the discussions, be assured that he is very interested in doing something. It may not be exactly what the inventor has in mind, but it's something. An inventor should not have any expectations as to what the deal might look like before it gets done. It may only lead to disappointment when it does not happen as expected.

Many curves have been known to be thrown in the process of making deals. I met one of my clients for the first time while she was on her way to close a deal for a couple hundred thousand dollars in start-up funding. An attorney had verbally explained to her the terms of the deal. These were acceptable, so she came from out of town to close the deal. The attorney and the oilman investor were there. It seems the terms in the written agreement were not even close to those discussed over the phone.

Nevertheless, they put a hard close on her. This was not a good way to start a business relationship. So my client, who had just gone through 24 hours of euphoria at the prospect of closing the deal, went through a week of depression when it did not happen. Try not to get your hopes up too high before the deal is done. Remember Yogi Berra's eloquent saying? "It ain't over til it's over."

On the other hand, the "No one can explain it as well as I can!" assumption may be totally false. Salespersons are an oft-maligned group, but if one is around he might come in pretty handy. Those with sales backgrounds are trained to explain features and sell benefits.

Finally, let's discuss the emotional and psychological attachment an inventor can have for an invention. To compare it to drug dependence or a religious quest would oversimplify it, but I think it is somewhere in the middle. The events that can lead to fanatical invention zeal are totally understandable, yet devastating in their cumulative effect on the project. Even if one perfectly positions his invention to just the right individual and has 25 glorious testimonials, he can mess it all up by allowing invention animism to rule.

Invention animism is a confusion by the inventor that his invention is himself. Any criticism of the product is, therefore, a personal attack on his very being. I guess if I had thought of an idea, struggled for years to perfect it, spent my life savings to develop and protect it, seen it change from the crude to the exquisite, dreamed about it, prayed over it, sacrificed friends and family for it, and owed money because of it, only to have someone unthinkingly pooh-pooh it, I might tend to be upset, too. Wait! That *has* happened to me. It wasn't a product though. It was a business. Come to think of it, that has happened to all of us in one way or another. If it hasn't, it is only because we have not lived long enough. Remember: The inventor is not the invention. The invention is not the inventor.

The inventor must learn to guard against invention animism. He has to learn that he is of far greater significance than his idea—no matter how much has gone into it. A creative inventor can always come up with another idea, but an idea cannot create an inventor. A fanatic has been defined as someone who redoubles his efforts after losing sight of his goals. My advice is to set your goals and concentrate on achieving them. Recognize that because people are different, they will have different opinions. Evaluate the criticism from the proper perspective. If there is something to learn, learn from it. If not, forget it. The key is to view the commercialization process as just business and not personal.

Recognize that because people are different, they will have different opinions. Evaluate the criticism from the proper perspective. If there is something to learn, learn from it. If not, forget it. The key is to view the commercialization process as just business and not personal.

SEVEN

Networking

"Mr. Watson, come here, I want you."

—Alexander Graham Bell

With those words a network was born. Today, the world communicates through a physically structured network of telephone and computer cables. Satellite dishes dot our lawns and office buildings. With networks we watch the news, attend a college class conducted hundreds of miles away, or just check on how the family is doing.

We use other kinds of networks with regularity. One of the most famous has always been the "good ol' boy" network. Chambers of commerce have a "business after hours" network where members get together and exchange business cards. Salespeople meet once a month to share leads with one another. The list is endless.

After learning how to position himself and his invention, an inventor should also begin to network. He should network with as many different persons and organizations as may have a direct bearing on the success of new products. As a matter of fact, the ability to successfully launch the product depends directly on the strength of that network!

The same organizations that move products for other companies can also provide solutions to the problems encountered during various stages of development and commercialization. Engineering organizations; marketing or sales associations; trade groups; manufacturing associations; economic development agencies at the local, state, and federal levels; and business incubator groups are all good organizations with which to get acquainted.

Network with as many people as possible who can add value to your project. For example, an inventor visits a manufacturer for the purpose of licensing his patent-pending tool. The manufacturer quickly sees that it is not synergistic with his equipment or market. He refers the inventor to the local Small Business Development Center office. The staff determines that a better prototype is necessary before presenting it to a potential licensee. The staff refers the inventor to a vocational or technical facility or college to determine whether building the prototype would make a good teaching project. If not, the staff locates several private-sector engineering companies that can make it. Once the prototype is complete and other marketing questions are satisfactorily answered, the tool is presented to another manufacturer that is better suited for licensing. The manufacturer decides that while he can easily produce the product, he is willing to do so only if a marketing firm can be located to properly launch and continue to sell the tool. The staff then locates a synergistic marketing organization and helps structure the deal.

While this is an elementary example, it illustrates the importance of cultivating a new product network consisting of those with varied backgrounds and fields of expertise. An inventor cannot do it all. To the degree that the inventor is successful in expanding his network, a successful new product launch will be more forthcoming.

An inventor cannot do it all. To the degree that the inventor is successful in expanding his network, a successful new product launch will be more forthcoming.

There is no better place to network these days than on the Internet and the World Wide Web. Internet subscription rates can run as little as $15 per month for unlimited access.

Many experts believe the Internet is just experiencing its initial justification. It is no longer doubted to be the wave of the future. With over 1,000 new subscribers every day, it is quickly becoming the most convenient and exhaustive networking tool in the world's history.

Let's say you would like to do a patent search. From the comfort of your home, just call up the U.S. Patent and Trademark Office's home page at: www.uspto.gov. From there, you can search for patents using key words, author name, assignee, patent number, patent attorney, or class and subclass. There are other ways to search, but these are the ones most commonly used. Although drawings and claims of the patent cannot be viewed at this time, the front page material and abstracts are there, and can be downloaded into your computer and printed.

Although a professional search is still recommended prior to submitting your patent application, you may be able to find enough information online to preclude further involvement in the original idea, freeing up time and resources to proceed with the next idea.

Should you have a question, subscribe to a newsgroup. There are currently over 16,000 UseNet Newsgroups, one for just about any topic you could consider. In the newsgroups, you can freely exchange any questions you may have, simply by posting a note in the particular newsgroup you wish to query. Your e-mail box will have replies in a day or two from people who may be able to help you. The Web is a compassionate place as well.

E-mail is an incredible resource. You are able to instantaneously generate a piece of mail through the Internet with real-time convenience, with no postage costs beyond your monthly fees! Most Internet service providers give you several megs of storage for your e-mail, and today's notebook computers and chip modems allow you to collect and send your e-mail messages virtually anywhere, even over hand-held cellular phones, or from the comfort of your motel or hotel room. On a recent flight I even witnessed an executive retrieving his e-mail from the telephone handset that is available on most domestic flights on the seat located in front of your own.

Perhaps one of the greatest advantages of the Internet is in data or information retrieval. Through a process known as "search engines" one can easily search entire libraries of files, downloading them as needed, just by entering a key word or search phrase into the search engine. You can use advanced key words or Boolean phrases to expedite your search. Each search engine will rank or score the number of matches it finds for your key word or phrase, and then go on to list in groups of ten or 20 of the most percentage points by "hyperlinks." Hyperlinks are always <u>underlined</u> in another color;

clicking your mouse on them quickly takes you to that article or home page.

Let's say for example that you needed to search for patent attorneys. You would go to a search engine such as Lycos or Alta Vista and type in the phrase. In a matter of seconds, you would receive a list of probably 20 pages with 20 attorney firms on each page, ranked according to relevance. The first nine pages may all be patent attorneys and the next 11 pages may simply be attorneys, because the search engine is programmed to search first for *patent attorneys* then *attorneys,* and then finally *patent.* It could well be that the last two pages could be all related to patents; the amazing thing is that each search engine is different, and the search criteria change daily.

Marketing on the Internet is indeed the wave of the future. Once connected, call up the Web site of the New Products Coalition at http://www.onpc.com. From this starting point and by using the links, you will begin to find every major information source on the Net that is of help to inventors. If you are not connected, ask a friend who is connected to give you a sample tour. Commercial online services such as America Online and CompuServe should be explored as well. CompuServe has an excellent Ideas and Inventions Forum hosted by Barbara Burnes that has as its only function an open forum dedicated to the inventive process; it serves the inventive community quite well. If you are connected to CompuServe, and haven't found the forum, simply hit "Go Ideas," and join in one of the many discussion groups or have a private chat with an expert in your field. America Online is perhaps the most easy way in cyberspace to access the newsgroups and subscribe to them.

If and when you decide to go online, feel free to e-mail me at tekscout@onpc.com.

EIGHT

Characteristics of a Successful New Product

"The man who deals in ideas that are ahead of his time is destined for oblivion, not success. Success most often goes to those who perfect innovations that are long overdue."
—**Harold C. Livesay**

Thousands of inventor inquiries were received during my five years at the Inventors' Assistance Program. With each inquiry we sent out a packet of information about the program. Within the packet was a form for the inventor to use to describe his idea or invention and its stage of development. After the form was returned to us a letter or a phone call was sometimes enough to help the inventor get through the next stage of development. If an interview was necessary, we would invite the inventor to our office or offer to meet with him the next time we were in his area. Of the total inquiries, we personally advised over 60 percent. Once we understood the idea concept, the question most often asked was, "Well, what do you think?"

Our opinion was being sought on its chances of success. This was certainly to be expected. Our answer, however, was usually unexpected. We generally did not know what to think. The marketplace was the only opinion that ultimately mattered. Our job was to advise the inventor in such a way that he readied his idea for input from the market. We acted as a kind of dating service for new products. We did everything we could to get them evaluated and commercialized by the marketplace, but we could not cause the market to fall in love with the product.

The definition of success varies from individual to individual. Therefore it is impossible to suitably define what success is to every inventor, much less predict it. Few new product ideas are ever launched or licensed. The others are for various reasons killed along the way. My working definition of success, therefore, is either having a licensing agreement in place or launching the new product with sustaining power. At the time of launch or licensing, the product has a reasonable chance to earn more money for the inventor than he has spent. The degree of success then depends upon many characteristics and factors working together in concert. Most of the reasons for success have nothing to do with the nature of the product, but everything to do with the vigor with which the product is marketed.

Preliminary Screening

I think it would be helpful to describe the screening process used by the Inventors' Assistance Program and now the New Products Coalition prior to presenting an invention to a potential licensee or joint venture partner. We sometimes refer to these potential funding sources as strategic alliance partners. The screening process is performed for one major reason: Because there are a finite number of potential strategic alliance partners, we have to make sure their time is not wasted. If we send them just anything, at any stage, they will eventually not wish to see any new ideas. If that were to happen there would be no reason to consult with inventors, because we would have no place to go for commercialization.

Does It Really Work?

There are various ways a reasonable person can be assured that a product or process does what is intended. Because most technologies are not "advanced technologies," the answer is usually obvious.

However, some determinations are very difficult, especially when the device claims a significant mechanical, chemical, or electronic improvement and does not have a working prototype. We have seen new pump designs, chemical formulas, and computer enhancements that could revolutionize their respective industries if actual performance met the innovator's expectations.

When the answer to the question "Does it really work?" is not clear from ideas drawn on napkins or even computer-assisted design (CAD) drawings, making sense of the project and obtaining necessary independent technical evaluations become a real challenge. This is made easier through technical evaluations graciously conducted by the University of Oklahoma, Oklahoma State University, and the numerous vocational and technical schools throughout the state, as well as private sector engineering firms and NIST's Energy-Related Inventions Program.

Is It Unique?

A general principle of product success is that it must solve a problem or fill a need better than its direct and indirect competition does. Direct competition for a home bread-making machine are other home bread-making machines. Indirect competition might be commercial bread manufacturers, bakeries, and those who like to make their own homemade bread. Strategic alliance partners, aware of the effects competition can have on a project, always look for some kind of proprietary position. A project's uniqueness usually is determined by a patent or patent-pending status, but could also be in the manufacturing technique or even in the distribution channels. Exclusivity is the most important consideration in determining royalty rates for inventors.

The examination of patents, trademarks, copyrights, and trade secrets enters into a project at some point. Generally, this analysis revolves around the patent search, the preliminary response from the patent examiner (if still pending) and/or the breadth of coverage granted by the issued patent. This, too, depends on where the project is in its development. Patent attorneys and agents are necessary ingredients. One of the first questions asked by a potential licensee or joint venture partner is "Who did the patent work?" Unless a professional has done the work, credibility of the project is usually lost. The second question asked is "Will the patent be easy to design around?" From this point, only a positive answer from a professional patent attorney or agent will move the project forward.

Also performed is a preliminary competitive analysis. Intellectual property rights do not guarantee success any more than firing a bullet guarantees hitting the target. If the product or process does not possess a unique advantage over the features, benefits, or pricing of the competition, the question asked is "Why produce it?" Would the market want a "me too" product? We use our online computer databases to begin the competitive analysis and include research accomplished by the innovator. The more the better. This analysis has proved to be a helpful springboard for the strategic alliance partner's own analysis and marketing strategy development.

Is There a Real Market?

In the television series *M.A.S.H.,* Hawkeye described the unit's procedures as "meatball surgery." He explained how they treated the wounded as quickly as possible, stabilized the patient's condition, then sent him to Seoul for more intensive follow-up. This description is close to describing our approach to market analysis— we perform a quick overview, then turn it over to the real experts in the private sector for their analysis. This results in an assessment of merit from those who also have the ability to commercialize the product, should it prove synergistic with their experience, abilities, and future goals.

To gain the interest of potential alliance partners, there usually has to be a preliminary and independent product analysis—even in rudimentary form. This is done through the use of new product surveys (see Appendix B) and testimonial letters from users or industry experts. In most cases, online computer searches quickly identify and retrieve relevant information describing the industry and market. The bottom line is that private sector firms do not want to hear an inventor's dreams or glorified estimates of market size. They want facts and quality information upon which decisions can be made.

A marketing firm, for example, may claim that a product will be successful based on experience gained through selling similar products. If the firm believes the market is sizable enough to warrant further expenditures to launch the product, then the project generally has found a desirable strategic alliance partner.

What Are the Manufacturing Costs?

Will a product be successful if the retail price is only twice the cost of raw materials and labor? It usually requires three or four times this amount to cover the overhead and an array of sales and marketing expenses, while still leaving room for profits. If the product can be made of plastic, is injection molding or vacuum molding the best choice? How much will the mold cost? What are all the possible distribution channels? Would it be best to use distributors or sell direct to the consumer? Many new product innovators overlook such critical questions. Accurate answers require experienced input from both manufacturing and marketing.

Determining whether sufficient margins exist is somewhat difficult in the earliest stages of development. Nevertheless by gathering material costs, estimating labor needs, and using surveys as an indicator of ultimate selling price, an assessment of price-competitive margins can be made. Establishing costs and margins is another reason why the early involvement of industry experts is critical. The private sector does not make a habit of overlooking costs while conducting an evaluation.

These are the first four of the five questions we ask ourselves before beginning to develop the funding mechanism to commercialize new innovations. Many more issues are embedded in these questions. Many that may seem trivial at first grow to be of considerable importance as the project moves toward completion. This is another reason why the early involvement of the coalition's manufacturing and marketing members is so important. Their experience with similar yet different products already on the market yields a vast amount of knowledge and advice—even if they choose not to license the product.

One screening question yet remains. It is the most important of the five. Is the owner of the intellectual property prepared to make a deal? This is discussed later in Chapter 10.

Secrets of Product Success

One opinion many potential inventors have as to what makes a successful product is that it must be needed by everyone; to live without it is unthinkable; it must be consumed quickly and repurchased frequently; it must cost pennies to make and sell for dimes. Examples of this description might be ballpoint pens, tissue paper, lightbulbs, toothpaste, toothbrushes, and soap. Some would-be inventors say they will not invent anything if it cannot be like one of these. It is certainly a worthy goal, but practically speaking there are just not that many more staple items left that need to be invented.

A record number of new products were introduced in 1990 to drugstores and supermarkets—15,879 of them. This breaks the previous record of 14,241 set in 1987, according to Marketing Intelligence Service. Although many will fail, some will survive many years. New products are like people: some die young, others live to a ripe old age.

What intrinsic qualities allow a product to live a long life? There is not much in the literature of new product development that gives us solid answers. Much of the writing is vague, esoteric, and "rah–rah" sales talk without depth. One thing is for sure—it first has to be born. An invention must turn into an innovation by being launched; then the consumer will be able to decide how long it lives.

Maybe we can get a longevity clue from those who purchase and resell products. The J.C. Penney Company, in its 1985 new product guidelines to buyers, may have given us a peek into what mass merchandising stores look for in new products. The paraphrased list below has probably been modified a bit by now, since it was circulated to employees during the company's change to a more upscale and fashion-oriented product line. But I'll bet it is not too different.

The new product:

- must be a new solution to a problem; not just a solution, but a new solution. It must be a clear solution to a problem and better than any other solution.
- must be easily understood and should not try to educate the consumer.
- must be obvious. Its needs to be self-evident. Marketing should not have to position it against competition.
- must be low tech and sell without a warranty.
- must use simple materials and manufacturing processes. There must be low tooling costs, and it must work.
- must have the right price point. An impulse purchase or gift item is ideal, and it should retail for $39.95 or less.
- must communicate consumer satisfaction; no fads allowed.

- must be positive and cannot be destructive, unsafe, harmful to the environment, sexist, etc.
- must stand alone; not part of a system.
- must have established distribution. It must have a known retail or catalog source.
- must be desirable and irresistible. It can be a "need" but should be a "want" as well.
- should not appeal to everyone or it might appeal to no one.

Where's the beef? How does one know if a product is desirable or irresistible? What is considered to be low tooling costs or low technology? Why should a retailer care about tooling costs? What is the difference between a solution and a clear solution? What percentage of customers should find it appealing?

Much more valuable clues are found from the following critique from a former Wal-Mart buyer and store manager (used by permission):

1. *Overall impact to the market.* How will the product impact the targeted market? Finding the answer consists of analyzing many complex questions. Many new products never make it through this stage. If a buyer questions the validity of the item to compete in the market due to weakness in any one of the following, the item's merit will probably be overlooked and the project shelved.

   - Market share is possible only if the item fills a particular need to the targeted market. That market could be categorized by age, ethnic background, or utility. The product must also be able to compete and vie for its share of the marketplace based upon its own merit and promotability.
   - Credibility of the item is very important. Will it enhance a department or detract? Design and packaging is very important here. It has to fit the basic mix of merchandise in which the retailer is involved. It may be something new and exciting, but if the credibility factor is slanted toward the negative, most buyers will reject it out of hand.
   - The projected life span of the product weighs heavily in any decision a buyer makes today. As inventories are trimmed and operations work with smaller budgets, a new product that will enjoy only a brief life span will probably not get the attention it deserves. Also the potential risk to the inventor is much higher with such an item

and his initial marketing efforts will be more expensive. "Fad" items are still marketed daily at tremendous risk to everyone involved, but most retailers of any magnitude have fine-tuned their merchandise mix to reduce investment, and each lineal foot of selling space is "modularized" or maintained by a strictly controlled mix of products that have a long market life. Don't expect them to rework their program to fit in a new item. The innovator must rework his product to fit their program. That is part of being an innovator.

- The amount of learning it takes a consumer to master a new item is an important criterion, and the buyer recognizes this. For example, a new game that is too complex in its instructions will not net returns an operation needs. Obviously something highly technical is targeted at a specific audience and not the everyday consumer, so it would be better accepted in a specific marketplace such as a specialty shop.

2. *Product availability.* This is very important for obvious reasons. If the innovator lacks the resources to meet the law of supply and demand, the product is doomed. More new products fail because of this than probably any other reason, and the buyers responsible for maintaining inventory levels will not cooperate if the sustainment capital is not there. A buyer must have the assurances that all purchase orders will be filled by specified ship dates. The first time those dates are not met, the item and the buyer can very quickly "just fade away."

3. *Gross profit.* Most new items that are introduced to a buyer should have a better-than-average margin than the department in which it will be merchandised. For this reason the innovator must operate from realistic royalty, shipping, and production figures, and should take the time (or spend the money) to obtain the necessary information before ever sitting down to negotiate. An item that will lower the overall gross margin of the department, and, likewise, the retail unit as a whole is simply not an attractive investment for the buyer. Expect the buyer to also look at the possibility of markdowns if the item should not perform as expected. If implemented, this action, too, will offset the margins if the product does not sell as expected.

4. *The product line.* It should be noted that today's buyers are interested in new products that have the ability to expand with new and creative ideas based upon the original concept of a design. Would a smaller or larger size, or variety of colors, or a multipack versus singular stimulate a higher turnover? Can it be offered in a different language to target a specific ethnic group within the trade area of the retailer? Alternative lines that feed off the original tend to make the new product more appealing to a prospective buyer. Crayola is but one of the many examples of this marketing strategy.

5. *Environmental impact.* In today's world of increasing and fluctuating pollution control measures, many items are deemed by buyers to be "not environmentally sound." Is the product biodegradable? Safe for consumption? Is there any health hazard? Has it been adequately tested and, if so, by whom? What is the extent of product liability the item offers? Will it meet government regulations? In the case of toys and games, are there small parts that could force a recall? With hardware items, are there sharp edges that could destroy packaging while in shipment or present a safety hazard to the consumer? All of these questions and many more will be asked by the potential buyer.

6. *Will the purchase adapt to the budget?* Every retail establishment operates on a system of numbers. Cost-to-sell ratios, sales per square foot, wages, advertising, and a host of other expenses that control the bottom line, which is *net profit!* Ideally any new product that is proposed to a buyer will fit within the framework of the budget and take nothing away from it. It should be packaged so that it is not easily pilfered. It must be able to withstand the test of time regarding shelf life. It must meet or exceed the department's expected rate of turns, while at the same time not tie up more than its share of square or lineal footage.

7. *Pricing feasibility and strategy.* Most buyers have been at their jobs long enough to know if the retail price of a particular item is feasible, and whether or not the market can stand that price. After all the above criteria are met, and there are many more, if the item is still priced beyond its perceived worth it is unattractive to the buyer. Somewhere a tradeoff will have to be made, and the buyer will not be the one to make it. To do so would lower the gross margin involved. A careful

study of existing competition prior to the initial presentation should allow you to adjust your numbers accordingly—if they can stand it. If not, you will have to reinvent the mouse-trap all over again by finding cost-saving alternatives.

Capturing the Giant

Now we are getting somewhere! My partner, Jim Harris, has also been doing work over the last several years getting new products into Wal-Mart and other large mass merchandisers. He calls his method the giant catching strategy.

During the course of structuring a new product for launch into the mass merchandising arena, most innovators of new products assume that Wal-Mart Stores, Inc., is the immediate objective for their product. As a retailing giant, Wal-Mart is indeed a desirable retailer in which to ingratiate a new product. I must explain to the prospective entrepreneur that Wal-Mart is probably nothing more than a fleeting dream, a "pie-in-the-sky" hope. There are several reasons for this.

Fine-tuned merchandise mix.   Most modern retailers have a computerized inventory control system built over decades of fine-tuning their merchandise mix. To put it bluntly, they already know what will sell! Any new product, unless successfully tested elsewhere, is an assumed liability. For that reason, 85 percent to 90 percent of all new products shown to the merchandising division are rejected out of hand. Why should they replace an established product that has a proven track record with a never-heard-of product? In essence, you are asking the buyer to dilute that share of a proven and known value with an unproven and unknown value. New product failures are not how buyers keep their jobs.

Budget.   Another consideration is the amount of "open-to-buy" the buyer has for his department. In other words, how many dollars does he have left in his budget to spend on product, whether new or old? Seasonal returns, advertising and sales promotions, department landed gross, interest on inventory purchased, and markdowns year-to-date all play a factor in determining the amount of available open-to-buy.

Timing and other factors.   Seasonal buying for an event during the forthcoming year begins *during* the same event in the current year, and perhaps as much as 40 percent of the buyer's annual budget is spent during the months following that season as it leads to the next. Juggling those dollars is a very complicated formula! Figure in the average turns per year, gross markup versus landed gross, net profit after budgeted versus actual markdowns, etc., and it further complicates the matter. Then figure how many square feet and the dollars per square feet (*sometimes even dollars per square inch!*) each *known* product will bring in order to conform to a shelf profile or gondola modular layout that will maximize and enhance his department's sales in order to come in at or over budget in all of the above except inventory, and one can readily see why a buyer may not really be interested in new product. His job is very complex. To keep it as simple as he can, he will want to stick with what he knows will sell— much to the chagrin of new product developers.

Can the giant be captured? There is not an easy answer. Mass merchandisers such as Wal-Mart must compete in order to maintain market share and sales momentum. Invariably this means keeping new products on the shelf. Certainly it means giving exposure to any new product they perceive is costing their company consumer sales. Sam Walton told me many times, "80 percent of your sales come from 20 percent of your merchandise," and his perception was uncannily accurate. This was at a time prior to computerization of major chains. Today he would probably say, "83.271 percent of your sales come from 21.00593 percent of your merchandise."

Computerization of inventory control has brought pinpoint accuracy. The smart product developer should realize the nature of the beast he is trying to tackle, and act accordingly. Just where and how does your product manage to fit into this equation? How do you position it where it can be envisioned as part of the 80 percent? Do you even want it to be there? These should be your basic questions. Then again the best question might even be, "Do you really *need* to capture the giant?

Possibly you do, but during the launch, probably not. Being aware of the rigors of entrenching a product in the "giant's lair" keeps me aware of the fact that viable options must be pursued— options allowing for a steady growth of market share, yet still with the vision of the giant as the ultimate goal.

By identifying and isolating smaller regional and subregional retail chains, and explaining you are not interested in showing your product to Wal-Mart or one of the other giants, you are offering a great incentive for that company to test your product. Even if they have only 300 retail units, you are gaining market share while creating a *positive* sales history. Then, utilizing this company's sales, approach the next one—maybe a regional chain with 600 retail units. There are many companies with 1,000 to 1,500 stores. Each is like a petal on a sunflower. The giant is in the middle, and it is the ultimate goal. The advantages of this market launch are numerous. By the time your product is being sold in a dozen chains smaller chains, the total retail unit base may easily exceed the giant's. You may even find you don't need him and his problems anyhow.

Also, keep in mind that by the time you are servicing 3,000 to 4,000 regional sales units, all the inherent problems that come with growth are usually solved. Your receivables are tracking your payables, and the market has told you in measurable terms exactly what it expects of you and your product. It is now thoroughly entrenched, hedging in on the giant's market, and can no longer be ignored. The option of "catching the giant" is now yours and yours alone. What a position to be in!

Entrepreneurs, while they can be creative, cannot be everything to everybody. It is my wish that all market-worthy new products have their shot at success. The probabilities of enjoying that success is limited only by the reasoning the entrepreneur puts into his marketing plan. Having said this, I strongly urge any new product innovator to seek competent and professional help in determining market direction and strategy. Realize your limitations, and that your product may be the best since shoes, but your chances for success are greatly diminished if you try to strike out on your own with the attitude that you are capable of "doing it all." There are probably those who have that ability, but they are very rare birds indeed!

Should you decide to attempt to capture the giant, I am not saying it cannot be done. But you will find your skills and ability to corner that giant will increase exponentially if you finely hone your marketing weapons on smaller game until you are ready for the "safari" of your life!

Among the scholars who write on the subject of new product development, one stands head and shoulders above the rest—Robert G. Cooper, PhD, a marketing professor at McMaster University, Hamilton, Ontario. Cooper has done a tremendous amount of research in large company environments on the subject of what has to happen to launch successful new products. Anything an inventor can read by Cooper on this subject will help provide much insight into the commercialization process. According to Cooper, almost 50 percent of the resources that this country's firms devote to innovation goes for products that are commercial failures. Maybe they, too, would benefit by reading Cooper.

Certainly a description of our screening activities do not tell the whole story of successfully commercializing new products, nor do the mass merchandisers' guidelines to their buyers. By examining Cooper's works and others, then synthesizing them with the experience of hundreds of products evaluated over the past eight years, we will further identify the most important characteristics of successful new products.

"Getting a product out to the public used to be a snap," writes Ron Gasbarro in the *Washington Post.* "When, in 1590, Dutch spectacles-maker Zacharias Janssen invented the microscope, he simply presented one to the archduke of Austria. The archduke, in turn, told his other archduke friends what a nifty gadget it was." The rest is history. The following is today.

The Commercialization Triad

To summarize, the three major characteristics of a successful invention are: quality, synergy, and research. These three ingredients merge to form a commercialization triad. This new product commercialization triad is very much like the "fire triangle." To have a fire, there must be oxygen, heat, and fuel. Should any one of these be taken out of the mix, there will be no fire. Likewise with invention commercialization: If any of the characteristics of quality, synergy, or research is removed, successful, long-term commercialization does not occur.

If any of the characteristics of quality, synergy, or research is removed, successful, long-term commercialization does not occur.

---

1. Quality.   Defining quality can be difficult. A company can have the finest quality control program in the world, but if the consumer does not perceive the product as quality and purchase it, is it a quality product? Quality is ultimately relative. It is relative to competition, price, needs, etc.

I spoke to a group of 25 preengineering students (all male) at Southwestern State University in Weatherford, Oklahoma, a couple of months ago. To help them see this perspective of quality, we first brainstormed to discover quality characteristics of a girlfriend. Whereas, one student preferred a blond, another preferred brunette or red-head. Brown eyes won out over blue or hazel. Then I passed out several new inventions not yet on the market, and we brainstormed for quality characteristics they would expect to see in these products. As for the products, red, white, and blue packaging was preferred by some, while gray and purple was preferred by others. The subjective nature of quality was obvious.

A visiting professor sitting in on the class who took the position that quality is measurable said, "You make it sound as if it is all a dollars game." I agreed with him. One of the most interesting characteristics of quality identified by the young men in the class for both a girlfriend and a product turned out to be that it should work as expected. A company not only wants to know if an invention really works, it wants to know if it works well. If it cannot produce a quality new product, it stays with what it is presently doing. The last thing it needs is a product that breaks down, needs overwhelming service, or puts the company at unnecessary product liability risk.

We have had several inventions that worked, but on further analysis, design flaws were discovered that caused it not to work well. One was a unique home security product that attached to the frame of a door. We were so impressed with the possibilities of this invention that we asked an architect consultant to evaluate the item. He thought it had definite potential with a few electronic additions and a total redesign, but he was not really wild about its chances. Undeterred from our mission, we located a designer, manufacturer, and distributor of similar products. He was pleased to evaluate it. He reverse-engineered the product and gave us his conclusion. While the product would work as the inventor had designed it, there was just one major problem: It allowed rain and snow to get into the mechanism. In freezing weather it would freeze up immediately, thereby trapping the occupants of the home inside. Further, he had no suggestions on how to design around this problem. The invention would work, but it would not work well. It did not pass the quality test.

Another that failed the quality test was a pickup truck security device that could be made for pennies and sold for dollars. We took it to several automotive accessory manufacturers and marketers for evaluation. It worked very well, just as the inventor had designed it to do; however, it was too hard to install. As an aftermarket item it had to be easy for the average pickup owner to attach to his truck. It was not only difficult, but to install it the pickup owner would have had to purchase an obscure tool costing ten times what the product would cost. This story had a happier ending. The inventor thought of a much easier way to install the unit. It now works just fine.

Product quality is a must. It must not only work, it must work well. It should be easy to use, but it also must be perceived to be of a high quality.

Quality reigns supreme! Product quality is a must. It must not only work, it must work well. It should be easy to use, but it also must be perceived to be of a high quality.

After Cooper's study of 203 new product launches was complete, he concluded, "Product superiority is the number one factor in success." The PIMS (Profit Impact of Market Strategy) research program was initiated in 1972 for the specific purpose of determining how key dimensions of strategy affect profitability and growth. From information gathered on some 450 corporations, authors Robert D. Buzzell and Bradley T. Gale wrote in their book, *The PIMS Principles*, "In the long run, the most important single factor affecting a business unit's performance is the quality of its products and services, relative to those of competitors." Tom Peters and Robert Waterman wrote an entire book, *In Search of Excellence,* about quality and how it positively affected the companies that placed it as a high priority.

This message is permeating the corporate world. Independent inventors should likewise hear the call. If not, their appeals for meaningful evaluations from those with the power to commercialize them will continue to fall on deaf ears.

2. Synergy.   Top quality is not the only characteristic of successful new products. Companies also ask if the new product works well in the firms' own environment. Is it a synergistic fit? Is the company itself well suited for the launching of the product? I made a mistake when we commercialized our first product about three years ago. I negotiated a licensing agreement on behalf of the inventor with a person who was not a synergistic fit. He had a marketing and sales background. He had the desire to be in business for himself. He had the intelligence. He had some money. He did great until just after the product's launch. Then, when the item did not jump off the shelf like we were expecting, he lost heart. Today, most of the first run of the product is gathering dust in a warehouse.

It takes more for new product synergy than that. It takes proven marketing experience and manufacturing expertise specifically in the invention's own field. Just as an inventor should hire a patent attorney who is knowledgeable in his type of patent, so too should he try to find a company familiar with his type of product. If he owns a chemical patent, he should find a chemical company. What would an electronics company know about the chemical business?

We have learned from my mistake. We now spend at least half of our time at the department searching for and getting to know companies. What we are looking for is possible synergy between a company and the inventor and his or her new product. Marketing synergy consists of the new product's ability to be understood by and incorporated into the selling arm of the company. It has to be able to flow through the existing distribution channels. The sales management and sales team should be confident in their ability to sell the item and excited about the prospect of doing so. Manufacturing synergy means that the engineering expertise has been in place and very little further education is required. Trained employees only need to retool to produce the product.

Manufacturing and marketing willingness and ability are still not enough though. There must be a financial commitment as well. In their 1988 article "Resource Allocation in the New Product Process," R.G. Cooper and E. J. Kleinschmidt report that "managers of successful projects committed far more dollars and manpower to marketing activities than was the case for failing products." They further state, "Managers of successful products spent considerably more on the front end stages of the new product process." (*Industrial Marketing Management,* 17, 1988.) If an inventor is serious about his invention becoming successful, his attitude about picking the right company should be "No bucks, no Buck Rogers." Of products we have licensed and that have since failed, the most common reason is the lack of financial resources necessary for staying power. One of the main reasons inventors seek license agreements is because they have exhausted their own finances and cannot obtain more capital. That is the wrong reason, but it is the most common one. We will look at this more thoroughly later in Chapter 10.

If an inventor is serious about his invention becoming successful, his attitude about picking the right company should be "No bucks, no Buck Rogers." Of products we have licensed and that have since failed, the most common reason is the lack of financial resources necessary for staying power.

---

3. Research.   Successful new products are characterized by thorough market research prior to completed development. One of the most important conclusions market research is expected to forecast is how well the product will sell. It is no accident that about half of the products licensed have already proven a market exists through actual test market sales. When a potential licensee sees the existence of a market, he feels his risk is reduced. If the market looks attractive in terms of size and expected growth, it gets even more exciting. The farther along a product is in its commercialization stages, the more likely it is to find capital or be licensed.

Cooper again confirms our experience. He writes:

> How well certain activities in the new product process are undertaken is strongly linked to new product success. In one study of 203 industrial product launches (123 successes and 80 failures), activities such as initial screening, preliminary market and technical assessment, and undertaking a detailed market study were strongly correlated with product outcomes. . . . In reviewing these results, note how the upfront or predevelopment activities stand out as activities that separate winners from losers. (Industrial Marketing Management, 17, 1988).

We have discussed the importance of market research in every chapter so far. The most important goal in preliminary market research is to gather as much information as possible on the industry and the competition. In Marketing 101 we learn about market research methodology. We learn that there are two basic kinds of research—primary and secondary. Primary market research is when we do things like surveys, testimonials, polls, and focus groups. In other words, it is information and opinions gathered for the first time directly from the public or other specially targeted entities. Secondary research is that which has already been gathered. Secondary research should always be done first. If what one needs to determine is already in print, there is no need to do it again through primary research techniques.

This is truly the information age. There is so much information available that numerous books have been written just to help one begin to gather it. Computer technology has made it possible for those in even the most remote areas of the country to tap into a wealth of information. There are only two things necessary to gather secondary market research—a library and access to the Dialog database. The larger public libraries and virtually all the academic libraries have access to Dialog.

Dialog is an online information retrieval service. Practically every subject imaginable is cataloged and ready to be downloaded for our use. It is based in Palo Alto, California. At the time of this writing it has 375 different databases within it, and it is growing at the rate of four or five new ones each month. Other helpful online services are DataTimes, NewsNet, Lexis/Nexis, and Dun & Bradstreet. Unless planning to do a great deal of research on different topics, there is no need to directly subscribe. Many libraries will perform searches for you at cost. Large cities have information brokers who know exactly how to get the information you need as quickly as possible. They are more expensive than doing it yourself or with the help of a librarian, but depending on your time constraints, they may be a good resource for your project.

DataTimes specializes in carrying the full text of major newspapers from around the country. Some of its information overlaps with Dialog, but there is enough differentiation that it too is well worth using.

NewsNet is mainly a compilation of industry-specific newsletters that cannot be found online anywhere else. These, too, can prove to be extremely helpful in your research when only information from expensive, narrowly focused newsletters will do the trick.

Lexis/Nexis is primarily a legal database. For one to get the maximum use from this system it would be helpful to be an attorney. However, we use it to retrieve the full text of legal journal articles and patents when we cannot wait a couple of weeks for them to arrive after ordering copies.

Dun & Bradstreet (D&B) primarily provides information on companies such as their history, officers, liens, lawsuits, and how well they seem to pay compared with the terms of the purchase. One of the great features about a D&B report is the background information on the officers or owners. This is difficult to find anywhere else. The up-to-date information it provides on litigation and bankruptcies has paid for itself many times over.

I wish I could adequately convey how necessary these services are to our work. We could not do our job of getting new products into the marketplace without access to these databases. Because there is no way we can be experienced in every possible industry, we subscribe to them to help us become "overnight experts." We have to know what is going on in the rest of the world outside of Oklahoma.

Dialog will probably be the most helpful for inventors researching their projects. Its databases cover business, science, technology, government, social sciences, and the humanities. Costs for each database vary. One year I calculated the average cumulative cost at around $4.30 for each minute of connect time. The business databases are more expensive than the rest, and 60 percent of the time those are the ones I search. For the inventor this should be viewed as an investment, not as just another expense. It should be seen in the same light as one's investment in building a prototype or filing for a patent. Two or three hundred dollars and an hour's worth of time should turn up a wealth of information that otherwise would have taken months to gather or might have been completely overlooked.

One thing online services do not do is books. There are occasions when one chapter in a book will give you just the information you're trying to discover. The online databases would in all probability miss it. That is why both the library and online services are needed: the library for books, and the online services for periodicals.

Dialog does, however, have some reference books—some very helpful ones—and turning on the computer sure beats thumbing through pages. Some of the reference books in Dialog are the *Thomas Register Online*, the *Encyclopedia of Associations*, *Books in Print*, and *Ulrich's International Periodicals Directory*. A couple of years ago we were evaluating a new product. It was a vampire bat feeder intended to hang on a tree or by a corral. This unit was supposed to keep the bats away from cattle by attracting the little critters to it instead. I thought surely if the vampire bat problem in the United States was at all significant there would be an association that might give me more information. So I logged on to Dialog, went to the *Encyclopedia of Associations* and searched for "vampire bats." I guess they are not a big problem, because there is nothing listed. I did come away enlightened for my efforts though. I discovered four associations of which I had previously known nothing: the Vampire Information Exchange, Vampire Research Center, Vampire, and the Vampire Pen Pal Network. Three of these, it seems, are made up of fans of vampire books and movies. The Vampire Research Center, however, conducts demographic studies of vampires through social-anthropological research known as vampirology. Further, it disseminates questionnaires (primary market research) to obtain information on people who believe that they or others they know are vampires. It is simply amazing what one can find during the course of market research.

Sometimes I cannot find what I am looking for, but 95 percent of the time I do. The *Encyclopedia of Associations* has helped a great deal, because if there is an association on a topic or field, the record will have the address, phone number, a contact, and a description of the association's mission. Associations save a lot of time when doing market research.

If I wanted to conduct a quick industry overview I would go to PTS PROMPT, Trade & Industry ASAP, and Business Dateline. PTS stands for Predicasts Terminal System. PROMPT is an acronym for Predicasts Overview of Markets and Technology and provides information in either abstract form or full text on companies, products, markets, and technologies for all industries. Trade & Industry ASAP gives us the full text from trade-specific and general business magazines and journals. Business Dateline provides the full text from around 200 business newspapers and magazines. This is a great one for learning company histories, biographies of owners, market figures, etc. Another great database is Trademarkscan. Let's say I had a new design for shirts and someone told me the Cambridge Classic shirt had the best fitting collars ever made. Where can I buy one? By searching Trademarkscan for "Cambridge Classic," I can quickly find the owner of the trademark and call the company. Another use, of course, is finding out if the name you have chosen for your product's brand name has been taken by someone else. That's important to know.

We have spent quite a bit of time on the subject of research, but it is important to take advantage of any and all information sources. I have seen many quality inventions, and I have seen these team up with synergistic firms, but not once have I seen an invention that has been researched through an online service. If preliminary primary and secondary research is so critical to the success of new products launched by large companies, how much more critical is it for the independent inventor? I believe that if all independent inventors would just do their research homework while they are building their prototype, we would see thousands more inventions commercialized each year. The invention that is well researched has a strategic advantage over one that is not.

If all independent inventors would just do their research homework while they are building their prototype, we would see thousands more inventions commercialized each year. The invention that is well researched has a strategic advantage over one that is not.

These are the items you should seek to address in your initial research:

Industry Information

- What is the industry's history?
- Is it growing or declining?
- Who are the key players? What are their annual sales?
- What are the barriers of entry into this industry?
- How large is the market?
- What are the government regulations?
- What are the trade associations?
- What are the industry publications?
- Where and when are the trade shows?

Customer Information

- Who are the customers?
- Where are they located?
- Why will they buy the product?
- What unique benefits does it provide?
- Why do they need or want those benefits?
- How much money will it save them?
- Will there be a foreign market?

Competitive Information

- What are the features and benefits of the competing products?
- Who are the major direct competitors?
- What are their sales?
- What is their market share?
- If there is no direct competition, why?
- What is indirect competition to the product?
- How are customers solving the problem now?
- What are the prices of competing products?
- How are they promoted and advertised?

Product Information

- What are the features and benefits?
- How does it work?
- How broad in scope is the patent?
- How old is the patent?
- Is service required?
- What kind of warranty should it carry?
- How is the product priced?
- Gather surveys and/or testimonial letters.
- Obtain bill of material estimates.
- Obtain quotes for assembly.

Well thought out answers to these questions should be enough to get the attention of anyone thinking of participating in the project. Indeed, as I mentioned earlier, had Edison done some research, one of his first inventions might not have been such a flop. Reasoning that Congress surely would want to get voting over with as quickly as possible and get on to more important business, he invented the automatic vote recorder. Little did he know how very comfortable congressmen were with the process and that they used the "excess time" for discussing other issues of the day and socializing. With his feathers thus singed, Edison determined to waste no further time inventing things that, however useful, did not have an immediate commercial application.

Nine More Characteristics of Success

Beyond the commercialization triad, nine additional characteristics of successful new products still remain. They might best be thought through with a specific invention in mind. These are not listed in any priority because every invention and every path toward commercialization is distinctive.

4. Unique benefits.   This characteristic is usually the first one questioned by interested examiners. They ask, "What makes this cup holder any better than all the others out there? What's the difference in using this wall-mounted storage rack and a nail or hook? Why should I buy this five-in-one tool when I can buy five single-purpose tools to accomplish the same thing?" They are really asking, "What are this product's unique benefits? How are they beneficial to me?"

Let's think downstream for a moment. After an invention is launched, the sales personnel will have to be able to clearly describe features and sell the benefits of the product. Customers observe features and buy the benefits. The whole process of buying and selling revolves around benefits. The more personal benefits a product carries, the easier for the customer to buy it.

Moreover, a good salesperson does not sell any benefits until he knows what benefits the customer wants. Why sell a benefit if the customer does not see it as one? When I was selling two-way radios to oil companies, one of the features of our system was that the tower's antenna was the highest object in the Arbuckle Mountains. The benefit was that one could communicate anywhere within a 60-mile radius. It was also unique because our competition's tower was much lower, so radios on his system could not talk as far.

Seems like a simple sale, right? Well, it wasn't. Even though our systems talked farther, sounded better, and cost the same, our competition had some features and "unique" benefits of his own. During his presentation he would explain how he was a hometown boy. The oil companies would benefit by being seen as good community citizens if they bought from him. Another "unique" benefit was that buying from him kept the money circulating locally. Why send it up north? He always forgot to tell them how he had already sent local money up north when he purchased his inventory. I was amazed how often his pitch worked.

When I was selling I would anticipate that my competition had already called on the prospect. My questions would concentrate on probing how much weight he gave to being able to use a system that had the maximum range, as opposed to gaining the perception of being a good local citizen. Fortunately most prospects decided on maximum range.

Isn't the goal of inventing to invent something people want? Researching the potential customer and competition prior to finalizing an invention's features and benefits is critical. Only then can one be sure he is inventing something that has unique benefits people will buy.

5. Saves money for the customer.   Consumers do not always buy the cheapest item. They buy the one with the highest value. Compared to direct and indirect competition, will the consumer be able to cost justify his purchase? Will he perceive his level of satisfaction such that he will pay the price? Will he get a better deal because higher quality justifies offering a longer warranty? Will he receive more benefits for the same price, or fewer? Products that save their customers' hard-earned money have a distinct advantage. I was recently involved in a new product launch for a men's travel accessory item. The product is called the Tie Traveler. This patent-pending invention spools two ties at a time into a plastic canister a little larger than a coffee mug. The suggested retail price is $9.95 and is easily cost justifiable because it does not allow creases to form across ties while folded in a suitcase. A traveling executive can appreciate the subtlety of not having a creased tie while making a presentation to 20 of his peers. Not only is the product cost justifiable from that perspective, it is justifiable from a comparison of competing items. According to the research, in the "less than $10 dollar" price range, any other direct competitor's item requires the tie to be folded, thus causing creases.

How does one determine an optimum retail price during the earliest stages of development? The sample survey in Appendix B contains a series of pricing questions we have used many times with excellent results. It can be used with new products still in the prototype stage of development and beyond.

6. Has testimonials.   Have you ever noticed how people seem to immediately reject anything new? The unfamiliar must be some kind of uncomfortable invasion that triggers caution, or even fear. If they can just figure a way to jettison this intrusion from their comfort zone, life can get back to normal. I have seen this in every industry except the fashion business. Fashion people thrive on changing styles. They crave to see new and different items. This is in direct contrast to other industries.

How does one overcome such negativism? It is not easy, but the best way we have found is through the testimonials of others. What do most television commercials have in common? Actual users of the product saying how wonderful it is. Why do they use these people to testify to the validity of their product? Because it works. S. Ram in his article entitled "Successful Innovation Using Strategies to Reduce Consumer Resistance" writes:

> *Prior to large-scale market introduction of an innovation, a firm may be able to use certain communication strategies within its control to generate market acceptance. Using print media or affiliated agents to disseminate favorable information about product performance or about favorable response to the concept from other customers seemed to reduce the amount of resistance to the innovation. (Journal of Product Innovation Management 6: 1, March 1989.)*

The testimonials or surveys gathered by an inventor are used for the purpose of gaining credibility and thus reducing resistance in potential funding sources. We have seen them work successfully over and over in finding licensees or other strategic alliance partners. They are an absolute necessity.

Caution: Do not skew the results! One inventor sent us about 25 or 30 surveys. While they were written in various styles of handwriting, the answers to one question were almost the same in 75 percent of the results. The question was, "What do you see as the foremost barriers to entry, if any?" The answer on an overwhelming number of surveys was something like, "Not being able to keep up with all the orders." We had never seen that kind of answer to any of the questions in the survey, yet here was a plethora of the same answers to the same question. Unfortunately, we could not present those surveys to a funding source with a straight face. We were seeking credibility—not incredulity.

7. Has sales.   Most products that are licensed, joint ventured, or receive an equity investment already have sales. I do not particularly like it, but that is the way it is. It is one of the truisms of new product development: The farther along a project is in its development, the more likely it is to succeed.

About half of the products that are launched fail shortly thereafter. It is usually due to poor management, lack of capital, or inadequate research prior to launch. The product itself generally has a market or it would not have sold at all. Proving the product will sell by actually selling it is simply the best way to attract further talent and capital to the project.

As Edward P. White wrote in *Licensing—A Strategy for Profits:*

> *There is little doubt that the invention of Workmate arose from the fact that Ron Hickman, the inventor, was, and still is, an ardent do-it-yourself enthusiast. He wanted to be able to do simple woodworking jobs in a home that had no workshop. By 1968 Hickman was convinced that he had a product (a collapsible, portable workbench) that was patentable and would have great practical utility. He therefore had the first provisional British patent specification filed and approached various British manufacturers, including Black & Decker, Stanley, Record, Burgess, Polycell, Salmens, and Marples. In most cases he managed to obtain interviews at a fairly senior level and made a full presentation of the hardware then available and demonstrated the jobs it could do. In all cases, the idea was rejected. In many instances the reason given was that it had no potential.*
>
> *As a result of these failures to find licensees, Ron Hickman decided to produce the bench himself. The manufacture of the parts was contracted out, but the assembly and marketing were done by a small team recruited for the purpose. The original Workmate appeared in 1968, and within four years sales had increased to 14,000 units a year, mainly by mail order.*
>
> *Ultimately, with Black & Decker, [the Workmate] achieved a worldwide market position. . . . First, however, he [Hickman] had to prove that his invention was, indeed, a marketable product.*

8. Low start-up cost.   Another characteristic of a successful new product is that it requires a very low investment to produce and sell it. This should be pretty obvious. The lower the start-up costs, the easier it is to find the money necessary to cover those costs.

Let's say we have two good items in the prototype stage sitting on our desk. One is an invention that will be produced by plastic injection molding. The other can be made in a cut-and-sew facility. The cut-and-sew item will make it to the market ten times faster than the plastic item. The reason is that the average cost of a mold to shoot the melted plastic into is generally between $20,000 and $40,000. The next time you are bored and cannot think of anything to do, go out to some monied folks and ask them to invest $30,000 in a mold to produce a new invention. It will make your day, and not in a pleasant way!

9. Commands strong margin.
Not everyone can write a software program that sells for $500 yet costs only five dollars to duplicate and package. Software has high margins. Many unique chemical products have very high margins costing $.25 a gallon to blend yet selling for five dollars. A computer may command a retail price 20 times its manufacturing cost when it is first rolled out. And why not? Prices are governed by supply and demand. If the demand is high and the supply is low, a true capitalist will want to earn whatever the market will bear, and then some.

David L. Kurts and Louis E. Boone write in their book, *Marketing*, "A recent study of marketing executives revealed that price currently ranks as the single most important marketing mix variable. Product planning and management is a close second, and distribution and promotion rank third and fourth, respectively." This seems to be saying that marketing managers place a higher priority on correctly pricing a product than on the product itself! What a sobering thought. A company's livelihood is dependent upon profits. Without profits there is no reason for its existence. It does not care about making an inventor rich. It does care about giving healthy returns to its stockholders.

Correctly pricing a product is no easy task. There is "cost plus" pricing, markup pricing, inflation pricing, competitive pricing, consumer pricing, price skimming, penetration pricing, low-ball pricing, loss-leader pricing, and opportunistic pricing, among others. Deciding which strategy to use depends on many factors in environments to which an inventor has never been exposed.

Skimming and penetration pricing are the two most common strategies used to launch new products. Skimming sets a high price for maximum short-term margins to recoup R&D or other start-up costs. When skimming, the product must quickly get to the market that is attracted to prestigious new products and can afford them.

Penetration pricing counts on setting a low price to capture a large market share. It depends upon a low amount of competition, high volume production, and a large untapped market.

Pricing, like patent searches, is no job for an amateur. The correct pricing of a product is more important to a company's survival than the product itself. There is always another product. Inventors should keep pricing and margin issues in mind while inventing. Expect them to eventually come up.

10. Fully developed.   Hardly anyone wants to invest in an R&D project. Until the tax laws change, this will be the norm. Investors have to see how they are going to make their money back plus a healthy return as quickly as possible.

None of the products commercialized through the IAP has had any R&D left to accomplish except for several plastic items that still needed a mold.

11. Has intellectual property.   A proprietary position is a virtual must with a product as opposed to a service. A patent or patent pending and a broad scope of coverage increases the chance of success. Other forms of intellectual property like secret food ingredients or copyrighted software also provide a necessary proprietary position. However, investors do not necessarily invest in just companies with products. Millions have been made by investing in service companies. In one study, by the Center for Entrepreneurial Studies, it was found that of ten criteria most frequently rated essential to a deal, only 29 percent of the venture capitalists listed having a proprietary position. Out of ten criteria it came in last!

12. Inventor has enough money for test market.   I am not pleased with the inventor having to bear this responsibility himself, nevertheless it is true. Most of the inventions that have been licensed, joint ventured, or received investments have established their efficacy with actual sales. The inventor is usually the one providing the money to get it to that point. There are research costs, patenting costs, prototyping costs, production costs, packaging costs, and advertising costs. The inventor and his or her family must decide if it is worth it.

Summing Up

We have had a couple of five-tools-in-one inventions during the past several years. One was for auto mechanics, the other for carpenters. Both were patented. Each inventor had some capital. They had been selling their product for a more than adequate margin. Both had videos to explain the features and benefits. In both cases the invention sold for less money than one would have to invest to buy five individual tools. Both inventors had extensive backgrounds in the field of their invention. Both had a few testimonial letters. Both were fully developed. The manufacturing could be easily set in motion. One of the strong benefits of the mechanic's invention was that it was safer to use than competing products. Yet both died.

The experts we contacted on behalf of each invention said they were overengineered, too hard to learn how to use, the potential users were satisfied with what they already had, and the units just did not look very "slick."

There are many multi-purpose tools in existence. Probably the most famous one is the Swiss Army knife. So why did these two die? Neither invention had the characteristics of perceived quality, research, or unique benefits. Therefore, neither could earn a place in a company's product line and, by doing so, qualify for the characteristic of synergy. While possessing eight of the nine lesser characteristics, they did not achieve the top three.

My guess is that both inventors, being experienced in their respective professions, simply felt that if they thought it was a good idea, so would their peers. In other words, they assumed they knew what the market wanted. Had they given an equal amount of attention to research as they did to prototyping and patenting, they might have saved themselves a lot of money and time. They may even have discovered something the market really wanted that they could patent.

Some of these characteristics may seem unfair. One might ask, "Why invent anything if I have to do so much market research? Why should I have to use my own capital or raise it to gear up to sell my product? Why can't my licensee or joint venture partner help complete the development? After all, haven't I already spent five grand for a patent?" These are legitimate questions for which there are only exasperating answers that vary from deal to deal.

R. G. Cooper reports that in 75 percent of his 203 projects "there was no detailed market study or marketing research undertaken at all. Yet a lack of market assessment has been consistently cited for years as the number one reason for new product failure." If research must be done and companies are not willing to do it, then the inventor himself must do it. It is just that simple. That's life.

The world will not beat a path to the inventor's door. The inventor must beat a path to the world's door.

The world will not beat a path to the inventor's door. The inventor must beat a path to the world's door.

These 12 characteristics are what we have found to be the most common characteristics of successful new products. I am certainly not implying that the only inventions ever commercialized possess each and every one of these 12 characteristics. I am saying that a correlation exists: To the degree these characteristics are incorporated into the invention, the chances of launching the product increase proportionately. Furthermore, the more each individual characteristic is fulfilled, the greater the invention's chances.

A baseball axiom states there are nine more ways a player can score from third base than from second base with less than two outs. If the base runner cannot score, it is better to be on third base—or second, or even first. The trick is not being left on base at the end of the inning. Most inventions, like most base runners, do not score. It is not necessarily because inventions are flawed; it is because inventors do not understand the intricacies of scoring. Getting to third base and then scoring depends much more on attaining the fulfillment of the above 12 characteristics than on an invention's patent claims or other special physical attributes.

NINE

Venturing

"For which of you, intending to build a tower, does not sit down first and count the cost, whether he has enough to finish it—lest, after he has laid the foundation, and is not able to finish it, all who see it begin to mock him, saying, 'This man began to build and was not able to finish.'

Or what king, going to make war against another king, does not sit down first and consider whether he is able with ten thousand to meet him who comes against him with twenty thousand? Or else, while the other is still a great way off, he sends a delegation and asks conditions of peace."

—Matthew 14:28-32

Venturing is building a company to manufacture and/or market your invention. It is one of only two ways to commercialize a new product. Volumes have been written in books, magazines, journals, and dissertations about starting and managing a company. Very few discuss it from the reference point of the inventor.

First, if the inventor feels he must venture to get his product to the market, he is misinformed. Secondly, if he does choose to venture, he is now in the position of having to invent again. He has already invented a product, now he has to "invent" a company.

As we discussed in the previous chapter, a product's alignment with a synergistic company is one of the three most important characteristics of new product success. If a synergistic company has already been "invented" by someone else, it seems a terrible waste of time to have to invent it again. This was one of Edison's mistakes. If he had not tried to build so many companies, it is likely he would have brought many more good ideas to life. According to Michael Peterson in his article "Thomas Edison, Failure" (*Invention and Technology,* Vol. 6: 3, Winter 1991), "He fell short as a businessman and spent much of his earnings in legal battles, protecting his patents and fending off unscrupulous competitors."

Venturing was too tough for Edison, and today it is still almost impossible. If the odds of having a successful invention are much worse than being a weekend winner at the Vegas blackjack tables, how much worse are the odds of success, if one must also "invent" a successful company to manufacture and market the invention? An inventor should think about how much he has learned while moving from the idea stage to whatever stage of development he is at now. If he multiplies this new knowledge by a hundred times, that is about how much more knowledge it will take to build a company that lasts.

Do not misunderstand me. It can and has been done. It is the American dream to start a company and make tons of money. The media have tantalized us for years with the successes of Edwin Land, George Eastman, Ken Olsen, Steve Jobs, and a host of other innovators. But the media do not report on all the companies that begin and then fail a year or so later. Why? It is not news. It's just normal. It is expected that a new company will soon fail because that is what usually happens. More than half of all new start-ups fail within three years—usually because of a lack of management expertise.

Venturing Quiz

We'll discuss some of the challenges in venturing your invention in a bit. But first take this self-test. It may save you the trouble of reading the rest of this chapter.

1. Do you feel that your invention will never make it on the shelves unless you do it all yourself?

2. Have you ever wanted to start your own business?
3. Have you ever had to fire anyone?
4. Have you ever managed a group of people?
5. Have you ever sold anything and made a living on a straight commission?
6. Have you ever had to collect receivables?
7. Have you ever had to juggle money from one account to another to meet payroll?
8. Can you put together a balance sheet?
9. Can you write a business plan?
10. Do you still have at least $20,000 you can afford to lose? (Ask your spouse, too.)
11. Do you have at least 60 hours a week to devote to starting up a new company?
12. Do you know through experience the difference between marketing and sales?
13. Can you really differentiate between yourself and your invention?
14. Would you be starting up your business primarily to make money?
15. Do you have a circle of acquaintances that have money willing to invest in deals?
16. Do you have experiential knowledge of Murphy's Law as it applies to business?

If you cannot honestly answer more than a dozen or so of these questions with a "yes," then it might be wise to forget about venturing.

What Venture Capitalists Want

If you feel you have passed the venturing self-test and still want to venture, serious consideration should be given to investment criteria in the venture capital industry. Venture capitalists, logically, know more about venturing than any one group. Their very existence depends upon making accurate judgments of an entrepreneurial company's future success potential. If they have a track record for investing in companies and are still in business, they have demonstrated their ability to pick winners.

New York University's Center for Entrepreneurial Studies mailed 150 questionnaires to venture capital firms consisting of members of the National Venture Capital Association and those listed in *Venture* magazine's "1983 Directory of Venture Capitalists." There were 102 responses returned. The word *essential* means the venture capitalist would reject the business plan regardless of any other characteristics, no matter how redeeming. The following are the results:

Ten Criteria Most Frequently Rated Essential

Capable of sustained intense effort	64%
Thoroughly familiar with market	62%
At least 10 times return in 5–10 Years	50%
Demonstrated leadership in past	50%
Evaluates and reacts to risk well	48%
Investment can be made liquid	44%
Significant market growth	43%
Track record relevant to venture	37%
Articulates venture well	31%
Proprietary protection	29%

An entrepreneur's ability for an intense effort, knowledge of the market, proven leadership, and ability to handle risk, combined with a background closely related to the venture and an ability to communicate well are the personality characteristics venture capitalists look for in a deal.

In addition, a venture capitalist wants a return of at least five to ten times the amount he invests within five years. He also wants the ability to get his money when he decides to cash in his chips. If he cannot get these things, he will keep his money in relatively safe investments.

Of all the possible marketing characteristics to choose from, these 102 venture capitalists chose a significant market growth as most important. Having proprietary protection—patents, copyrights, trademarks, and trade secrets—came in last of the most essential items. However, it came in as the most important product characteristic if a product was to be involved in the venture. The most important conclusion to draw from this study is that venture capitalists do not generally look for inventions in which to invest. Venture capitalists want to make money, so they look for talented management.

There is a wide gulf between being an inventor and being an entrepreneur. Just as there are comparatively few inventors in the world, so are there few real entrepreneurs. The person who is able to combine being an inventor with being an entrepreneur is extremely rare. Chances are that if an inventor was cut out to be an entrepreneur, he would have started more than one business before he ever had an invention.

I have a picture on the wall in my office of a balding gentleman with a beard. The caption quotes him as saying, "Venture capitalists don't give a damn about my technology. All they are concerned about is my management team." And why not? Venture capital companies are responsible to invest other people's money and receive a healthy return. They know that management—not products—provides that return. Whatever products or services the company might offer is secondary to the experience and quality of the management team. Private investors and venture capitalists have told us over and over, "I'd rather invest in a company with a mediocre product and great management than one with mediocre management and a great product. I don't care if the deal is the cure for cancer."

Private investors and venture capitalists have told us over and over, "I'd rather invest in a company with a mediocre product and great management than one with mediocre management and a great product. I don't care if the deal is the cure for cancer."

Challenges

Next to the management problem, everything pales in significance. Good people will make things happen. Without quality management experienced in your invention's industry, there are some problems that will be encountered that you will not be able to cope with successfully. I call these "challenges."

While many books on venturing seem to exhort one to recklessly "go for the gold," I think it would be enlightening to discuss some of the challenges of entrepreneuring. Inventors seem to have never heard anything about them; I find myself repeating this information over and over to new inventors.

Failing to run the gauntlet successfully on even one of these challenges has the potential to cause a start-up business to fail. Breakdowns with two or more simultaneously can be devastating.

The Business Plan Challenge

What is the first thing a budding entrepreneur is asked for when he goes to the bank or Small Business Administration for a loan? The loan officer wants to see his business plan. We are often asked what such a plan should look like. While there are no pat answers or a single magical formula, certain points need to be made in every business plan to gain the attention of funding sources.

A business plan has a four-fold purpose:

1. It should be used as a tool to obtain the capital your business needs.
2. It should serve as a guide in operating the business once the funding is in place. It should be a "living" document—that is, one that can be modified as the business adjusts to new markets, additional products, and improved production.
3. A business plan serves as a mechanism for the entrepreneur to think through issues about which he may not have considered.
4. The final purpose of a business plan is for the benefit of the funding source, who reasons that if someone cannot put together a good, logical plan he certainly cannot run a business.

There is nothing necessarily wrong with paying a consultant to help with the plan. There is everything wrong if the plan is not your own. The consultant is not going to manage the business; therefore, the plan should not be his. You have to agree to every word in it. You have to explain and defend it after the presentation. Just as you are the author of a patent, so too must the business plan be yours.

Good business plan consultants can be hired in Oklahoma starting for around $3,000. It goes up from there depending on the amount of work needing to be done. If it requires research, for example, the cost increases proportionately to the researcher's expenses and fees. The consultant is being paid for his knowledge about what should go into the plan and his abilities in communicating your thoughts on any given subject. He is not being paid to guarantee the inventor will get funded. When used as a tool for funding, keep in mind that the plan's primary job is to open doors. Beyond the content of the plan (which is its most important element), it should look good. First impressions are critical. If it does not pass this test, it will be thrown away. It only makes sense that a document that is clean, bound, and laser printed stands a much better chance of getting read over one that is printed on a dot-matrix printer and stapled with coffee stains on the cover.

A 20- to 30-page plan is plenty. It should be able to be read at a single sitting. One longer than that will only serve to discourage the reader.

Many fine books are in print on the subject of how to write a business plan. There is none better than David H. Bangs' *Business Planning Guide* (see Bibliography). He is a former banker and knows from experience what should be in a plan. Particularly strong is his method of explaining how to do the financials and the meanings and relationships of all the numbers. If you decide to write the business plan yourself, get the book!

The Marketing Plan Challenge

The business plan is only the first challenge. While an abbreviated marketing plan should be included in the business plan, it is also necessary to write a more thorough marketing plan. It is in the execution of the plan from which success will flow. Without sales nothing happens. A detailed plan to generate sales must now be constructed to set the company on the right track toward generating cash flow.

In 1979 and 1980, *Business Week* described the marketing strategies of select successful companies. The results of these strategies were evaluated later by *Business Week*. Some of the results were quite successful, but these are listed to show how even large, well-funded companies can make mistakes.

Company	*Strategy/Results*
Adolph Coors	Regain lost market share and become a national force in the beer industry. Largely unsuccessful due to weak marketing clout.
Campbell's Soup	Diversify away from food. Abandoned by new CEO who successfully expanded into new food products.

Company	Strategy/Results
Church's Fried Chicken	Build modular, efficient fast food outlets aimed at the lower end of the market. Failed because upscale chicken restaurants captured most of the market growth.
Exxon	Diversify in electrical equipment and office automation, offset shrinking U.S. oil reserves by investing in shale oil and synfuels. Failed because of poor acquisitions, management problems in office automation, and falling oil prices.
Shaklee	Streamline product lines and become the leading nutritional products company. Ran into trouble due to recession and sales-force turnover.
Toro	Capitalize on brand recognition and reputation for quality in mowers and snowblowers by expanding into other homecare products. Failed because of snowless winters and distribution mistakes; new management changed strategies.
Trailways	Survive in the bus business by striking alliances with independent carriers and persuading regulators to hold Greyhound to 67 percent of intercity bus traffic. Failed because of deregulation and Greyhound's market-share war.
Union Carbide	Reduce dependence on commodity chemicals and plastics and build up six faster-growing higher-margin lines. Deep economic slump hit all chemical markets and delayed sale of undesired businesses.
U.S. Home	Use economies of scale in land development and financial clout to take a commanding position in home building. Ran into trouble when interest rates rose and home sales sank.
Wang	Become the leader in the office-of-the-future market by introducing new products to combine data and word processing. Largely unsuccessful because of rise of personal computers.

The question has been asked, "If these companies had a plan and failed, why should anyone go to the trouble of writing one?" One answer lies in realizing that these companies had other ways of making money, that is, other profit centers. The new venture usually has only one. It has only one chance to succeed. In order to enhance that one chance, an exhaustive marketing plan must be created. It is not enough just to have several pages of the business plan devoted to marketing. Those few pages should serve as the foundation for the "grand" plan.

Just as with the business plan, there are many books on how to create a marketing plan. Any help one can get from a book on the subject is far better than winging it. So buy one or check one out from the library, but as an inventor, and someone probably inexperienced in marketing, you must understand what has to go into a thorough marketing plan. Should a consultant be retained, the cost will generally be about the same as for a business plan.

Following is an outline of the 12 major topics a marketing plan must contain:

1. The consumer
2. Product strategy
3. Distribution strategy
4. Pricing strategy
5. Promotion strategy
6. The industry
7. The competition
8. Political environment
9. Cultural environment
10. Economic environment
11. Legal environment
12. Technological environment

Corporate Paperwork Challenge

When inventors desire to form a company, the most common structure they seem to choose is the corporation as opposed to a sole proprietorship or partnership. To incorporate in Oklahoma, the fee is only $50 and the forms can be ordered from the secretary of state. Other states have similar procedures.

Additional items to check on include an employer's identification number from the Internal Revenue Service. This number must be obtained if the company pays wages to one or more employees and is required on its tax returns, statements, and other documents.

In addition to federal income taxes and Social Security taxes, there are state and local taxes to consider along with many other kinds of taxation that vary from state to state.

If employees will be required, workers' compensation insurance must be paid. Each state has different requirements for meeting this obligation.

Then there may be licenses or permits on all the federal, state, and local government levels a company must apply for and receive before a business can legally operate. With all this paperwork to handle after the company gets going, along with the paperwork necessary for suppliers, customers, and funding sources, it might be best to incorporate to protect oneself from being personally liable for the company's debts. Just in case something goes wrong. Right? Not necessarily.

Inventors know little about a legal maneuver popularly called "piercing the corporate veil." It allows a judge to tear down the corporate shield and hold stockholders personally responsible for debts. Inventors pay the $50 filing fee, incorporate themselves without advice from a corporate attorney, and assume that all is well. There is more to it than that.

Consider the case of John, who decided it would be easier to launch his invention if he incorporated and assigned his patent to the company. After handling that chore himself and saving a few bucks in attorney fees, he decided he needed some equipment for the company. Nothing fancy, just the basics: a computer, a fax machine, and a copier. He could purchase them from one store with a lease purchase. The lease would allow him to keep his working capital to gear up for manufacturing and marketing. Most of the working capital would go for ordering raw materials. The invention would virtually sell itself, so there was no need to budget very much toward selling the item.

The bank had assured John he could get a loan for his manufacturing equipment and he already owned a building, so he decided to go ahead and purchase the office equipment. As he was filling out the forms, he noticed his corporation had to submit a financial statement going back three years. Because he had only just incorporated, the company did not have three years of financials. It did have the patent as an asset. Surely it was worth the $20,000 lease.

He discussed the problem with the store manager and was told it was no big problem. He could just give them a personal guarantee. But what about the patent? Could it not be used as collateral? No. It had no worth to the store. If John's company does not pay back the loan, where would the store's management go to sell such an intangible asset? They were in office equipment sales, not intellectual property. John was beginning to wonder why he had incorporated. After all, the company owned his "baby," and no one valued it anywhere close to the value he placed on it.

So what's a personal guarantee? The store manager explained that it is a pledge of John's personal assets to be used as collateral. "Just fill out this credit application form, and we'll be on our way." John had excellent credit, except for the time he lost his job and missed a couple of house payments, but those were easily explained. Besides, he was putting up his car and household furnishings as collateral. The store manager and John finally made a deal. The equipment would be delivered the next day. Now that John was almost ready to do business, he had to finalize the contract on his manufacturing equipment. Without that he could not make the product. He went to see his banker to get the loan. What? You want to see my business plan? John now had a use for his new computer. Fortunately, he already knew how to type. Unfortunately, he had never turned on a computer, much less operated one. Some of his working capital had to be used to pay for lessons. More had to be spent to take care of his family while he wrote it.

Four weeks later, he returned to the bank with his business plan in hand. His banker liked the plan. He said it gave him and the bank examiners a certain comfort level they would not have without it. "Now just fill out this application, and we'll be on our way." Not again. To make a long story short, John ended up taking out a second mortgage on his home for the $50,000 worth of equipment.

Eight months later, his invention had not sold like John thought it would. There were some significant sales, but not enough. He had been so busy handling the manufacturing, he was not able to devote enough time to selling. He owed his suppliers $25,000, and had accumulated $100,000 in inventory that few wanted to buy. Wal-Mart said the packaging was not quite right. Sears said the market had changed since he first talked with them a year ago. And Kmart did not want it at all without a clear two-year history of sales.

John had been paying some of his bills out of his personal checking account and others out of the business account. It had been too much of a pain to do it the way he knew he should. Besides, who would know the difference?

John developed a cash flow problem. He began robbing Peter to pay Paul. He reasoned that what little money was coming in had to go toward paying the second mortgage. He could not lose his home.

John's company went under. His attorney was able to strike a deal with the office supply store. John found a job to cover his second mortgage and otherwise put bread on his family's table, and the corporate bankruptcy would take care of the $25,000 debt to his former suppliers.

In court, the supplier's attorneys tried to demonstrate that John's corporation was not really a corporation at all. Even though the proper incorporation forms had been filed, there were no additional records of corporate decisions in the corporate book. No stock had been issued. There was no building lease agreement between John and the company. Further, there had been no adequate attempt to separate the company's income and expenses from John's personal income and expenses.

The judge ruled that John's company was not a real corporation. The supplier's attorneys had pierced the corporate veil. By the company filing bankruptcy, it was not going to absolve John from the debts incurred by the company. He was personally liable for them. Eventually, he had to file personal bankruptcy. There is much more to incorporating than just filing the initial forms. One might say that a corporation only exists from the paperwork reflecting its activities. If that paperwork is not done correctly, there is no corporation. Properly incorporating does limit personal liability, but there are more ways to "pierce the corporate veil" than discussed above. A prospective entrepreneur should always hire a good corporate attorney to help explain, structure, and maintain corporation status.

Personnel Challenge

A decade ago, one of the most popular mail-order books was one about how an employee could be an independent contractor. He could now be self-employed and entitled to all the benefits thereof. Employers liked the idea, too. It was a way to eliminate payroll taxes, workers' compensation insurance and benefits, and to do away with all the bookkeeping burdens that result.

I guess the powers that be determined they were missing out on taxes that were rightfully theirs, so they cracked down on this method of avoiding taxes. Assuming that one can run his business by calling employees "independent contractors" is a great mistake. You cannot just hire someone and label him as an independent contractor.

Two companies I know of ran into difficulties last year using this independent contractor technique in hiring employees. Many inventors, determined to start their own business, have insisted they would be using independent contractors to keep their taxes down. But the government does not care what a company calls its workers. It does care about the nature of the worker's relationship to the company. If independent contractors are determined by the IRS or state tax collectors to, in fact, be employees, the employer has serious problems. For one thing, withholding taxes are now due and payable, and the IRS considers it to be the same as embezzlement when a company does not pay its payroll taxes.

I want to be very clear about this. Tax collectors collect. That is their job. The more they collect, the faster they advance in their chosen profession. They only enforce tax laws, they do not make them. They are not in social work. They do not practice economic development. Getting into tax problems, especially payroll tax problems, is the kiss of death for a business. Once it starts, it hardly ever gets better. If someone builds a business around his invention, many people will depend upon him for their livelihood. Many have families to support. Having to lay off employees or shut down a company due to tax problems would be extremely unfortunate.

If you are thinking of using independent contractors in your business, think twice. Read the following factors used by the IRS to determine whether one is an employee or independent contractor, then see your tax attorney or CPA for advice.

Common law factors used to determine workers' classifications. The IRS uses 20 common law factors to determine whether workers are employees or independent contractors (see Internal Revenue Manual, 4600 Employment Tax Procedure, Exhibit 4640-1).

Workers are generally employees if they

1. must comply with employer's instructions about the work;
2. receive training from or at the direction of the employer;
3. provide services that are integrated into the business;
4. provide services that must be rendered personally;
5. hire, supervise, and pay assistants for the employer;
6. have a continuing working relationship with the employer;
7. must follow set hours of work;

8. work full-time for an employer;
9. do their work on the employer's premises;
10. must do their work in a sequence set by the employer;
11. must submit regular reports to the employer;
12. receive payments of regular amounts at set intervals;
13. receive payments for business and/or traveling expenses;
14. rely on the employer to furnish tools and materials;
15. lack a major investment in facilities used to perform the service;
16. cannot make a profit or suffer a loss from their services;
17. work for one employer at a time;
18. do not offer their services to the general public;
19. can be fired by the employer; or
20. may quit work at any time without incurring liability.

Grant Challenge

Free government money? "Get your fair share by ordering my book." How many times have we seen that on television? One inventor became upset with me when I told him I did not know of any grants that might apply to his invention. Of course, the television salesperson told him to get upset whenever a bureaucrat claimed ignorance. This implied that we really did know where they were and how to get them. We just were not telling. Finally, I told him that if I knew of any such grants I would already have them and be working in the private sector becoming a millionaire.

Can you imagine how much publicity would be generated if there were anywhere near the number of grants some would have us believe? When is the last time you read in the paper about an inventor receiving a grant? Is it because inventors do not apply? No, it is because very few grants exist in the first place. As we discussed in the chapter on evaluations, the U.S. Department of Energy gives grants to worthy energy-conserving inventions that pass two NIST evaluations. With this grant there are three big caveats:

1. It must be an energy-conserving device.
2. It must pass NIST's evaluation.
3. It must compete with many other inventions for the award. There is not an unlimited amount of grant money in this program.

Most grants have similar limitations. They are not just doled out the moment an application is received. Let's take a look at one of the most popular grants people hear about all the time—the Small Business Innovation Research (SBIR) grant. The SBIR program began in 1982 with the Small Business Innovation Act. It set aside 1.25 percent of the annual R&D budgets of any agency with such budgets of $100 million or more. During fiscal year 1991, 11 government agencies identified topics needing research and solicited proposals from the private sector. They were the U.S. Department of Defense; National Aeronautics and Space Administration; the Environmental Protection Agency; Department of Energy; Health and Human Services; National Science Foundation; Department of Agriculture; Department of Transportation; Nuclear Regulatory Commission; Department of Interior; and Department of Education.

The Small Business Administration oversees annual amounts now totaling over $450 million. It was designed to help encourage the development of new technologies with commercially viable applications by the private sector. It provides for Phase I awards up to $50,000 and Phase II awards of up to $500,000. Phase I is the proposed research. Phase II is for more research and prototype development. Phase III is the commercialization aspect, and capital must come from the private sector to launch new products and technologies created from the government-funded R&D awards of Phase I and Phase II. Government procurement contracts are possible.

In the first place, SBIR is not a grant as grants are traditionally understood. It is a contract with the federal government to perform research on topics selected by the government agency. The money is not free. They expect something in return. Secondly, SBIR money is for research in the idea stage. If one already has an invention ready to launch, he cannot qualify for commercialization funding through this program.

The amount of commercialized new products and processes coming out of the SBIR program has been minimal at best. Many of the same companies are award winners over and over again. They do the research, then go back to the till and do some more, but either forget about or are unable to commercialize the fruits of their labor.

Overall the SBIR program can be very helpful to companies with research facilities whose long-term research and development goals are somewhat parallel to those of one of the 11 participating federal agencies. It is one of the few sources of seed capital available today for new product research and development. To be included on the mailing list of SBIR solicitations, write to the Office of Innovation, Research and Technology, U.S. Small Business Administration, SBIR, 1441 L Street, NW, Washington, DC 20416.

For the inventor trying to market his invention, this program is generally a waste of time. The funds from Phase I and II are only to be used for research and development, not for commercialization. It is also expensive to file a proposal. On the average it costs between $4,000 and $8,000 to put together a package for consideration. Usually only existing companies can hope to qualify. Facilities and credentialed expertise need to be apparent in the proposal. Those with higher degrees in the subject of research needed by the government agencies understandably get a more favorable reception from the SBIR reviewers.

There are many people with connections to government agencies that issue grants. Most government employees are honest and hardworking. If they are responsible for funding grants, that is how their job performance is evaluated. I have never heard of a single government employee being rated by how many citizens he has lied to.

There are always caveats to receiving grants. These are little-known facts about a specific grant or any other funding source that make a big difference. They are not commonly known because the popularizers of these programs seem to forget to make the qualifications clear. If they did, it might hurt the sales of their books. One should always strive to understand the caveats as early as possible. They serve as early warning signals not to waste one's time. Before getting excited about the possibility of receiving a grant, would it not be helpful to know that it would only be awarded to a single welfare mother of three or more children in her care living within a ten-mile radius of Chicago?

There are two important truths about grants: The first one is there are not nearly as many available to inventors as what television book salespeople would have us believe. The second one is that if an inventor spends too much time looking for grants, he will likely miss commercializing his invention while he pursues shadows.

There are two important truths about grants: The first one is there are not nearly as many available to inventors as what television book salespeople would have us believe. The second one is that if an inventor spends too much time looking for grants, he will likely miss commercializing his invention while he pursues shadows.

The Challenge of Finding Capital

Unless the inventor is already wealthy, he must somehow raise money to launch his venture. As with grants there are always caveats among the numerous funding sources around the country. In other words, funding sources all have different criteria they look for in a business loan.

Many lending institutions offer debt financing—commercial banks, federal and state loan programs, asset-based lenders, and factorers. These organizations look at many criteria before a loan is made. In general, the criteria are:

- Collateral value
- The financial condition of the borrower
- The profitability of the borrower
- The borrower's capacity to repay
- The reputation and integrity of the borrower
- The management ability of the borrower
- The bank's expected rate of return
- The bank's internal credit policies
- Conditions in the borrower's industry
- General economic conditions
- Federal and state banking regulations
- Federal and state industry regulations

If the bank cannot make the loan, they will sometimes refer one to the Small Business Administration. An SBA loan guarantees up to 85 percent for the loan to the bank. The inventor will still need collateral, and there is more paperwork, but quite a few SBA loans are made each year to those companies with more than two or three years of operating history.

Different kinds of SBA loans exist. The SBA 7(A) is the most well known. The loan can be used for working capital; the purchase of machinery and equipment; the purchase of buildings; or to convert, construct, or expand facilities. The caveat? A new company may be required to have 30 to 50 percent equity already in the company.

The SBA 504 loan program is another lending fund and is administrated by private Certified Development Companies, each with a specific geographic territory. This type of loan offers a 100 percent guarantee for the long-term (up to 20 years) financing of land, buildings, machinery, and equipment. The caveat? None of the money can be used for working capital.

Another possible funding source is the Farmers Home Administration's Business and Industrial Loan Program. It can provide up to a 90 percent guarantee. These loans can be made in any area or community of 50,000 or less population, and preference is given for projects in rural communities and towns consisting of a population of 25,000 or less. It finances working capital as well as fixed assets. The caveat? A tangible balance sheet equity of at least 20 to 25 percent is required for new businesses.

Then there are asset-based lending institutions where a business may borrow against its inventory and receivables. Factoring companies may also help. Instead of borrowing against receivables, a factorer will actually purchase them at a discount, then collect the full amount from the purchaser as his profit. This type of financing is certainly not the type inventors need to start a venture; nevertheless, it is mentioned as something that might be needed later. If you have a good relationship with your local bank, it may also provide a limited amount of receivable financing. Beneath this top layer of funding sources are the individual state programs. In the 1970s, ten or fewer states had programs set up to finance their businesses. Now over 45 states use some of their economic development budget for business financing. While most of this is for established companies in need for expansion capital, some states provide financing programs of which an inventor/entrepreneur might qualify. Some of these are highly structured with specific guidelines and rules. Others are more informal and flexible. The only way to determine whether your project might qualify is to check it out. The addresses and phone numbers of each state's lead economic development agency is in Appendix C. It might also be advisable at this time to contact your closest Small Business Development Center (SBDC) office for assistance.

Small Business Development Centers know much more about their state's financial resources than this book can discuss. The closest SBDC should be an inventor's first place to look for financing assistance. The staff will be able to determine very quickly whether a project might qualify or whether it would be a complete waste of time to apply. If the latter is the case, at least the inventor knows he would be spinning his wheels and can look into other sources.

According to the Corporation for Enterprise Development, the following states offer seed capital funds: Arkansas, Connecticut, Florida, Illinois, Indiana, Iowa, Kansas, Louisiana, Michigan, Minnesota, Missouri, Montana, Nebraska, Ohio, Oklahoma, Oregon, Pennsylvania, Tennessee, and Wisconsin.

The definition of seed capital as used here is "state investment funds, generally in the form of equity participation, providing very early, and generally small amounts of financing to help entrepreneurs prove the viability of a product or business concept not yet in the production stage."

From the same organization the following states offer product development finance: Alaska, Connecticut, Hawaii, Illinois, Indiana, Iowa, Louisiana, Massachusetts, Michigan, Minnesota, New Mexico, North Carolina, Ohio, Oklahoma, Pennsylvania, Rhode Island, Texas, and Utah.

Product development finance is defined as "high-risk financing for new product or production process development, generally provided to mature firms and repayable through royalties tied to product sales. Such financing permits states to encourage innovation and modernization in mature firms without exposing the firm to undue risk." (From "The 1990 Development Report Card for the States," published by the Corporation for Enterprise Development.)

An interesting fund was recently established in Texas called the Texas Product Commercialization Fund. Its purpose is to help Texas businesses bring innovative, technology-based products or processes to the marketplace. The funds can be used for working capital, machinery and equipment, construction, acquisition, or renovation of buildings. Generally the business must have some type of private-sector investment (either an investor or lender) matching the Texas Department of Commerce's investment, and the business must have at least 10 percent equity. The maximum loan term is three years. The amounts that will be loaned are between $25,000 and $200,000.

The Texas legislature directed preference be given to businesses developing energy related products or processes, grantees under the SBIR program, businesses formed to commercialize research funded in part with state funds, and businesses receiving assistance from Texas' SBDCs. Complete details can be requested from the Texas Department of Commerce.

This is great. Even though it is debt financing that few inventors will qualify for if they are trying to build a new company, it shows that the state of Texas is interested in commercializing new products. The information I have received does not indicate the product has to be developed in Texas, so there might be some Texans with whom one could joint venture or license their technology. If one could find a synergistic company in Texas, the availability of this loan program just might make the difference in a go or no go decision.

This information came to me from a contact at a Dallas SBDC office and serves as a good example of how the SBDCs around the country are in the know about significant programs of benefit to inventors. At the time of this writing, the program is still so new it has not yet made its first loan.

In addition to the first and second layers of financing are the venture capital companies and private investors. To identify venture capital companies, probably the best single source is *Pratt's Guide to Venture Capital Sources.* Most libraries should have this reference book. It not only lists all the known venture capital firms, but it provides much good background information on the venture capital industry.

Unfortunately, there is no such book for all the private investors or "angels" across the country. (I have not yet concluded whether they are so named because they go about doing good or because they are so hard to find.) They are usually current or retired businesspersons who have extra money they are willing to invest in venture deals. How much they are willing to invest varies according to how deep their pockets are and how much of their hard-earned money they are willing to risk. A good network is the only way to find them. SBDCs or your state's Department of Commerce might be able to help.

Having discussed all these possible sources, traditional funding sources like banks, state programs, federal funds, and venture capital funds are generally unavailable for inventors of new products and start-ups. These sources justifiably invest only in experienced management and established companies. Specific products or processes are of secondary consideration. Many new product ideas, therefore, are left out in the cold regardless of the products' future value.

For every project traditionally funded there are at least 20 or 30 seed and start-up ventures that are considered and do not qualify for financing. Yet a significant number of these ventures involving proprietary products would become successful if only the proper resources could be located for the project.

The real solution for creating more capital sources for inventions lies in the formation of networks dedicated to forming strategic alliances with existing manufacturing and marketing firms. These companies together represent the largest of all new product development and commercialization "funds." Strategic alliances are licensing agreements, joint ventures, R&D partnerships, shared manufacturing agreement, or even customized marketing and sales agreements. Established firms are much more likely than an inventor or inexperienced entrepreneur to have cash flow, personnel, equipment, expertise, and leveraging power to complete development work and launch a product.

In Oklahoma we identified over 500 companies wishing to commercialize new products through strategic alliances. Although forming strategic alliances is complicated, unique with each project, and requires aggressive hands-on effort, it has proven to be successful—judging from the more than 50 projects launched so far. Strategic alliances have been shown to be far more effective at new product commercialization than in building companies around a single product. We will take up the subject of licensing in Chapter 10. For now let's take a quick look at the joint venture as a possible vehicle for commercialization. We have handled some new product projects that already had either manufacturing or marketing capability, but did not have both. Either the inventor was a manufacturer without marketing expertise or the inventor had an entrepreneurial background but was unable to raise the capital necessary to produce the product. As an inventor with either of these two skills, a joint venture might be possible. The key to a joint venture is that each party needs the other to achieve the common goal of commercializing the product.

It was recently discovered that a plastics manufacturer in northeast Oklahoma was acquired from its Fortune 100 parent company in a leveraged buyout. The new owners were three local citizens. One was the former company's plant manager. The plant had a very successful record and was recognized for its quality product. The parent company had to sell it because one of its other subsidiaries had lost a significant court case and needed cash. While acquisition negotiations to buy the company were pending, the parent laid off about half of its employees. During the first year of operation under new ownership the company kept up with its orders from one or two major customers. The company had a tremendous amount of excess capacity and a trained labor pool to draw from in the community, but it had no additional orders. It desperately wanted to grow, but it did not feel it had the cash to hire a marketing team and launch a marketing campaign to increase its business.

When we were apprised of the situation we were able to use our network of marketing companies to locate one willing to expand the company's markets. Further, it would do it for a percentage of sales and no up-front fees. This was a critical aspect, because the company had no working capital to formulate and implement a strategic marketing plan. While the details (and there were a significant number of them) are confidential, a joint venture agreement was finalized between the two companies.

Both received what they wanted—more business. While both had some capital, neither had enough to make the plan work independently of the other. Both had knowledge and skills that the other party did not possess. Should large orders result from the joint venture, the manufacturing company had a line of credit to draw down on to order the raw materials and pay the employees until the customers' checks were received.

There are many definitions of joint ventures, but the best one I have found is an enterprise owned and operated by a small group of businesses for a specific business or project for the mutual benefit of the members of the group. A joint venture can be used to develop new markets, develop a new product or technology, pool resources to develop a distribution facility, qualify for capital, or bid on a government contract. It can be with a foreign partner to keep manufacturing costs low.

It is possible for a joint venture to be negotiated whenever an inventor has more to offer to the project than just the intellectual property. If he brings to the table specific marketing experience or manufacturing ability, management expertise, or financing, it is possible. If not, well, that's why licensing agreements were invented.

Securities Law Challenge

I was at an invention commercialization seminar in eastern Oklahoma. One of the inventors had his business partner with him. Over several years the business partner had invested several thousand of his own dollars to develop a working prototype. In addition he had gotten other smaller investors to put money in the company. Later he was talking about how much had been spent on the project to date, and it did not seem to add up. Finally I asked him how many investors were in the deal. He said, "Over a hundred!" I was stunned. I asked him if he had gotten advice from a corporate or securities attorney before he sold the stock. "No, it wasn't necessary. They all believed in the project and wanted to invest." I just shook my head and told him he had better hope our securities administrator didn't hear about it. State and federal securities laws are enacted to protect unsophisticated investors. There are limits to the number of people that can invest in a company. There are laws that limit what a pro-moter can and cannot do and say while raising money. There are laws that apply once the money is raised.

Raising money is serious business. It has to be done right or someone could go to jail.

Raising money is serious business. It has to be done right or someone could go to jail. You should always get an attorney's or an investment banker's advice before incorporating and selling shares in your company—or any other kind of security. Most disturbing about the above project was the fact that the business manager had raised his money in spite of several experts in the field telling him that the invention violated several fundamental laws of the universe and would never work. Blind faith is never a healthy reason to invest time and money in a project. Once mental assent is given to the valid-ity of blind faith, it only makes it easier for one to become a victim of any number of fraudulent activities. It seems that blind faith is just as active in the business world as it is in the religious world. Maybe we would be better off if we more readily appreciated Missouri's motto—"Show Me!"

Due Diligence Challenge

Inventors with seemingly great inventions who try to build a company face another roadblock called due diligence. Due diligence is a term borrowed from the Securities and Exchange Commission. It is performed when the inventor seeks either debt or equity financ-ing. In performing due diligence the funding source makes a "due diligent" effort to confirm that the company is telling the truth in its business plan or other documents. Because the main concern of debt funding is the type and amount of the collateral, less due diligence will be performed to get a loan than in an equity agreement.

An equity transaction occurs when someone puts capital into the company in exchange for equity, for example, stock ownership, patent ownership, or both. Because the only way for an investor to get his principal back plus a return is through the growth of the company, he has to make sure that what he is investing in is worth it. If an inventor is planning to make such investments sometime in the future with earnings from his invention's successful commercialization, he will want to do the same thing. So expect it.

A venture capitalist or sophisticated private investor will want to make sure of the ownership of the patent, the scope of its coverage, and whether there might be other authors not listed on the patent. He will also want to verify all the details in the business and marketing plans. He will want to know how the assumptions were arrived at to form the basis of the financial projections. He will want to talk to your banker, accountant, attorney, suppliers, sales representatives, customers, landlords, and even friends and enemies.

The due diligence process can be an extensive and grueling investigation. It increases in its intensity as the project's perceived risks grow. An investor will leave no stone unturned. He is looking for snakes hiding under the rocks that might cause him to lose his investment. He will focus on the management of the company for the reasons discussed above.

The Insurance Challenge

If you are going to venture expect to apply for general insurance on your company as well as to obtain products liability insurance for your product. The following is a list of some of the information and questions your insurance agent will need to propose the best possible coverage.

GENERAL INFORMATION

1. Type of organization:

2. Year founded:

   State of incorporation:

3. Subsidiary of another company?

   Name of parent:
   % of ownership:

4. Controlled by another company?

   Explain:

5. What is your Standard Industrial Classification (SIC) code?

6. Provide a general description of your business:

7. Describe major service(s) and/or product(s):

8. Is stock publicly held?

   Exchange?
   Has there ever been an unfriendly takeover attempt?
   Estimate of probability that one may occur in future:

9. Is company currently in an acquisition mode?

   General description of types of targets:

10. Have you acquired any other organizations in the past 25 years?

11. Has your company sold any of its subsidiaries or divisions?

12. Do you have operations outside the U.S., Canada, or Puerto Rico?

13. Does your organization joint venture with other organizations?

    Describe types, typical method of insuring:
    List any current projects:

14. List directors, officers, and stockholders:

15. Has the company espoused a policy on whether or not it will indemnify its employees with respect to liability for serving on these boards?

GENERAL INFORMATION (continued)

16. Does the company purchase directors and officers liability insurance?

17. What is the company's
    - cost of capital?
    - actual internal rate of return?
    - target internal rate of return?
    - effective income tax rate?

18. Describe your organization's tax posture?

19. Do you have an investment interest in any other operation or business?

20. Indicate how long your organization has been under its present management:

21. Length of time at present location?

PRODUCT LIABILITY SURVEY

1. List all current and discontinued products:

2. Can each unit of product be readily identified by a serial number?

3. Can products be traced to their ultimate destination?

4. Is there a products recall plan in force?

    Discuss estimated cost. Comments:
    Has it ever been used?

5. Is any part of the manufacturing process subcontracted?

    Describe:

6. What is company philosophy toward insurance of its distributors and vendors?

    If you are a distributor, are you insured by manufacturers?

PRODUCT LIABILITY SURVEY (continued)

7. Do your distributors modify, package, or service the product?

   Explain:

8. Are any products sold outside the U.S.?

   List countries, product, and uses:
   Annual sales: $

9. Do you sell foreign-made products in the U.S.?

   Describe:
   Annual sales: $

10. Are there plans to introduce any new products in the next 24 months?

    Describe:

11. Are any of the products:

    ❏ used in automobile manufacture?
    ❏ used in watercraft manufacture?
    ❏ used in aircraft or spacecraft manufacture?
    ❏ flammable?
    ❏ explosive?
    ❏ poisonous?
    ❏ subject to spoilage?
    ❏ corrosive?
    ❏ carcinogenic?
    Explain:

12. Are outside design/engineering firms used in the development of your products?

    If yes, do you verify their insurance coverage?

13. Are any products ever designed or manufactured to customer specifications?

    Details:

PRODUCT LIABILITY SURVEY (continued)

14. Are any products ever

    - installed on customer premises by your employees?
    - serviced or repaired on customer premises by your employees?

    Details:

15. Are any products tested and approved/certified by outside laboratories (e.g., Underwriters Laboratories, American Gas Association)?

16. Are instruction manuals, labels, warnings, etc., reviewed by your risk manager and legal counsel?

    Are they also printed in another language to fit either an ethnic or foreign market?

17. Are detailed research, design, and testing records maintained?

    Comments:
    Are records kept of any reported product malfunctions?

18. Is there an ongoing quality assurance program?

    Details:

19. Regarding suppliers of component parts:

    - Is each part identified by a serial number?
    - Is their quality control program evaluated?
    - Is proof of insurance required and maintained?
    - Is there a hold harmless in your favor?

    Comments:

20. Do any of your subsidiaries sell their products to other subsidiaries (e.g., component parts)?

    Explain, obtain annual amount of intercompany sales:

21. If house brands are sold (retailers), identify manufacturer(s) and packager(s):

Summing Up

I have attempted to show how very difficult and exasperating it can be to venture a new product. The above represents only a small portion of what must be considered when venturing. Very little about entrepreneuring is taught or written from this perspective. This is no mystery. Positive thinking sells better than negative. However, those who counsel with those willing to risk their life savings and their mental health to realize a dream must understand those folks are vulnerable. They should accept the responsibility and duty to explain the other side of venturing. There are more than enough who glamorize it. I have not intended to kill anyone's dream. This chapter has been written to warn and inform inventors about the numerous and, for most of us, insurmountable challenges in commercialization through venturing.

One must "count the cost" not only in terms of money, but in the toll it will take on the entrepreneur and his family. Too many good new products have gone by the wayside because those venturing them could not see it through for one reason or another. By holding the belief that venturing is the only way to market an invention, one could very well be taking the first step toward a dismal future. But do not despair. There is another solution—licensing.

TEN

Licensing

"There must be a beginning of any great matter, but the continuing unto the end until it be thoroughly finished yields the true glory."

—Sir Francis Drake

I recently met a man named Frank who lived in a small lake resort community. He had moved there after retiring from a major aerospace company. Frank is now well over 70 years old, and his mind is sharp as a tack. He has earned one patent and has several others pending from his designs of improved boats and boat trailers. These modified designs make water sports even more pleasurable for those who fish, water ski, or just like to ride in boats.

The fame of Frank's boat and trailer designs has spread far—not exactly far and wide, but more like far and narrow. By this I mean vacationers from all over the country who see their friends with Frank's boats and trailers quickly call him up and place an order.

Years ago, Frank made an offer to a local manufacturer. Would the manufacturer pay Frank a 5 percent commission on any orders Frank brought to him? "Absolutely," replied the manufacturer,

135

amazed by his luck. So on the strength of a handshake, the deal was done. A rather significant number of Frank's boats and trailers have now been sold. So many, in fact, he has earned about $50,000 on sales of approximately one million dollars.

What a way to live. Frank has a spacious home with a beautiful view overlooking a sky-blue lake. He has built a successful boat distributorship to supplement his retirement income. In addition, his own boats and boat trailers earn him royalties while he invents even more new and improved designs.

Frank is now beginning to feel his mortality. While thinking of what might happen to his family after he is gone, he felt something must be wrong with the way he had structured his invention business. He had spent most of his $50,000 royalty income traveling to boat shows, contracting with an advertising firm to make videos of his products, and paying for product liability insurance. "They were a write-off, anyway," Frank explained. He felt he had to spend the money in order to sell more of his boats and trailers. Why did Frank feel uncomfortable? Statistically, he had beaten the odds. He had won. Nevertheless he was troubled. After a million dollars in sales and nothing in the bank to show for it, he should feel deeply troubled.

His problem was simple—he did not understand licensing. He had heard that 5 percent was generally a fair royalty and sometimes a fair commission for a salesperson. But he did not know the standard terms of agreement for either licensing or sales contracts. For example, he did not know that it was normal for an inventor to receive a 3 to 7 percent royalty for licensing his intellectual property only—without having to pay for any marketing expenses. He just did not know that it should be the responsibility of his licensee to bear the cost of such things as advertising, insurance, and sales. Frank had been providing all these freely to the manufacturer. While thinking he was licensing, he had actually ventured his products. He had won the battle of successfully launching his new products, but he had lost the war of earning the profits that should have been his.

This chapter is about licensing—the second way to commercialize an invention, and the one I would choose if I were an inventor. Licensing should be chosen not because one runs out of enough capital to venture or because one cannot raise the capital to venture it; it should be a well thought out decision made before the inventor throws what little money he might have down the drain trying to build a single-product company.

For the winning inventor, understanding licensing should be as natural as getting out of bed in the morning. Licensing, as will be explained, significantly reduces the inventor's risk and financial exposure. Taking the combined statistics of new business failure and new patent failure into consideration, it should be seen as the preferred funding mechanism for the commercialization of products protected by intellectual property.

What Is Intellectual Property?

Article 1, Section 8, of the U.S. Constitution granted Congress the power to promote the progress of science and useful arts. From reading the entire section it would make perfect sense for the brief pericope to conclude with the word *Arts.* However, with 18 additional words it became the only power given Congress in Section 8 that spells out precisely how the power is to be carried out. From those 18 words, U.S. copyright and patent systems were born. Furthermore, those 18 words spell out that the first to invent and the first to write are to be rewarded—not the first to file, as is the case in every other country in the world with a patent system.

Oliver E. Allen's article in the September 1990 issue of *American Heritage,* titled "The Power of Patents," summarizes the history of patents:

> *The system started on a small scale after the first patent act became law in April 1790. The first patents (No. 1 was issued on July 31 of that year) had merely to be okayed by two of the three officers of the patent board: the Secretary of State, the Secretary of War, and the Attorney General, who were expected to perform their patent work in addition to executing all their other duties. By 1802 a more formal arrangement was needed, and a separate Patent Office was set up under the jurisdiction of the Secretary of State. So great was the flood of applications that the office allowed inventors to omit any claim that their devices or processes were novel; all they had to do was register them.*

Today the U.S. Patent Office has grown into the largest single depository of technical information in the world. It is cluttered and cumbersome to use. It is understaffed. It is not entirely computerized like Japan's new billion-dollar system. Nevertheless, it is the best in the world, and without it, America would not be the only super-power in the world.

When I first heard the term *intellectual property*, I had to laugh. I thought of one of the old horror movies depicting a mad doctor's laboratory with human brains in jars lined up one after another on shelves. I later learned that intellectual property is no laughing matter. Quite an industry is built up around it. Companies could not function without intellectual property. Millions are spent each year defending intellectual property claims in court. In the 1980s patent litigation rose 50 percent over the previous year. In case after case judges have ruled in favor of the inventor. The original inventors have won multimillion dollar judgments for inventors of the laser, delayed windshield wiper, and the semiconductor to name but a few. Several years ago, the courts ruled against patent owners about 80 percent of the time. Today the courts have realized that unless the inventor is protected there is no reason for a patent system. They now rule in favor of the patent owner about 80 percent of the time.

Some who have gone through the patenting process say they will never file for another one. They will just venture the product themselves without any protection and try to be the first to the market, hoping this strategy will be good enough to sustain their product in the market long enough to earn a significant profit. After all, they reason, are there not many products being sold today with no patent protection? This feeling should be expected considering the high number of granted patents that never make money for the inventor. The problem with this view is that most inventors do not have large synergistic manufacturing and marketing companies with vast distribution channels waiting to launch a new product. Just being first to the market does not guarantee the product will prevail over the inevitable competition.

IBM is hardly ever the first to the market with new technology. It seems to wait for someone else to perfect the technology. Then it waits for the market to indicate its readiness. Then and only then does IBM use its marketing muscle to sell its version of the item.

Should you determine that launching a new product without patent protection is the course you will take, you should also recognize that without the involvement of a synergistic company, failure is almost assured. And without a proprietary position it is virtually impossible to find such a company. It simply is wrong to assume that earning intellectual property protection is a waste of time and money. This assumption usually is based on an emotional response to a negative experience that likely would not have happened in the first place if the inventor had known more about the issues involved in new product commercialization.

There are basically four kinds of intellectual property: patents, trademarks, copyrights, and trade secrets. All can be licensed. Formal federal procedures exist to gain the first three. Each state has its own laws regarding trade secrets, but all courts require you to demonstrate a diligent effort to keep the secret privileged information available to only those with a need to know. Three kinds of patents exist: utility, design, and plant. Some describe these as a monopoly. Others say patents are not really a monopoly, but do give one the right to sue someone else who manufactures and/or markets the item without permission of the owner. Without getting into semantic ambiguities that confuse the issue, patents are grants by a government to the inventor or inventors that exclude others for a limited time from making, using, or selling the invention in the country that grants the patent. Brief descriptions of the rights granted by each of the three patent types follow:

1. A *utility patent* is obtained for processes (chemical, mechanical, or electrical procedures), machines, articles of manufacture, and compositions of matter. These patents address the workings of the articles themselves, protecting their functional, rather than aesthetic, qualities. These carry a 17-year term from when the patent is issued.
2. A *design patent* is obtained for an invention of a new, original, and ornamental design for an article of manufacture. Its stress is on the beautification in manufactured articles hoping to increase their desirability and satisfy the aesthetic sense of the purchaser. Design patent protection extends only to an item's appearance, not to its functional aspects. These carry a 14-year term from when the patent is issued.
3. A *plant patent* may be granted for a distinct and new variety of a cultivated asexually reproduced plant, including mutants, hybrids, and newly found seedlings.

Patents must be novel, useful, and nonobvious. Novelty refers to its newness. It cannot have been previously patented, invented, or discovered. If it has, it is judged to be "anticipated by prior art" and denied protection.

Being useful (having utility) means the invention must actually work or otherwise be useful, though it need not be better than what is available. Utility is seldom a problem, except in the area of chemical process patents. If the invention passes being novel and useful, then it still must be nonobvious. This standard dictates that a patent may not be obtained if the differences between the subject matter sought to be patented and the prior art are such that the subject matter as a whole would have been obvious at the time the invention was made to a person having ordinary skill in the art to which said subject matter pertains.

The nonobvious standard has proven to be a subjective test that is applied in varying ways by the U.S. Patent and Trademark Office and the courts, with varying results. It is estimated that 60 percent of all patents invalidated by the courts are ruled to be obvious.

A trademark is any word, name, symbol, or device or any combination thereof adopted and used to identify goods and distinguish them from those manufactured or sold by others. It protects the consumer from deception and confusion, and it serves to guarantee the products. It cannot be a generic term, for example, milk, coffee, or bread. It can be arbitrary, suggestive, or descriptive, however, the closer it is to arbitrary the better. Examples of arbitrary trademarks are Kodak and Lux. They have no meaning by themselves. George Eastman thought of the Kodak trademark using the "trial and error" method. He said he knew a trade name should be short, strong, and not mean anything. The letter K was one of his favorite letters, so he decided to start and end his trademark with it. He tried many combinations of letters between the two *ks* before he settled on the name of Kodak.

Supreme Court Justice Felix Frankfurter once commented on the importance of trademarks:

> *The protection of trademarks is the law's recognition of the psychological function of symbols. If it is true that we live by symbols, it is no less true that we purchase goods by them. A trademark is a merchandising shortcut which induces a purchaser to select what he wants or what he has been led to believe he wants. The owner of a mark exploits this human propensity by making every effort to impregnate the atmosphere of the market with the drawing power of a congenial symbol. Whatever the means employed, the aim is the same—to convey through the mark, in the midst of potential customers, the desirability of the commodity upon which it appears. Once this is attained, the trademark owner has something of value. If another poaches upon the commercial magnetism the symbol has created, the owner can obtain legal redress.*

Trademarks can be protected by common law, state law, and federal law. For example, if the mark is used first in commerce, it is protected by common law only within a 20-mile radius. If it is registered with the U.S. Patent and Trademark Office and sold in at least one other state, it is protected in all 50 states regardless of whether it has actually been sold in those states. One can file for a trademark if he intends to use it within three years. Formal registration can occur only after it is used in commerce. A trademark may become even more valuable than a patent. It should be registered as quickly as possible.

Having said this, let me add that it actually may be a waste of time and money for an inventor to register a trademark without input from the licensee (the one who licenses the intellectual property). The licensee may not like the name or artwork. He may dislike the trademark so much that he would not consider licensing the item. A licensing agreement can be worded to allow the licensor (patent owner) to own any trademarks that may be obtained in order to market the product.

Copyrights protect original works of authorship that are fixed by a tangible form of expression. They include literary works; musical works; dramatic works; pantomimes and choreographic works; pictorial, graphic, and sculptural works; motion pictures and other audiovisual works; and sound recordings. Computer programs are considered literary works. Copyright registrations are not filed with the U.S. Patent and Trademark Office, but with the Library of Congress.

Did you know that if you hire an artist to design the package in which your invention will be sold, the artist owns the copyright? I know—that does not sound correct. It just seems as though it should belong to whoever paid for the artwork. However, remember the Constitution protects the authors, not those commissioning the work. If someone paid an inventor $2,000 a month as an independent contractor to produce a new mechanical design that turned out to be patentable, the inventor would own the intellectual property unless he assigned it by written agreement to his client. If no written assignment existed, the inventor could actually prevent the client that paid him to invent it from using it. The same is true with copyrights. This is effective automatically unless a written contract states otherwise. It is called a work-for-hire contract. You should consult your attorney for more information.

Trade Secrets

Patents

Trade secrets are also considered to be intellectual property if an appropriate effort has been made to maintain secrecy. A court would not exactly consider a soft-drink formula or a barbecue sauce recipe to be secret if it were tacked up on the break-room wall.

While all states have their own trade secret laws, a movement is underway to standardize on the Uniform Trade Secrets Act. About 20 states have actually adopted it in their statutes. The Act includes methods, techniques, and "know-how."

Generally a court will look into a company's security procedures; employment agreements; confidentiality agreements with employees and independent contractors; noncompete contracts with employees; and the company's employee handbook for evidence of a diligent attempt to keep trade secrets a secret.

Inventors with patents pending should treat them as trade secrets. It is not public information until a letter of patent is issued. Patent-pending status that is adequately protected as a trade secret can be helpful in giving pause to any would-be competitors of your product if they see the appropriate "patent-pending" markings. The reason for this is they do not know what claims have been filed. This can give a product a significant marketing advantage lasting two or three years, and maybe more if the proceedings are drawn out. Although infringement proceedings cannot begin until after the patent is issued, they fear they might have to cease and desist in the manufacture and selling of the item if they violate any claims.

While in the process of locating and negotiating with potential licensees, it is best not to reveal your patent-pending number to anyone. No one except you and your attorney or patent agent need it. I have heard stories of patent-pending numbers getting into the wrong hands. From having this number, it is said one can take it to the patent office, pull the pending patent, and discover exactly what claims have been filed. I have never personally been involved in this kind of situation, so I cannot judge whether it can actually occur, but if this has happened even once, it is once too often.

By the same token, the claims listed in your pending patent filing should never be revealed during the search for a licensee. He does not need to see your claims until just before he is ready to sign the licensing agreement. Then he should be willing to sign a confidentiality agreement with a noncompete clause prior to examining the specific claims.

It is not unusual for a potential licensee to insist that evidence be given that a patent filing actually is pending. The inventor should be willing to provide the receipt from the patent office and all the filing information except the patent-pending number and the claims. The potential licensee could also be referred to the attorney handling the filing. He will want to talk with the attorney anyway about the possible scope of coverage and whether he has begun debating with the patent examiner.

A potential licensee will insist on this proof because he knows some may allege that a patent is pending when in reality the inventor has only some drawings stashed away in the closet. To some inexperienced inventors, *patent pending* means only that they intend to file someday when they raise enough money.

But there is another reason a prospective licensee would want to see what has been filed with the patent office (less the number and claims). Not being a technical person, I tend to enjoy reading the background section of the patent filing. It enables me to get my mind around the project quickly. The same is true for a licensee. He has to quickly get some sense of what he may be licensing, and this is one way to do it.

If the pending patent is treated as a trade secret, the only way a competitor might logically decide to offer a similar product is to hire an attorney to analyze the features of your product. Then he must perform a patent search and offer an opinion on how the claims might have been constructed and the chances of patentability. Based on this advice, the competitor may decide to launch his similar product or wait until the patent is granted to make the decision. They usually decide to wait.

"Know-How" Can Be Licensed

An inventor should always, if possible, license his "know-how"—not just his technology (patent). Know-how is work that has gone into the project that is not necessarily patentable, yet is important to the project's success. If the inventor has done his market research and identified all the competitors and the potential markets, located suppliers of raw materials, and obtained price quotes for those raw materials, then that work represents know-how. It gives the licensee a jump start in gearing up to launch the product; therefore it adds value to the project and should be a negotiating point with the licensee. Other know-how might include technical drawings, formulas, use instructions, assembly instructions, patterns, customer lists, surveys, artwork, or even manufacturing knowledge.

For the inventor (licensor) "know-how" is an important element in the licensing agreement. Let's say a pending patent filing is finally denied by the patent office a year after it has been licensed. The claims were judged to be obvious by the examiner. Yet the product had been selling well for several months and the first royalty payment, hopefully the first of many, is coming due. If only the technology had been licensed, the inventor would be dependent upon the licensee "doing the right thing" and continuing to pay his royalty. The licensee would in no way be obligated to pay the inventor, because he licensed the patent, which was not granted. The inventor has no recourse but to go into business himself, along with anyone else wanting to compete. This same scenario would occur if the patent was challenged and judged by a court to be invalid. The licensee would no longer be legally bound to pay the licensor any royalties on sales.

The solution to this might be to license not only the technology but also the know-how. The majority of the total running royalty could be for the technology and a smaller percentage for the know-how. If the total royalty is to be 6 percent, 4 percent could be applied to the patent and the other 2 percent could be for know-how. It is a point of negotiation between the licensor and licensee. But the inventor should understand that know-how royalties may continue for as long as the product sells. This is true unless a time limit is negotiated, the know-how becomes public domain, or if someone else is awarded a patent on the trade secret. This is in contrast to licensing just the patent, because these royalty payments are no longer owed to an inventor after the patent expires.

Licensing "know-how" is a nebulous subject. Let me repeat this caveat: Do not sit down and draft a licensing contract based on this book alone. Advice from competent intellectual property counsel is very important. Get it before signing any agreement.

Patents, trademarks, copyrights, and trade secrets—these are what are collectively referred to as intellectual property. They are assets created by one's mind, and all can be licensed. All four could even be included in a single licensing agreement.

Licensing Agreements

Two basic types of licensing agreements exist: exclusive and nonexclusive. The most well-known is the exclusive licensing agreement. With this type of agreement, the licensee receives by contract from the inventor (licensor) the right to manufacture, use, and/or sell the product exclusive of anyone else—including the inventor. Some say this is actually an agreement not to be sued for manufacturing, using, or selling the product, but I've never seen a contract worded like that.

Nonexclusive licensing agreements allow the same right to manufacture, use, and sell the covered invention, but anyone who possesses such a license must compete with others holding the same agreement. May the best one win!

The exclusive licensing agreement does not have to cover worldwide territories, every possible market, and all applications. It is not unusual for an exclusive license to be limited in some way, usually by geography, market, or field of use. To be considered an exclusive license, there must be a provision for at least some exclusivity. A licensor could be granted the rights to sell only in the United States or even west of the Mississippi River. He could be licensed only for England, France, and Spain. These would be exclusive licenses with geographic limitations.

It is possible for an inventor to exclusively license his invention to be manufactured and sold only in the health care market. The licensee might be a hospital supply distributor covering the Southwestern states. He knows all the other major hospital distributors around the country, and he anticipates that if the item is successful in the states he covers, it will sell anywhere. Then there is the exclusive license limited by the field of use. Had you been the inventor of Velcro, you might have decided to issue licenses on the type of products on which it would be used. Velcro has many applications. Some uses are as fasteners for men's and women's clothing, athletic equipment, and office equipment. So it might be possible for one to issue an exclusive licensing agreement only for lingerie sold through beauty shops in Russia. That might not be considered a very valuable license with all those kinds of restrictions. Nevertheless, it still would be an exclusive license, because no one else could manufacture and sell the same lingerie through beauty shops in Russia.

One more worthy of mention is sometimes referred to as a sole license. This grants an exclusive license to the licensee with one exception—the inventor. This can be handy if the inventor has a limited capacity to produce and sell his invention and realizes a transition will have to be made within a year or two. It could allow the inventor to launch his product on a small scale to an easy niche market while also allowing his licensee to gear up for a full-blown manufacturing and marketing effort.

Licensing agreements can take many forms; like inventions, each is different. There is no sure way to say one form is always better than another. It depends on the situation. However, one general truth can be stated about licensing agreements: They are most valuable to potential licensees and easier to negotiate when there are minimal limitations. Using the example above, a licensee would much rather be able to sell lingerie not only to beauty shops in Russia, but to every retailer in the world that buys and sells women's clothing. He would also like the right to sell directly to the consumer through magazine advertising or catalogs.

An inventor once told me there was no way he was going to license his invention for 5 percent. After spending 15 minutes or so explaining the pros and cons of licensing, he belligerently asked, "Why in h*** should I have to give up 95 percent of my deal?!"

I am still trying to think of a more tactful way in which I could have responded. At first I was just stunned, then I almost fell out of my chair in hysterical laughter. Here was a man with no capital who insisted on building a multimillion dollar company to manufacture and sell his invention; yet he could not understand the concepts of gross sales, net profit, or the capital necessary to generate them. In concluding he was being asked to give up 95 percent of his project, he failed to consider that he was also giving up virtually 100 percent of the headaches and risk that go with manufacturing, marketing, and financing. Unfortunately, this was another good product never launched because the inventor did not or would not understand licensing.

There are certainly some challenges in licensing. If it were easy everyone would be doing it, and everyone would be rich. It is hard work to find a qualified potential licensee. Once one is found, the deal can be difficult to negotiate. How do two separate entities arrive at an equitable royalty rate? The inventor might lose control over the implementation of his own invention. The deal might fall apart shortly after it is made, leaving the inventor to start all over again.

On the other hand, if he is successful in finding a licensee, he probably has funded his invention much more quickly through licensing than if he had tried to raise venture capital. He has kept his continued financial exposure and risk to an absolute minimum. His product will be launched more quickly. He can go on to something else and enjoy maybe 10 to 20 percent of the item's net profit as a royalty.

Finding Licensees

One thing we have learned over the years is that it is generally a waste of time to work with large companies to license inventions from independent inventors. They can talk a great game, but when it comes to actually making a deal, it rarely happens. Most of their interaction with inventions from independent inventors is for public relations purposes. Some popular writers claim that large companies are the only way to go—that one can make more money from a large company's failure than from a small company's success. They can back up their view from personal experience, but that has not been my experience. I cannot see how it would be the norm.

Chase after large companies only if you enjoy running gauntlets. I and my colleagues have spent many hours in discussions with large companies on more than a few inventions and have gotten nowhere. The reasons given are too numerous to list, but they all mean one thing: They are not interested. Finding small manufacturing companies and marketing firms that wish to grow has been far more successful than waiting on and negotiating with large companies.

Chase after large companies only if you enjoy running gauntlets. I and my colleagues have spent many hours in discussions with large companies on more than a few inventions and have gotten nowhere. The reasons given are too numerous to list, but they all mean one thing: They are not interested. Finding small manufacturing companies and marketing firms that wish to grow has been far more successful than waiting on and negotiating with large companies.

Our experience is confirmed elsewhere. In their article, "World of Small-Firm Licensing," Marcia L. Rorke and David S. Lux write:

> *Licensing agreements tend to work best (and are arrived at more easily) when the language and culture of the licensor and licensee are similar. The "corporate culture" barrier is almost always a factor in the difficulties individual and small business inventors face as they try to license to very large corporations. For small businesses and individual inventors, technologies handed off to a small-firm product champion who understands applications, technical implications, and the market stand a far better chance of success than those that enter large corporate product development efforts. (Les Nouvelles, December 1990.)*

Finding those who are interested is the trick. Networking is part of the commercialization triad of research. Gathering this information makes a critical difference between success and failure. The online databases discussed in Chapters 7 and 8 are invaluable. Some states may have surveyed their manufacturing and marketing companies for interest in new products. Licensees are out there, and they can be found.

We traditionally think of manufacturers only as potential licensing partners. The truth of the matter is that most of the inventions we have licensed have been to marketing firms who then subcontract the manufacturing. Let's face it: Most inventions can be made without much trouble. It is not difficult to find someone to make a mold for a plastic item or cut and sew a clothing accessory. Many manufacturers will do custom work. Those that do usually have little or no marketing expertise. But marketing expertise is the number-one most important attribute of a potential licensee. He must have the ability either to market the product himself or easily arrange for the marketing. It would be a good idea for an inventor to focus his efforts first on sales and marketing firms as licensing candidates. Secondarily look for manufacturers in the invention's general field, but only if they are marketing companies first, and manufacturers second.

Following is a case history from a book entitled *Licensing—A Strategy for Profits,* by Edward P. White. It relates how the inventor of the Designer Blocks technology found his licensees. It testifies to the importance of consulting the *Encyclopedia of Associations* during preliminary research:

The primary source for information about the concrete block industry is a trade association called the National Concrete Masonry Association. This association holds a major convention each year which is attended by 2,000 to 3,000 people. I was informed by my patent attorney that the patent would issue about four weeks before the convention. We purchased exhibit space at the convention and scurried like crazy to put an exhibit together. At the convention I met with other suppliers who suggested the best prospects in the various regions. I also reviewed the program to see who chaired committees, served on the executive board, etc., to get an idea of who the leaders in the industry were. We also advertised in the program that this was a newly patented product. So many of the leaders also sought us out because they knew how important it is to be first with new products in their respective markets. Others were interested in simply typing up the new idea.

At any rate, ours was the first new product in the industry in several years, and we were able to generate a lot of interest at the first convention we attended, even though the industry was in a pretty severe recession.

Licensing—A Strategy for Profits, commissioned by the Licensing Executives Society, is a very good overview of the licensing process. Its case studies and bibliography are particularly helpful for those wanting to learn more about licensing.

Royalties

When first beginning to think about the possibility of licensing, inventors seem more concerned about three issues above all others. It is good that inventors are most concerned about these questions because if there are misperceptions about them, the agreement surely will be killed one way or another before negotiations can even begin. They are:

1. What will my royalty be?
2. How much up-front money will I receive?
3. How can I keep the company from sitting on my idea and not doing anything to commercialize it?

Royalty rates are governed by two overriding concepts. The first is that an inventor brings technology to a company that the company has not had to develop itself. It is possible that the company may have had to spend millions of dollars conducting research and development to arrive at the inventor's technology. On the other hand, an employee of the company may have developed the idea while conducting his normal daily activities. In this case the invention probably would have been automatically assigned to the company.

Second, an inventor's royalty rate is governed by the expected profits to the company. Notice carefully the words "profits to the company." Companies are interested in profits to an inventor only if it means that through giving profits to the inventor the company itself will earn profits in direct proportion to its risk. It is critical that the inventor understand this risk factor. The manufacturer, marketer, or financier actually licensing a patent risks significant dollars to commercialize it. Inventors do not seem to appreciate this fact while considering what royalty rate would be acceptable to them.

Licensees have risks too. One potential licensee I know made a list of risks his company was willing to assume in licensing a new product for the automotive aftermarket. Both the company and the inventor realized it would take a year or two to gear up and begin selling at a significant pace. It certainly is not an exhaustive list, but the company was trying to help the inventor understand that if only one of the following events occurred, the project might very easily have to be abandoned—after the company sunk $40,000 or $50,000 into its commercialization:

- The next recession could damage the market for cars and accessories.
- The next inflationary period's high interest rates could hurt demand for cars and accessories.
- Gasoline prices could rise and kill desire for cars and travel.
- A similar and less expensive product could be launched during ramp-up (preparation to launch a product).
- A similar but less expensive product could be launched during ramp-up by a firm with larger financial resources.
- A different product filling the same need could be launched during ramp-up.
- A different product that fills same need could be launched during ramp-up by a firm with larger financial resources.

- A better-financed competitor could launch his product and block access to distribution channels by bundling his product with the rest of his product line.
- Manufacturers might begin building as standard items in new cars an alternative solution.
- As the time of the launch languishes during this negotiation, the odds of its success diminish.
- The patent could be attacked by litigation at any time.
- Key patent claims could be denied as a result of litigation.
- The company might have to litigate infringement at any time.
- The product may either not sell, not be developed correctly, not work properly, or have no market demand.
- Advertising campaign might turn out to be more expensive than expected.
- Advertising campaign might turn out to be more lengthy than expected.
- Market demand may not meet expectations.
- Anything less than total success looks bad and will negatively impact the company's reputation and future business.
- Initial distribution strategy could fail.
- New government regulations could increase the cost outside consumers' buying ability.
- Undetected yet existing government regulations could increase the cost outside consumers' buying ability.

It certainly is true that an inventor has a great deal of time and money invested in his invention. But when proposing a licensing agreement, the inventor must also put himself in the licensee's shoes to understand his risks.

A potential licensee will ask the following questions as well:

- What are the continued development costs to get to launch?
- What are the start-up costs?
- Can we design around the patent so we do not have to pay a royalty?
- Will improvements be developed quickly after the launch?
- How much will the improvements cost?
- How much training will the sales force require?

Taking into consideration these two broad concepts of research/development and risk/reward makes it easier to understand that across all classes of technologies—chemical, metal, mechanical, electrical, etc.—most royalty rates fall between 3 and 7 percent (depending on expected high or low gross profits) of whatever the money the licensee receives from sales. This can turn out to be between 20 and 30 percent of the net profit of the invention.

A royalty rate should be closer to or even higher than 7 percent if the expected gross profit margin will be high, and closer to or lower than 3 percent if the margin is anticipated to be low. It should be based on gross sales. Basing the royalty rate precisely on the company's net profit from the sale of the item is ambiguous and subject to interpretation. Gross sales are usually referred to in a licensing agreement as "net sales." It is usually defined as all income from selling the invention received by the company, minus costs for packaging for shipment, shipping, and taxes. For example, if a company is selling your invention direct to the consumer through a direct mail marketing campaign, it would receive income not only for the invention, but also to cover the costs of postage, packaging, and taxes (if the product was sold in the same state as the licensee's sales headquarters). Even though it is income to the company from the sale of the item, it is income necessary for doing business. The licensee will not be able to keep any of this money, so the inventor should not expect to receive a royalty from it.

However, other packaging costs such as header cards and blister packs usually are absorbed into the net sales price. The packaging really sells many consumer goods, not necessarily the elegance of the product itself.

These are general guidelines for determining a royalty rate; the two parties must consider many other additional factors. There are even formulas for determining royalty rates, but to get both parties to agree to the presuppositions that establish those formulas is in my opinion a waste of time. Like most consumer purchase decisions, most deals are made on the basis of emotion than on cost justification. Trying to impose such formulas on a potential licensee in order to justify a certain royalty usually will kill the deal immediately or create arguments that will kill the deal later. It is enough that all agree to the general rule that says that 3 to 7 percent of the gross should go to the inventor, as long as that represents an expected share of 20 to 30 percent of the net profit on the item. If the net profit is expected to be significantly higher than normal for other products in its field, then the royalty rate should go higher than 7 percent.

How does the inventor know what the normal net profit should be for items in his invention's field? The answer lies again in the third point of the commercialization triad: research. Start with the company that sells it the last time, the one selling to the consumer. One could use the survey form in Appendix B to determine how much profit he expects to make. Then trace it to the manufacturer from there. From whom does he buy it? How much does he make?

Should this prove impractical, go to the type of store from which you would expect a consumer to purchase your product. Go to the section of the store you anticipate would stock it. Look for items that would be good companion products, for example, paint brushes for paint, or shoe polish for shoes. Find a companion product with a patent number. Take that patent number to one of the patent depository libraries and pull the patent. The inventor's name and address should be on the patent. Call or write to him: Ask him how the industry works. He probably will know a great deal about it. He also might be willing to share with you how he got his product into the market. He may even be willing to help you license your product to his licensee. You cannot tell what may happen until you try. The worst that could happen is that he may for some paranoid or selfish reason refuse to help you.

I am sure there are many differing views to this approach of establishing a royalty. I have not been able to determine a better frame of reference upon which to begin the licensing process. My experience has been as a neutral party trying to help negotiate a win-win deal. I have resisted companies that try to take advantage of inventors, and I have resisted inventors who insist on ridiculously high royalties. I would love to see a magic formula that everyone could agree with from the beginning. Then we could just plug in the numbers, arrive at a royalty, and everyone would be happy. But that will never happen because every invention, every situation, and every person involved in the process is different.

Up-Front Payments

The next issue inventors are most concerned about is up-front money. Many have heard stories of huge up-front payments or outright purchases of patents. Just as the media have focused on successful inventor/entrepreneurs, so have they reported licensing agreements only having large up-front payments. They do not report all the licensing deals without up-front payments. Neither do they mention that the up-front payments may have been payment for the inventor's raw materials. They also do not disclose that the up-front money was actually a cash advance against future royalties. Neither do they report about how the inventor, having received cash at the signing, paid heavy federal and state income taxes, and how it lowered the royalty rate the inventor could have received had he not insisted upon up-front money.

Even in books written to help inventors we read that an inventor should always get money up front. Having an investment in the invention is supposed to somehow guarantee the company will spend extra special time on its commercialization. This advice is both reckless and dangerous. It is reckless in that there are just too many factors influencing licensing decisions to impose such a dogmatic rule. Finding a qualified potential licensee is difficult enough without killing the deal by demanding up-front money. There is nothing wrong with trying for it, but keep in mind that most up-front payment demands, if successful, end up lowering an inventor's royalty rate. It also siphons off cash that could have been used to gear up for manufacturing and marketing, thereby increasing not only the licensee's risk, but also the inventor's own risk of seeing his product on the shelves.

Usually inventors will make more money by thinking of the income to be earned in the long term. Why? Because inventors who demand up-front money make it harder to negotiate with a potential licensee. The harder it is to negotiate, the less likely it is the product will ever see the light of day. An inventor who demands up-front money is less likely ever to receive any money from his invention.

Up-front money is hardly a guarantee of success. It may even lead to failure. The advice to always collect up-front money is also dangerous. I can tell you the story of an inventor who spent over $10,000 for two patents on one product. After two attempts at venturing, he would not license his invention without up-front payments covering the cost of his patents and what he had lost trying to venture. To this day he is still waiting for a licensee to pay him an up-front fee. After three years he has not sold even one of his items. He had read a book telling him to only license his invention if the licensee was willing to pay up-front money. He spent all his family's money on patenting fees, but he was too stubborn to wake up to the real world, so he could not get a return for his family. The potential for causing other people to suffer makes this kind of advice dangerous and irresponsible.

Minimum Royalty Payments

Finally, inventors are concerned about how to prevent a licensee from doing nothing with the licensed technology. This can be answered in two words: you cannot. If a company chooses to do nothing after licensing, there is absolutely nothing one can do to make it commercialize the technology. Knowing this, there is a routine clause that should go into every licensing agreement. Exclusive licensing agreements should always specify minimum annual royalties paid to the inventor each year. If these royalties are not met, the inventor should have the right to find another licensee or renegotiate the contract.

We licensed one invention this way that turned out to be a terrible mistake. I warned the inventor three times of the necessity of having minimums in the agreement. The licensee would not hear of it. The inventor was so sold on the licensee's ability to perform that he adamantly told me that if this licensee could not sell it, no one could. They then signed the licensing agreement against my advice.

Guess what? After the first year none sold, and the inventor contractually had no rights to his invention. He had signed all manufacturing and marketing rights over to someone without any performance guarantee. He might as well have assigned the ownership of his patent away for free. The inventor himself does not even have the right to sell his own invention. Even worse, the inventor's licensee offered the invention for sale by approaching several distributors on the possibility of their committing to a minimum purchase. This made the invention public and may have hindered its patentability due to the one-year rule. The one-year rule simply stated is that the inventor has one year to file his patent after the invention is made public.

As with royalty amounts, there is no magic formula to use for determining minimum annual royalties. They must be negotiated on a win-win basis. The amount cannot be so high as to discourage the licensee nor so low that it would be easy to just pay the minimum and keep it off the market. The licensee and the inventor must come to a reasonable amount by estimating the degree of difficulty in bringing the product to the launching point, then estimating annual sales from there.

Again, this is where an inventor's research will come in handy. If he has thoroughly researched the market, this should not be too complicated to estimate with input from the company. Generally both parties are so excited about the product's chances for success that the tendency will not be toward conservatism. Both parties should keep in mind that few new product launches go without a hitch, so allow for this.

Minimum royalties are usually graduated upward over the first three years. Depending on the product and research, an agreement might call for $3,000 by the end of the first year, $4,000 during the second year, and $6,000 each year thereafter. This allows for the licensee to gradually ramp up his manufacturing and marketing efforts.

Sometimes the inventor will also license his patent during the first year for 7 percent, then 6 percent during the second year, and finally 5 percent during the third year and each year thereafter. This provides the licensee with a double incentive to perform. Not only does the licensee's royalty percentage decrease, but his product costs go down due to higher volume. The more he sells, the higher the margin he realizes.

Royalties, up-front money, and annual minimum royalties are the items most asked about and most hotly debated. I am sure that if I were to spend four more years finding licensees and negotiating agreements, I would have even more experiences from which to draw. Nevertheless, these are my observations and conclusions on these three issues based on my experiences to date.

Other Licensing Considerations

There is more that needs to be thought through in a licensing agreement. These additional points can have an important effect on the three we just discussed: control, sublicensing, litigation of infringement, maintenance fees, accounting, improvements, and indemnification.

Control

Concern about losing control over implementing the technology often is a major reason why some inventors carelessly reject licensing in favor of venturing. They see it as giving up their baby to a stranger. I can think of dozens of cases where this has been the primary reason for new product failure. We have found excellent licensees for inventors and negotiated the licensing agreement between both parties prior to them even meeting, only to have the inventor refuse to sign the licensing agreement. With pen in hand, they just could not force their signature onto the page.

Regrettably this scenario has serious consequences that affect others, besides the inventor. The potential licensee has gone through the process of evaluating the invention and forming a strategic manufacturing and marketing plan. As the product's champion, he has involved his people all the way down the line and spent significant time away from his other duties and money for attorney fees, shipping samples around the country, telephone calls, and possibly travel expenses, to name a few of many possibilities. If the inventor refuses to sign the previously agreed-to contract, few have the ability to just say, "Well, that's okay. I understand." They may say it, but really they are quite angry. They have lost time, money, and face. Should the inventor return later with a new attitude, the potential licensee will not want to discuss the prospects of licensing again. Who can blame him? Who in their right mind would want to go through all that again, only to have it fail again? Further, the people helping the inventor lose credibility. So much so that the prospective licensee will think twice before agreeing to look at another invention. The inventor's failure to follow through, then, hurts other inventors, because had this one been successful, the licensee would have launched more products later on. The cascade of negative effects is devastating.

Some people do not seem to realize the importance of doing what they say they are going to do. They feel they have the right to change their minds after making a commitment. Beguilement seems to be a right exercised all too frequently. It is unfortunate how this mentality is given new philosophical and ethical life by those in leadership positions. But those who practice crawfishing must also suffer the consequences of the loss of their personal credibility and reputation. It is tough enough just doing business. We should be able to depend on people to keep their word. Those who do not feel compelled to follow through on their commitments should be jettisoned from the project. If they are allowed to continue, they will only cause grief later.

The Inventors' Assistance Program (IAP) staff had to learn the hard way from these situations. We learned to ask the hard question, "Is the owner of this patent really willing to license it?" This seems to beg the question. Most might say, "Of course, that's why an inventor develops a new product or process—to make a deal!" Inventor expectations, however, are rarely mirrored by those of a prospective licensee. A business alliance can become very difficult to negotiate should an inventor envision a joint venture, the prospective partner only wants a manufacturing subcontract, and the IAP staff feels that a licensing agreement would be most effective. The staff tried to prevent these time-wasting scenarios by qualifying both parties prior to scheduling a meeting.

Fear of losing control of an invention can have other negative consequences for the inventor. I am aware of several occasions in which an inventor has refused to license his invention and insisted upon a joint venture. He thought he would have a larger role to play in the project than if he just licensed it. On each occasion the inventor has received much less than if he had licensed.

Two inventors of the same accessory item discovered a company getting ready to launch a perfect companion item to their invention. The company had the manufacturing, marketing, and financial resources needed to launch both products at the same time. The company offered the inventors a fair licensing agreement, offering to buy the inventors' mold at the price they paid for it, plus a healthy royalty on sales. The inventors refused to license, saying they did not want to give up control.

Now the company really wanted the product, but had no use for the inventors. Their backgrounds in no way would add value to the project. So the company rewrote the contract and deleted all reference to the term *licensing*. The company bought the mold, financed the manufacturing and marketing effort, but profits from the sale of their invention would not be paid to the inventors until after the investor (the company) recouped his investment. The percent of net profits now going to the inventors was less than if they had licensed for 5 percent of the gross sales. With the new contract they are now getting paid less, and that income will begin only when the total investment is paid back out of sales. In essence they are paying more than twice for the mold to get their invention launched. They paid for it the first time out of their own pockets, now they are paying for it again (along with the marketing costs) from the delayed participation in net profits. Further, the inventors' risk is much higher than in licensing, because the company may not ever realize any net profits on the item. The company, not the inventors, controls how capital is expended. How this money is spent determines the net profit on their invention.

This happened for one reason: The inventors did not understand licensing. They were prejudiced against it from the beginning. It certainly was not the company's fault. It offered them a straight-up deal, which the inventors rejected. But the company wanted the item, so it offered them a deal the inventors liked. They played semantic gymnastics, took advantage of the inventors' ignorance of business, and got a better deal for the company. The inventors did not understand that in licensing there are generally accepted norms that have been traditionally established, norms that dictate the approximate royalty an inventor should receive, and norms that dictate the amount of risk the inventor should absorb. In venture capital deals, there are no such well-defined norms. Whoever can make the best deal wins.

Intelligently giving up control is not the same as losing control.

Unless an inventor has more to offer than his patent, something in the way of financing, manufacturing, or marketing, there is no reason for the company to consider anything other than a licensing agreement. If the inventor insists on a joint venture or some other kind of alliance without licensing, he is playing with fire.

The concept of licensing should not be seen as losing anything—much less control over implementation. It should be seen for what it really is—intelligently gaining the necessary funding to launch the invention. In contrast to venturing, a start-up company gives up control one way or another with a venture capital or private investor equity deal. Very few people with money will give an inexperienced inventor seed or start-up capital without having control over how the money is spent. How the money is spent directs the operations of a company. In a licensing situation, capital will still be expended on labor, materials, marketing, and sales—yet without the inventor being personally at risk.

Sublicensing

Sublicensing occurs when the licensee licenses the product to yet another company. If the inventor grants an exclusive worldwide license for all markets and all applications to his licensee, he may elect to sublicense his foreign rights to a foreign company. This conceivably could reduce costs if the invention is manufactured and sold in a foreign country. A licensee may wish to sublicense simply because he has found a company that can better commercialize the invention. He may wish to joint venture with another company and use a sublicensing agreement as part of the deal. There could be many other reasons to sublicense.

The ability to sublicense increases the value of the licensing agreement for the licensee. Most licenses and literature I have read suggest that the inventor should never grant sublicensing rights without his approval. Our experience has taught us exactly the opposite. A licensee will not want to get permission from an inventor to expand his market. If he feels he can make more money by sublicensing, he will want the ability to exploit it without having to worry about whether the inventor is in favor of it.

The inventor usually is not in a position to determine whether a sublicensing agreement will increase his royalty earnings. He just is not privy to all the facts. Why should he care, as long as the licensee is selling product and at least meeting his minimum royalties? To require inventor permission before sublicensing will only serve to strain the relationship between the inventor and his licensee. The licensee will feel he is at the mercy of an amateur in his business. If the inventor persists in this, it could easily become a deal killer.

With this understanding, the inventor should receive the same royalty on sales from a sublicensee that he would have received had the licensee sold the product. Further, he should split equally with the licensee any fees received from the sublicensing agreement. For a sublicensing agreement to occur the licensee will have to see potential income on the transaction. For example, if the royalty rate is 5 percent, the licensee may try for a sublicense at 7 percent, thus earning a 2 percent royalty from sales. If he can earn more from this arrangement, so can the inventor.

Having made the case for a licensee's freedom to freely choose a sublicensee, a situation may arise where the only way a market can be penetrated is to lower the inventor's royalty. Should this situation arise, the inventor must be consulted and be allowed to approve or disapprove the deal. The licensee should also be willing to accept a lower percentage.

Let's say two years after the new product was licensed and launched, the licensee was able to establish a strong connection somewhere in Europe. The European connection has access to distribution channels throughout the continent. With higher manufacturing costs, higher costs of raw materials, and other considerations it is determined that only 5 percent of net sales can be paid in royalties from the sublicensing agreement. If this is the case, then the only contractual option would be for the licensee to pass along the entire 5 percent to the inventor and earn nothing. Because it would not be desirable for the licensee to earn nothing from his own arrangement, the royalty from these sales should be renegotiated. The inventor must decide whether penetrating this European market is worth a reduction in his royalty percentage. By reducing his percentage, the inventor may actually earn much more from his intellectual property.

Litigation of Infringement

In addition to sales and sublicensing revenue, a third possible way to earn money from a license is in the litigation of infringement. The inventor probably does not have a lot of money to litigate with, so it is in his best interests to grant to his licensee the first right of refusal to sue a competitor for patent infringement. The split of any income after attorney fees should be 70 to 80 percent to the licensee and 20 to 30 percent to the inventor. If the licensee declines after a reasonable period, the inventor then has the right to pursue it, with the split reversed. Both parties should agree in the contract to support the other and cooperate with each other in the event of litigation.

Maintenance Fees

Maintenance fees (taxes) are required on active utility patents; design patents are not affected. These taxes are due three times during the 17-year life of the patent. This gives the inventor time to begin receiving revenue from his invention. If he does not receive or plan to receive enough revenue to justify paying these taxes, Congress feels the invention should belong to the public. The inventor, not the licensee, usually is responsible for paying these taxes, because the inventor actually owns the patent. Both the inventor and licensee should be aware of this requirement because the patent becomes public domain and protection ceases to exist if the fees are not paid. Any competitor could then manufacture and sell the invention with impunity. There generally is a provision in the licensing agreement to the effect that should the inventor decide not to pay his maintenance fee, he will notify the licensee. The licensee then has the option of paying it.

Accounting

The inventor should also provide for the ability to audit his licensee's records once a year. While this generally should not be a problem, it can become one once the revenue begins to flow. The inventor should not retain just any accountant to perform this function. He should hire only those experienced in auditing royalties.

Improvements

The contract should allow for improvements made by the inventor or the licensee. A year after the product is launched, a customer may make a suggestion that improves the invention. There should be a provision in the licensing contract to incorporate this change into the product with royalties still paid to the inventor just as if he had come up with the suggested change. If the licensee develops the improvement and it is patentable, then the licensee pays for the patent work and grants a royalty-free, nonexclusive license to the inventor. The same goes for the inventor, should he invent a patentable improvement. Improvements add life to the invention, so a favorable environment should be negotiated in the contract to encourage continuing development.

Indemnification

Indemnification should be granted to the inventor by the licensee. The inventor is not responsible for what the licensee does or does not do, so he should not be held accountable should the licensee make a mistake. In the event of an infringement suit from another patent owner, the inventor should not be held liable for any more than his royalty income. Further, the agreement should require products liability insurance be carried at all times by the licensee and listing the name of the inventor on the policy. This costs very little extra, but provides a great deal of comfort.

This is a brief overview of licensing—the alternative to venturing. It is hoped that owners of intellectual property now feel there is a legitimate alternative to having to build a company around the new product in order to get it commercialized. Your patent attorney should never be far away when negotiating licensing agreements. Patent attorneys are professionals who deal with intellectual property rights for a living. They are far better than nonprofessionals at knowing the ins and outs of licensing.

Having said that, it needs to be recognized that having an attorney negotiate a licensing agreement could actually be counterproductive to getting the deal done. This is not intended to be "lawyer bashing." On more than a few occasions I have seen potential licensees shy away from situations involving negotiations with attorneys. They say they do not wish to spend the money to hire one just to equalize the playing field. Maybe they are afraid too many concessions will have to be given if they turn over the negotiating to lawyers. For whatever the reason, it has been our experience that attorneys generally should not be retained for face-to-face licensing negotiations. It is less intimidating for many potential licensees. The inventor (or preferably his agent) can always say he must consult with his attorney before agreeing to any of the points. The attorney will know what is normal and what is not. The inventor must make up his own mind whether to accept or reject each clause in the contract.

Win-Win Deals

A good licensing agreement provides both the inventor and the licensee with the ability to make money through sales, sublicensing, and infringements, and it rewards the two parties according to the risk they accept.

If one feels that he has been shortchanged a year or two down the road, it will only serve to destroy the enthusiasm of the offended party. A mere contract cannot create the necessary vigor a licensee must have to implement the commercialization of the invention to its maximum potential. Neither can a contract motivate an inventor to continually strive to create improvements in his invention or keep a sharp eye out for infringers.

A licensing agreement is, in effect, a partnership to exploit the market for the financial benefit of the inventor and the licensee. Each party should approach the negotiation of the licensing agreement with the best interests of the other in mind. Equitable agreements on the points discussed in this chapter should be the most important goal, not just getting the best possible deal for one side. I realize this must sound terribly idealistic or even naive, but an inventor should at all times guard against the licensing negotiation being conducted in an aura of enmity. After many negotiating sessions I have discovered a startling fact: If one is genuinely concerned about the well-being of the other party, it shows. It shows so much that it facilitates the making of a win-win deal.

Summing Up

Licensing is the best method for commercializing your patented or patent-pending invention. As a rule, most inventors simply do not have the manufacturing and marketing experience necessary for successful venturing. The best licensing candidates are smaller companies with distribution channels already set up. Finding qualified licensees only takes homework, persistence, and a much smaller amount of capital than venturing. There is also far less risk than in venturing.

The best licensing candidates are smaller companies with distribution channels already set up. Finding qualified licensees only takes homework, persistence, and a much smaller amount of capital than venturing. There is also far less risk than in venturing.

Understanding how licensing agreements are structured, what the norms are, and striving for a win-win agreement are the most important licensing concepts to grasp. (For more information on the subject, see the sample licensing agreements in Appendix B, and study them closely to see the differences in language and stipulations.) No two licensing agreements are ever alike. Think through the ways in which each clause might influence the commercialization of your invention.

Finally, no matter how big a company may be or how many resources it might have available to launch your product, the odds are still against the invention's success. Even after licensing the product it can still fail; and as we have discussed earlier, most do fail. Throwing cold water on hopes and dreams is not my favorite pastime, but please do not set your expectations too high. Licensing simply is an alternative funding mechanism to venturing. You are hoping someone who has already invented a company and has been successful with it will use his or her manufacturing, marketing, management, and financing resources to cut your risks in taking your product to the market. Rarely are there big winners. Sometimes there are good returns on the investment. But more than half of the projects will die from extenuating business circumstances that simply could not have been anticipated at the time of signing the licensing agreement. Anyone who says differently is either naive or untruthful. Nevertheless, if the product makes it to the market, at least you will have accomplished your goal of allowing the market to speak.

ELEVEN

Ten Ways to Invention Suicide

Sanctity of life is a major social, political, and theological issue. The sanctity of new product life should become a major topic of discussion in inventor organizations throughout the country. During the past eight years of launching new products, I have seen many ways inventors cause the unfortunate and premature demise of their own inventions. I have not listed all the ways an inventor can "do his product in," I have listed the most common ones. I have termed these methods to be "suicidal" in light of the fact that so many inventors have trouble distinguishing their inventions from themselves.

1. The Paranoid Inventor

All too often an overly suspicious inventor refuses to discuss his invention with those who might add value to his project. While at the U.S. Department of Commerce we used to get calls from those wanting help in commercializing their idea. When we asked them what it was, some would say, "I can't tell you." We would then explain that we could not offer assistance without knowing about the project. After working on over 1,000 projects I know of none that were stolen.

There are four good reasons for this lack of thievery:

1. Most ideas are not very good ones anyway. Only about 20 percent that we saw were worth spending time trying to develop.
2. Everyone has different interests, and one man's treasure is another man's junk.
3. Most people are basically honest.
4. Most dishonest people still would not steal another's idea for fear of getting caught and risking litigation. None of the people I deal with in the private and public sectors wishes to have his or her reputation destroyed by being known as an idea thief.

This does not mean an inventor should not be discreet or that those helping inventors should not take appropriate measures to safeguard the information given them. But there is, in my opinion, far less pilfering of inventions than is commonly reported.

It has been my experience that most of the stories we hear about ideas being stolen come from those who have thought of an idea years ago, did nothing to commercialize it, and then discovered it, or something close to it, being sold. Sometimes, too, theft stories are told by those who specialize in inventing products that have already been invented. They do not believe it possible that someone could have had the same or similar idea.

The inventor must find a balance between trusting no one and trusting everyone. Somewhere between the two extremes are those who have the need to know in order to help move the project forward. Those are the ones with whom to freely share. Sometimes a confidentiality agreement is appropriate, but sometimes it is not feasible. By federal law, the evaluators with NIST must sign such an agreement. At the Inventors' Assistance Program (IAP), we did not sign them. Nevertheless, we took appropriate measures to safeguard ideas. Further, we initiated legislation exempting financial records and trade secrets (covering an inventor's records) from the state's Open Records Act. The legislation has been on the books for several years, so invention information is not accessible to the general public.

The inventor must find a balance between trusting no one and trusting everyone. Somewhere between the two extremes are those who have the need to know in order to help move the project forward. Those are the ones with whom to freely share.

The way to keep your invention as safe as possible is to keep your logbook up to date or to file a disclosure document with the U.S. Patent Office or to have your patent attorney otherwise establish your invention's date of conception. Then get your patent-pending status as soon as possible after conducting thorough research in proving to yourself that your idea is unique. This research should be a combination of a professionally done patent search and marketing research.

The New Products Coalition does not accept any project unless it is at least in the patent-pending stage (if the intellectual property to be transferred is a patent). We ask the inventor not to reveal to us or anyone else his patent-pending number or the claims that were filed until interest in shown by a potential licensee or joint venture partner. Once interest is established, then a confidentiality agreement is signed so the claims and/or any possible improvements can be reviewed and freely discussed. This is the acceptable way of doing business in the early stages of technology transfer.

2. The Omnipotent Inventor

I once visited with a very bright computer technician/programmer who had a great idea. It was a modem board that would also allow a computer to send fax messages. He was really excited about its possibilities because there was nothing like it on the market. He wanted to venture his idea and turn it into a billion-dollar computer accessories company. I had read of such a device being developed by Apple, and so I asked him if he had read anything about it. He admitted hearing about Apple working on a very similar product to his, but it was not identical.

I then asked a few hypothetical questions. "Assuming Apple launches their version soon, would not IBM be quick to follow? And what about all the modem and clone makers in the computer business? Would not all these be an incredible array of competitors?" His answer was, "I'm not afraid of those guys."

Here was a young man with an idea. He had no prototype, no capital, no manufacturing experience, and no marketing experience, yet here he was, saying he was not afraid to build an organization to compete directly against existing companies like IBM and Apple. Further, he had no plan. He only had an idea for a new product.

There is no question this inventor could eventually learn to wear all the hats necessary to start a company. He would have to have the right opportunity, the right education, and the right mentors. The problem was that his new product was not going to wait. By the time he had all the experience he would need for an undertaking of this magnitude, the world would be sending 3D images over fiber optics. He had about as much chance of success as a 300-pound belly dancer.

His feeling of omnipotence told him he could do anything. Communicating that to others made him appear foolish. No investor has time for foolishness.

3. The Greedy Inventor

Holding out for up-front money or a ridiculously high royalty reduces the inventor's chances of receiving any revenue from his invention. I have discussed this in Chapter 10, but I mention it here again because so many inventors bring death to their projects by insisting on one or both of these features in their licensing agreements.

Holding out for up-front money or a ridiculously high royalty reduces the inventor's chances of receiving any revenue from his invention.

A young man came to us with a beautifully made prototype of a key ring especially for women. We loved it. While the inventor waited in my office, I showed it to a dozen of the women in the office, and with one exception they said they would buy one immediately upon seeing it in a store. Further, they would be willing to pay between five and seven dollars for it.

I returned and reported the results to the inventor. It was obvious to the inventor that he had a winner. We began discussing what had to happen before he could make money from his patent-pending invention. He had no money and no experience. All he had was the idea.

As I began to discuss licensing with him, he decided to venture it himself. He did not want to settle on 20 to 30 percent of the net profit. He wanted all of it for himself. There was nothing I could do to convince him otherwise. A year later he came in to see us again. We thought he had finally realized he needed to license, but he was only wondering if we could help him raise the money for his project.

This is an example of how both greed and a feeling of omnipotence can kill a deal. We had a potential licensee lined up who could afford to pay for the mold and the packaging and quickly introduce the item into the correct distribution channels. In addition to the inventor's normal royalty on net sales, the licensee would have been willing to pay the inventor a commission on his sales if the inventor had joined the company's marketing department. To this day, nothing has happened to get the invention commercialized.

4. The Impatient Inventor

We have seen impatience work against projects in several ways. It seems to evolve into cutting corners, badgering a potential licensee for a decision, and giving up prematurely.

Most inventors do not do enough research to establish who the future customers are, what and where the markets are, who and what is the competition, appropriate distribution channels, packaging design, and background information on prospective licensees. The sloppy sales technique of throwing mud against the wall and hoping some of it sticks seems to be the preferred modus operandi of many inventors.

Performing research may take longer to get the invention ready to present, but it gives it a fighting chance to succeed by increasing the probabilities of finding a licensee. If one's goal is to actually get one's intellectual property licensed—not just go through the motions—then extensive research will decrease the amount of time it takes to consummate the licensing agreement. It separates the amateurs from the professionals.

Impatience has on several occasions revealed its hoary head and killed licensing deals in progress. In one instance we had located a company with a great distribution network for several applications of the invention. The company was sold on the product and could not wait to get it into their system. The firm was taking its time in considering how to word the licensing agreement because it had never before licensed an invention. After a couple of weeks the inventor began badgering the vice president daily for a decision. The company broke off negotiations. The reasoning was that if this inventor was such a pain during the presigning process, she would only get worse afterward. They feared she would be calling every day wanting sales reports and updates on strategies, and they did not have time for that.

There is a balance between hammering a company for a decision and reasonably expecting to be updated on the progress. The IAP staff was getting those updates and helping the potential licensee understand licensing. The inventor would not accept the fact that we were doing all that could be done for her with this firm, so she took matters into her own hands and promptly killed the deal.

A friend and I have a running joke. When someone is procrastinating in making a decision, we act stunned that the rest of the world is not on our time schedule. We cannot understand why we are not the center of everyone else's universe.

Finally, the lack of patience has caused inventors to give up too soon. It is not unusual for it to take several years to find a licensee. It is not unusual for the first licensee to fall on his face and not be able to meet the first year's minimum royalty payments. It is not unusual to have to find another licensee when this happens.

The lack of patience has caused inventors to give up too soon. It is not unusual for it to take several years to find a licensee. It is not unusual for the first licensee to fall on his face and not be able to meet the first year's minimum royalty payments. It is not unusual to have to find another licensee when this happens.

Major reasons for this seem to be lack of research by the inventor and company, unforeseen market changes, and unexpected changes in a company's priorities. When a company licenses a patent, it is very excited. The potential seems to be tremendous. Then reality hits. It will require significantly more work than first believed. It will require more money than first believed. After this truth soaks in, the company may decide it was not really the right one to license the invention. These mistakes are difficult to admit. They are unfortunate events in the quest to commercialize inventions; nevertheless they happen. An inventor should realize that just because a particular company may not have been the right one to license to in the first place, it does not necessarily mean the invention is no good. Another, more synergistic company has to be found. Just as no one can tell whether an invention will sell before consumers have a chance to buy it, no one can know for sure about whether the licensee is the right one until he has been given a chance to perform.

5. The Empty-Nest Inventor

A mature adult is one who has learned to let go of many of life's events. Not learning this can cause serious mental problems that affect our personalities. Among other stressful events, we learn to let go of our children when they leave for college, our loved ones when they pass away, our mistakes and emotional hurts, and problems encountered in past jobs. We are thankful for what we have received and learned, but we have to let go and get on with our lives.

Not being a psychologist, I will not dwell on the empty-nest syndrome. I am as vulnerable as most in wrestling with the problem of letting go. Nevertheless I see it over and over as an impediment to commercializing inventions. It is totally understandable. If I had spent years developing an idea, then patented it and believed that millions would buy it, I too might not want to let go of the project. I would want somehow to keep it close to me so I could cherish it. I certainly would not want a stranger to come along and mess it up.

How does a carpenter let go of his cabinet? How does a painter let go of his painting? How does a home builder sell the house that just took six months to build? Inventors are not the only ones who have to let go of their creations. Be willing to let it go. It is the only way for others to benefit from it.

6. The Emotional Inventor

Emotional responses that cause the destruction of an invention ultimately stem from the affliction of invention animism. Again, invention animism occurs when an inventor attributes his very self (soul?) to the invention. He cannot disassociate himself from his creation. If it is criticized, the inventor takes it as a personal affront. Make no mistake—invention animism is a deadly disease. Through emotional outbursts of anger and resentment, it kills a large percentage of ideas and inventions.

When an inventor cannot take constructive criticism about his invention, people do not want to be involved in the project. They have better things to do than interact with defensive people. They do not see the invention as being the inventor. They see it as just another deal. The more emotionalism that comes from an inventor, the more quickly a project is dropped.

The inventor must not see his invention merely as a reflection of his being. My theory is that invention animism leads to the empty-nest syndrome, which leads to the emotional responses that put a licensing deal in jeopardy. These three work together. If the inventor is aware that these seem to occur naturally with all inventors (and with those in other professions, too), he should be able to better guard against them.

7. The Deaf Inventor

Many inventors do not seem to hear what others say. They have their minds made up and they are inflexible. If someone knowledgeable in the industry suggests the price might be too high or makes a suggestion for an improved feature, these inventors just do not hear it. Instead of listening to those who have experience, in their minds they are already talking to someone else who will have a better attitude toward the product.

Two examples come to mind. One inventor had his energy-conserving device evaluated by NIST. NIST said the invention would not do what the inventor claimed. Instead of the inventor convincing NIST of their "mistake" or otherwise disproving the evaluation, all this inventor said was that NIST did not know what it was talking about. The technical evaluation had fallen upon deaf ears. Another example involved an inventor who paid a marketing firm $12,000 for a marketing feasibility report. The marketing firm interviewed many potential customers, store buyers, and other industry experts, conducted focus groups and gathered a huge amount of online secondary marketing information. After the results were analyzed and written up, the conclusion was that the product could not be manufactured at a cost allowing it to flow smoothly through the distribution channels. In other words, the public would not pay the ultimate retail price for the product.

The inventor did not hear that conclusion. Due to his deafness, the inventor is, to this day, promoting his project by handing out copies of the negative findings to prospective investors.

8. The Flake Inventor

Being a flake inventor can result from adopting any number of a variety of eccentricities that serve to upset the people with whom he is dealing. Usually the person feels the inventor has wasted his time or money in some fashion. Specific examples I have witnessed are making up survey results, lying about who is the real inventor, blaming others, spending an investor's money unwisely, and not following through with a commitment.

The project that galls me most happened about two years ago. Three men came in seeking $250,000 to build a manufacturing facility for the production of heavy equipment. They had no money of their own, no manufacturing experience, and no business plan. But they had managed to build and sell several of the units. They wanted the capital to gear up for mass production. They said they had orders for a thousand more.

Knowing they would not qualify for debt financing, I asked if they would be interested in a joint venture with a heavy equipment manufacturer. They said they would. I then presented the proposal to a company looking for new products. The company spent several days costing the product and figuring how the deal might work. The solution was that the three inventors would turn over the existing orders to the company, freeing the inventors to develop and implement the continuing marketing and sales strategy. The company would handle everything on the manufacturing side, including billing. For this the company wanted a 20 percent gross profit margin, instead of the usual 15 percent. With this arrangement the inventors would get $720,000 to be split equally between them. All future sales would be handled the same way.

The inventors declined. They said they felt the company was asking too much to make 20 percent instead of the normal 15 percent. Just for giving their existing orders to the company they would have split $720,000! In my opinion this was the epitome of flakiness.

9. The Procrastinating Inventor

Procrastination shows who is serious and who is not. For many inventors, finding a licensee is just an enjoyable hobby. We try to identify hobbyists as quickly as possible and move them out of the system. By doing so we will be able to spend time with those who really want to get their deal done. Some people have been playing around with their idea for years and will not license it or walk away from it. It is almost as if they have nothing better to do.

In order to achieve our mission the IAP staff must move with the movers. With hundreds of inventions in our pipeline at various stages of development, we have to quickly determine what step should next be accomplished. It may be intellectual property protection, prototype development, market research, or testimonial solicitations. We cannot commercialize the invention unless all the necessary elements are present. It is the inventor's responsibility to do the legwork necessary to get his project to the point at which it can be licensed. Because we cannot spend time with procrastinators, it is less likely for them to get their invention commercialized.

In the private sector an inventor also has to strike while the iron is hot. Once a project has been introduced to a player, the longer it takes to get the information he needs to make a decision, the less likely it is he will license it. The excitement cools quickly if nothing is stoking the coals. Seldom is the procrastinating inventor successful.

In the private sector an inventor also has to strike while the iron is hot. Once a project has been introduced to a player, the longer it takes to get the information he needs to make a decision, the less likely it is he will license it.

---

10. The Inventor Who Fears Success

I have trouble understanding this last method of invention sui-
cide. I can at least identify with the previous nine while refusing to
embrace them. How can one be afraid of success? When I was growing up playing baseball and football, success was the ultimate goal.
Being the best we could be was nice, but winning the big one was a
sweet, gratifying high. We worked hard to win. We deserved to win,
we expected to win, and win we did. By the time my high school
class graduated, we must have accumulated 10 or 15 district and
state championships. Each was a wonderful experience.

Not being able to relate to this so-called fear of success, one
might wonder why I think it exists. I have already admitted to not
being a psychologist, but I believe the fear of success is in some people because there is no other explanation for their actions. Very intelligent people have pulled stunts that are just too dumb to be dumb.

An inventor embezzled money from his own seed investors. Another inventor widely sought publicity for his invention, knowing
the real inventor lived in his home town. A small business owner
bought himself a new Lexus with his company's payroll taxes.

Some say these people feel they do not deserve success. Some say
they were brought up in an abnormal family environment. Some say
they do not want the added responsibilities that might come from
winning. Whatever might be the cause, one who has this problem
should not be trying to commercialize his invention. He should first
seek therapy or otherwise work through his problem. Many other
people will have to roll up their sleeves and get involved to successfully launch a new product. Those willing to do so are hard to find,
and their efforts should not be sabotaged by an inventor who sub-
consciously or consciously wants to kill his invention.

CONCLUSION

For many who have created new product ideas, the principles set forth in this book may be a shock. It might be surprising to learn that marketing a new product is usually more difficult than creating it. It may also be startling to think that an inventor must beat a path to the door of the world, not the other way around. But these new product development truths should not be so unexpected. There has to be a reason why so many (98 percent) patented inventions are languishing in a mire of inactivity or lost in a maze of futility.

An independent inventor's competition is much larger than he or she might believe. Companies looking for new products do not just call up inventor clubs and ask to see some deals. The ones with resources for such detective work search high and low for technologies that might be synergistic with company goals. They search the patent files, federal government labs, universities, foreign patents, venture capital firms, bankruptcy courts, business brokers, state economic development and technology agencies, manufacturers, business incubators, innovation centers, and even patent attorneys.

The commercialization triad of quality, synergy, and research is achieved only rarely. Part of the reason is that inventors do not know the triad must exist for successful commercialization to occur. Second, inventors spend too many unproductive hours and dollars trying to venture when they do not have the expertise to do so. A marketing frame of reference is key to commercialization.

Finding solutions for independent inventors is the purpose of this book. Many of these proposed solutions are neither simplistic, nor are they easy to implement. They are not necessarily systematic, because there are no magical formulas that apply to every project. But, it is to be hoped that, through the understanding of just one additional ingredient in the art and practice of commercialization, an inventor will eventually see his discovery appreciated by the public.

While thoughts in this work were directed primarily to independent inventors, the principles can also be applied by government research facilities, university laboratories, and private sector firms. They, too, must become much more imaginative in orchestrating the commercialization triad.

Sample Materials

Sample Confidentiality Agreement

This Agreement made and entered into by and between _____
_____ (hereinafter referred to as INNOVATOR),
and _____ a company [or an individual] con-
sidered for the purposes of this agreement an expert in the field of
_____ (hereinafter referred to as EVALUATOR);

WHEREAS INNOVATOR is in possession of certain confidential and
proprietary information and/or intellectual properties relating to
project applications for _____ (hereinafter referred
to as "confidential and proprietary information of INNOVATOR"); and

WHEREAS EVALUATOR is desirous of receiving such confidential and
proprietary information of INNOVATOR for the sole purpose of evaluating same.

NOW, THEREFORE, in consideration of the premises and the mutual
promises and covenants of the parties, the parties hereto have agreed
and do hereby agree as follows:

I.

EVALUATOR will not, without the prior written consent of INNOVA-
TOR, use or disclose to any other person, firm, or corporation any information disclosed to EVALUATOR under the terms of this
agreement. EVALUATOR shall be under no obligation to maintain confidential any information which:

(a) EVALUATOR can show was in its possession at the time of disclosure thereof by INNOVATOR to EVALUATOR and was not acquired,
directly or indirectly, from INNOVATOR or others with whom INNO-
VATOR has a contractual arrangement; or

(b) was acquired by EVALUATOR from another who had no confidential commitment to INNOVATOR with respect to same or did not
acquire such information, directly or indirectly, from INNOVATOR; or

(c) becomes, through no fault of EVALUATOR, a part of the public
domain by publication or otherwise.

II.

All plans, drawings, photographs, prints, computer programs, samples,
data, equipment, formulae, parts, models, or other documents or materials furnished by INNOVATOR to EVALUATOR shall remain the
property of INNOVATOR and same shall be deemed in the custody of
and as bailment to EVALUATOR only for the limited purposes specified
herein and shall be returned to INNOVATOR, along with any copies or

reproductions thereof, upon demand by INNOVATOR. EVALUATOR will not, without the prior written consent of INNOVATOR, use, simulate, disclose, reproduce, or copy, or permit the use, simulation, disclosure, reproduction, or copying of any of such documents or materials.

III.

Nothing contained in this Agreement or any disclosure hereunder shall be construed as granting to EVALUATOR any license or other right in or to the information so disclosed or to any patent or patent application relating thereto.

IV.

This Agreement shall be interpreted, construed, and enforceable in accordance with the laws of the State of Oklahoma regardless of the place of execution hereof or the place of performance of any portion hereof.

IN WITNESS WHEREOF the parties hereto have executed this Agreement in duplicate on this   day of   ,   .

EVALUATOR

By:

Title:

Sample Licensing Agreement

Exclusive Licensing Agreement

This Agreement, made this   day of   ,   , by and between David Cain, (LICENSOR) and Strategic Marketing Alliances, Inc., (LICENSEE).

WITNESSETH THAT:

WHEREAS LICENSOR is the owner of an invention known as Boom Box Shut-Ups, shown by attached patent-pending documentation, Exhibit "A" hereto, hereafter referred to as the Invention, and

WHEREAS LICENSEE is in the business of marketing and manufacturing apparel accessories and contract sewing and desires to add the invention to its product line.

NOW, THEREFORE, in consideration of the mutual covenants and agreements set forth below, the parties agree as follows:

Article I—Definitions

(1) "Patent Rights" shall mean all United States and foreign patent applications relating to the Invention and any improvements thereto made by LICENSOR, and all patents which may issue on any of said application(s).

(2) "Licensed Equipment" shall mean the apparatus Boom Box Shut-Ups.

(3) When Licensed Equipment is sold or rented by LICENSEE separately from any other equipment, "Net Sales" means the total monies received by LICENSEE for sales or rentals of the Licensed Equipment, less packaging for shipment, transportation charges, and taxes.

(4) When Licensed Equipment is sold or rented by LICENSEE in combination with unlicensed equipment and the sales price of the Licensed Equipment is not separated from the unlicensed equipment, "Net Sales" shall mean a portion of the total monies received by LICENSEE (less packaging for shipment, transportation charges, and taxes) from the sale or rental determined by multiplying the total monies received by LICENSEE by a fraction that is the cost of manufacture of the Licensed Equipment divided by the total cost of manufacture of the total equipment sold or rented.

Article II—License Grant

(1) LICENSOR hereby grants, bargains, sells, and conveys unto LIC-ENSEE the exclusive right and license to manufacture, use, and sell Licensed Equipment covered by the Patent Rights throughout the world, subject to the terms and conditions set forth herein, including the right to grant sublicenses.

(2) Whenever possible, LICENSEE shall inform LICENSOR regarding the grant of any sublicense or joint venture; provided, however, LIC-ENSEE retains the sole right to control the terms and conditions of any sublicense, subject to the terms of this Agreement, along with the identity of any sublicensee.

Article III—Royalties and Records

(1) LICENSEE shall pay LICENSOR earned royalties of five percent (5 percent) of Net Sales of Licensed Equipment sold by LICENSEE. These provisions shall apply whether the Licensed Equipment is made by or for LICENSEE.

LICENSOR may terminate this agreement after the first twelve-month (12-month) period and on each anniversary thereafter of this Agreement by giving written notice if the LICENSEE has not paid LICENSOR the following minimum amounts:

Year One	$3,000
Year Two	$6,000
Year Three and Thereafter	$9,000

In the event that LICENSEE shall transfer any Licensed Equipment covered by the patent rights to a third party owned in whole or in part or controlled in whole or in part by LICENSEE, for a consideration less than that for which the same transfer would by made to an unrelated third party, LICENSOR shall receive his royalty based upon the Net Sales which would have been received in an arms-length transaction. In the event LICENSEE should resell Licensed Equipment, a royalty shall be required only upon the first sale.

(2) The royalties required to be paid herein, shall be paid quarterly in United States dollars converted at the official current rate at the date of transaction for foreign sales, with each royalty payment being due within thirty (30) days following each calendar quarter for the Net Sale in the immediately preceding calendar quarter.

(3) Simultaneously with the royalty payments required, LICENSEE shall advise LICENSOR in writing the identification of the Licensed Equipment and Net Sales with respect thereto made during the quarter covered by the royalty payment.

(4) LICENSEE shall keep books and records of all domestic and foreign transactions relating to this Agreement in accordance with commonly accepted accounting practices, and LICENSOR or his designee shall have the right to inspect and audit such books and records at any time during regular business hours; provided, however, such right shall not be exercised more than once during each calendar year during the term of this Agreement.

Article IV—Technical Assistance

(1) Promptly upon execution of this Agreement, LICENSOR shall supply LICENSEE with all readily available technical information in his possession relating to the design, construction, and use of the Invention (including any marketing and sales information) that has not already been supplied to LICENSEE.

(2) LICENSOR shall, during the life of this Agreement, keep LICENSEE advised of all improvements to the Invention made by or for LICENSOR, along with the identification and content of any applications shall become a part of the Patent Rights.

Article V—Warranties

(1) LICENSOR warrants that he has the right to grant the License to LICENSEE by this Agreement.

(2) LICENSOR does not warrant that Licensed Equipment does not infringe the patent rights of third parties, but does warrant that to the best of his knowledge, Licensed Equipment designed by LICENSOR, at the date of this Agreement, does not infringe upon the patent rights of any third parties of which he is aware.

Article VI—Marking

(1) LICENSOR, to the extent of his knowledge and ability, shall keep LICENSEE advised of the identification of all United States and foreign pending and issued patents covering the Licensed Equipment being manufactured by LICENSEE.

(2) LICENSEE shall include an appropriate patent marking on all Licensed Equipment and appropriate associated LICENSEE equipment made and sold or leased by LICENSEE or any sublicensee.

Article VII—Litigation

(1) In the event LICENSEE is sued for infringement of one or more patents owned by a third party as a result of the sale or use of Licensed Equipment, LICENSEE shall have the right to withhold one-half (½) of all royalties due and owing to LICENSOR under this Agreement, during the course of such litigation for use in payment of attorney fees and expenses in defending such litigation. At the conclusion of such litigation, LICENSEE shall promptly pay LICENSOR the balance, if any, of withheld royalties not used in payment of attorney fees and expenses in defending such litigation.

(2) In the event of any infringement by any third party of any patent included within the Patent Rights, LICENSEE shall have the first right, at its expense, to enforce by appropriate legal proceedings such rights against such infringer. All recoveries for past infringements, including damages, royalties, or settlements (other than sublicense fees which may be received) shall be divided eighty percent (80 percent) to LICENSEE and twenty percent (20 percent) to LICENSOR after reimbursing LICENSEE for all of its not otherwise reimbursed, out-of-pocket costs, attorney fees, and expenses of the legal proceeding. In such proceeding, LICENSOR shall, as requested by LICENSEE, become a party-plaintiff and assist LICENSEE, as requested by LICENSEE, and at LICENSEE's expense. LICENSEE shall consult with LICENSOR with respect to the terms of any settlement contemplated.

(3) In the event LICENSEE shall fail to initiate appropriate legal proceedings, or agree to do same, against an infringer within one hundred twenty (120) days after receipt of a written request from LICENSOR to do so, LICENSOR may prosecute the infringer on his own behalf and at his expense. In such case, all monies recovered by LICENSOR, after reimbursing LICENSOR for his costs, attorney fees, and expenses, shall be divided eighty percent (80 percent) to LICENSOR and twenty percent (20 percent) to LICENSEE. LICENSEE agrees to proceed diligently in deciding whether to initiate legal proceedings.

(4) In any litigation initiated by either party under the authority of this Agreement, the other party may, at his or its own expense, be represented by his or its own counsel in an advisory but not controlling capacity.

Article VIII—Sublicenses

(1) All sublicenses shall be in writing, and a true and correct copy thereof shall be provided to LICENSOR promptly after execution of the sublicense.

(2) Each sublicensing agreement shall contain provisions for royalty rates, time and manner of reporting and payment of royalties, audit, and termination no more favorable to the sublicensee than those included in this Agreement. Each sublicense shall contain the express provision that the sublicense will terminate upon termination of this Agreement.

(3) LICENSEE shall promptly pay to LICENSOR (a) one-half (½) of all fees paid by sublicensees for the grant of a sublicense and (b) royalties on Net Sales of Licensed Equipment by each sublicensee at the rate specified in Article III upon receipt of royalties by LICENSEE from each sublicensee.

Article IX—Termination

(1) Unless sooner terminated as provided herein, this Agreement shall remain in full force and effect until the expiration of the last patent included in the Patent Rights.

(2) LICENSEE may terminate this Agreement at any time on ninety (90) days' prior written notice to LICENSOR, but no such termination shall affect royalty obligations or liability in litigation obligations, arising prior to such termination.

(3) In the event that LICENSEE shall commit breach of this Agreement by not paying monies due hereunder in a timely fashion, LICENSOR, without waiving any other remedies available to him, may terminate this Agreement upon thirty (30) days' prior written notice. If LICENSEE shall cure the breach within such thirty-day (30-day) period, however, the notice of termination shall be rendered null and void and this Agreement shall remain in full force and effect.

(4) LICENSEE and all sublicensees shall cease manufacturing Licensed Equipment at the time this Agreement may be terminated either by LICENSOR or LICENSEE, but shall have the right to sell all Licensed Equipment made before termination with payment of the appropriate royalty.

(5) The waiver by either of the parties of any breach of any provision of this Agreement shall not be construed to be a waiver of any succeeding breach of the provision or a waiver of the provision itself.

Article X—Filing and Maintenance of Patents

(1) LICENSOR shall file and prosecute patent applications on inventions included in the Patent Rights hereunder at his own expense and shall have exclusive control over said applications. LICENSOR shall at his expense file such applications in the United States and in all other countries that the parties agree are important. In the event LICENSOR does not proceed with any particular patent on Licensed Equipment being made by LICENSEE, LICENSEE may proceed to do so and deduct the cost thereof from royalties due LICENSOR hereunder.

(2) All maintenance costs for issued patent rights under which LICENSEE is the licensee shall be paid by LICENSOR. LICENSEE shall notify LICENSOR when it has no further interest in any patent requiring maintenance payments.

Article XI—General

(1) In the event any of the terms of this Agreement, in the opinion of either party, become inappropriate or oppressive, the parties agree to negotiate in good faith with respect to an appropriate amendment of this Agreement.

(2) This Agreement shall be deemed made and entered into pursuant to the laws of the United States of America and the laws of the State of Oklahoma.

(3) All notices hereunder shall be in writing and except as provided below, shall be mailed first-class mail, postage prepaid, addressed as follows, or at such other address as either party shall from time to time designate:

If to LICENSOR:
David Cain, 7069 Cleopatra, Muskogee, OK 74403

If to LICENSEE:
Strategic Marketing Alliances, Inc., 4900 Richmond Square, Suite 100, Oklahoma City, OK 73118

If notices are under Article IX they shall be by certified mail, return receipt requested.

(4) This Agreement and all of the rights and obligations hereof shall be binding upon and shall inure to the benefit of the successors and assigns of LICENSEE and the administrators, executors, heirs, and assigns of LICENSOR, LICENSEE shall not assign this Agreement to anyone other than a successor of substantially the entire business of LICENSEE

relating to the manufacture of Licensed Equipment without the written approval of LICENSOR, which approval shall not be unreasonably withheld.

(5) This Agreement constitutes the entire understanding and agreement between the parties hereto in respect of the subject matter hereof, integrates all prior understandings and agreements with respect thereto, and may not be altered, amended, or modified in any manner except by written agreement of the parties.

IN WITNESS WHEREOF the parties hereto have caused this Agreement to be executed as of the date first written above.

By: _____

Strategic Marketing Alliances, Inc. (Licensee)

By: _____

David Cain (Licensor)

Notary

My Commission Expires: _____

Sample New Product Survey

Boatack™

We need your help. New products need input from those knowledge-able in the industry and marketplace. Would you help us by completing the following brief survey? Enclosed is a stamped, self-addressed envelope for your convenience.

To your knowledge, is there or has there been anything else on the market like the Boatack?

If yes, what?

Without considering price, would you or your customers want to purchase the Boatack?

If not, why?

What would be the best construction material for the Boatack?

How would the Boatack sell in comparison with others like it?

How might it be improved?

Would you purchase the Boatack if it were on the market? Why or why not?

From where do you usually purchase items like this?

Pricing

What price is so low that you would question the quality of Boatack?

What price would lead you to believe that you got a good deal?

At what price would you begin to question the value of buying?

What price would be so high that you would not buy?

What is your normal gross profit margin on these type of items? (Use only if your survey targets are retailers, wholesalers, or distributors.)

What do you feel are the main benefits of the Boatack?

What do you feel might be the foremost barriers, if any, to the Boatack being purchased?

Inventor Assistance Organizations

This list may help you solve problems such as prototype development, finding a good patent attorney or agent, advice about what to do next, etc. It is based on the best directory of organizations I could find, and comes from the Pacific Northwest Laboratories. Because we are a highly mobile society, the organization's contact person, the local area code, or in a few cases, even the nature of the company's mission may have changed by the time this book goes to press. If the person for whom you are looking cannot be found or is not experienced with your particular concern, just ask for a referral and go from there.

Alabama

Director
Near SBDC
PO Box 168
Huntsville, AL 35804-0168
205-535-2061; Fax: 205-535-2050
small bus@hsvchamber.org

Gary Hannem
Director
SBDC
Auburn University
108 COB Lowder Bldg.
Auburn, AL 36849-5243
334-844-4220; Fax: 334-844-4268
ghannem@business.auburn.edu

Wilson L. Harrison
Director
UAB Office for the Adv. of
    Dev. Industries
1075 13th St. South
Birmingham, AL 35294-4440
205-934-2190; Fax: 205-934-1037

Carolyn Long
Account Executive
Univ. of North Alabama
SBDC
Box 5250
Florence, AL 35632-0001
205-760-4629; Fax: 205-760-4813

Alaska

Jamie Kenworthy
Exec. Dir.
Alaska Science/Tech. Foundation
4500 Diplomacy Dr., #515
Anchorage, AK 99508-5918
907-272-4333; Fax: 907-274-6228

Charles Christy
Database Admin.
Alaska Tech. Transfer Assistance
    Ctr.
430 W. 7th Ave., Suite 110
Anchorage, AK 99501
907-274-7232; Fax: 907-274-9524

Pamela Middaugh
Exec. Dir.
Alaska Inventors & Entrepreneurs
    Assn., Inc.
PO Box 241801
Anchorage, AK 99524-1801
907-276-4337; Fax: 907-276-4337
inventor@arctic.net

Clyde Johnson
Director
Kenai Peninsula SBDC
PO Box 3029
Kenai, AK 99611-3029
907-283-3335; Fax: 907-283-3913

E. Wall
Lead Subcenter Dir.
Univ. of Alaska SBDC
430 W. 7th Ave., Suite 110
Anchorage, AK 99501
907-274-7232; Fax: 907-274-9524

Arizona

Deborah Elver
Pgm. Coord.
Cochise College
SBDC
901 N. Colombo
Sierra Vista, AZ 85635
520-515-5478; Fax: 520-515-5437
elverdeb@tron.cochise.cc.az.us

Susan Moore
President
Inventors Assn. of Arizona
2201 N. Camino Principal, Suite 4
Tucson, AZ 85715
520-296-4464; Fax: 520-290-8164

Jennee Miles
Director
Mohave Comm. College
SBDC
1971 Jagerson Ave.
Kingman, AZ 86401
520-757-0895; Fax: 520-757-0836
jenmil@pops.mohave.cc.az.us

Linda Andrews
Regional Dir.
Pima Community College
SBDTC
4905A E. BRd.way Blvd., #110
Tucson, AZ 85709-1260
602-748-4906; Fax: 602-748-4585

Christina Gonzalez
Manager
SBDC
1414 W. BRd.way, #165
Tempe, AZ 85281-6941
602-966-7786; Fax: 602-966-8541

Rich Senopole
Director
SBDC
117 E. Gurley St., #206
Prescott, AZ 86301
520-776-2373; Fax: 520-778-3109
sba_rich@sizzle.yavapai.cc.az.us

Dr. Rita C. Manak
Director
Univ. of Arizona
Office of Tech. Transfer
PO Box 210158, Rm. 515
Tucson, AZ 85721-0158
520-621-5000; Fax: 520-626-4600

Arkansas

James T. Benham
Arkansas Science & Technology
   Authority
100 Main St., Suite 450
Little Rock, AR 72201
501-324-9006; Fax: 501-324-9012

Janet Nye
State Director
Univ. of Arkansas at Little Rock
SBDC
100 S. Main St., Suite 401
Little Rock, AR 72212
501-324-9043; Fax: 501-324-9049

California

The Dream Merchant Magazine
John Moreland
2309 Torrance Blvd., Suite 104
Torrance, CA 90501
310-328-1925; Fax: 310-328-1844

Tiffany Haugen
Director
Accelerate Technology
SBDC
4199 Campus Dr. #240
Irvine, CA 92715
714-509-2990; Fax: 714-509-2997

Kenneth Romano
CACT Director
CACT—Sierra College
5000 Rocklin Rd.
Rocklin, CA 95677
916-781-0433; Fax: 916-781-0410
ramano_ke@email.sierra.cc.ca.us

Bradford L. Friedman
Law & Tech. Advisor
California Invention Center
California State Univ.
675 Sharon Park Dr., # 237
Menlo Park, CA 94025
510-885-3805; Fax: 510-885-8039
cic@csuhayward.edu

Lawrence J. Udell
California Invention Center
School of Business & Economics
California State Hayward
Hayward, CA 94542-3066
510-885-3805; Fax: 510-885-2039

Denise Arend
State Dir. of SBDC
California Office of Small
Business
801 K St., Suite 1700
Sacramento, CA 95814
916-322-5790; Fax: 916-322-5084

Carole Enmark
Director
Cascade SBDC
737 Auditorium Dr., HA
Redding, CA 96001
916-247-8100; Fax: 916-241-1712

Randy Mason
Program Mgr.
Central California
SBDC
430 W. Calowell, #D
Visalia, CA 93277
209-625-3051; Fax: 209-625-3053

John Christensen
President
Central Valley Inventor's Assn.,
   Inc.
PO Box 1551
Manteca, CA 95336-1551
209-239-5414

Brad Mix
Business Consultant
Coachella Valley SBDC
501 S. Indian Canyon, #222
Palm Springs, CA 92264
619-864-1311; Fax: 619-864-1319

Sherm Fishman
Contra Costa Inventors Club
295 Stevenson Dr.
Pleasant Hill, CA 94523-4149
510-934-1331; Fax: 510-934-1132

Bob Smith
CEO
Experimental Cities, Inc.
"A Flash of Genius"
PO Box 731
Pacific Palisades, CA 90272-0731
310-276-0686; Fax: 310-274-7401
gmarcus@igc.apc.org

Steve Schneider
Program Coord.
Idea to Market Network
PO Box 12248
Santa Rosa, CA 95406
800-ITM-3210; Fax: 707-584-4161

Debbie Trujillo
Manager
Imperial Valley SBDC
301 N. Imperial, Suite B
El Centro, CA 92243
619-312-9800; Fax: 619-312-9838

Teri Corrazzini Ooms
Exec. Dir.
Inland Empire SBDC
2002 Iowa Ave., Suite 110
Riverside, CA 92507
909-781-2345; Fax: 909-781-2353

Michael Roessler
Asst. Dir.
Inland Empire SBDC
2002 Iowa Ave., Suite 110
Riverside, CA 92507
909-781-2345; Fax: 909-871-2353

Martha Regan
Co-President
Inventors Alliance
5666 Arboretum Dr.
Los Altos, CA 94024
415-967-0220; Fax: 415-967-0720

Jim Mitsuoka
President
Inventors Forum
PO Box 8008
Huntington Beach, CA 92615-8008
714-253-0952; Fax: 714-836-5609

Greg W. Lauren
Coordinator
Inventors Forum of San Diego
11190 Poblado Rd.
San Diego, CA 92127-1306
619-673-4733; Fax: 619-451-6154

Alan A. Tratner
President
Inventors Workshop Intl.
1029 Castillo St.
Santa Barbara, CA 93101-3736
805-962-5722; Fax: 805-899-4927

Maggie Weisberg
Partner
M&M Associates
PO Box 1020
Fort Jones, CA 96032-9712
916-468-2282; Fax: 916-468-2238

Melvin L. Fuller
Partner
M&M Associates
VVC Productions
PO Box 1020
Fort Jones, CA 96032-1020
916-468-2282; Fax: 916-468-2238

Gillian Murphy
Director
San Joaquin Delta College SBDC
814 N. Hunter St.
Stockton, CA 95202
209-474-5089; Fax: 209-474-5605

Charles Robbins
Director
Sawyer Center
520 Mendocino Ave., Suite 210
Santa Rosa, CA 95401
707-524-1770; Fax: 707-524-1772

Director
SBDC
4275 Executive Square
La Jolla, CA 92037
619-453-9388; Fax: 619-450-1997
sbdc@smallbiz.org

Director
SBDC
560 Wall St., Suite J
Auburn, CA 95603
916-885-5488; Fax: 916-823-2831

Paul Hischar
Manager
SBDC
375 S. Main St., Suite 101
Pomona, CA 91766
909-629-2247; Fax: 909-629-8310

Teresa Thomae
Director
SBDC
6500 Soquel Dr.
Aptos, CA 95003
408-479-6136; Fax: 408-479-6166

Sherm Fishman
Exec. Dir.
Small Entity Patent Owners Assn.
295 Stevenson Dr.
Pleasant Hill, CA 94523-4149
510-934-1331; Fax: 510-934-1132

A. Wayne Snodgrass
President
Small Manufacturers' Institute
6000 J St., Suite 83053
Sacramento, CA 95819-6122
916-278-4877; Fax: 916-367-3270
wsnodgrass@aol.com

Jeffrey Johnson
Director
Weill Institute
SBDC
1706 Chester Ave., #200
Bakersfield, CA 96330
805-322-5881; Fax: 805-322-5663

Colorado

Lewis Kontnik
President
Colorado Bio/Medical Venture
   Center
1610 Pierce St.
Lakewood, CO 80214
303-237-3998; Fax: 303-237-4010

Jim Reser
Director
Fort Lewis College SBDC
1000 Rim Dr.
Durango, CO 81301-3999
970-247-7009; Fax: 970-247-7623
reser_j@fortlewis.edu

Suiteve Madone
Exec. Dir.
Fremont County D C
402 Valley Rd.
Canon City, CO 81212
719-275-8601; Fax: 719-275-4400

Director
Greeley SBDC
1407 8th Ave.
Greeley, CO 80631
970-352-3661; Fax: 970-352-3572

Director
SBDC
School of Business 105
Alamosa, CO 81102
719-587-7372; Fax: 719-587-7522

Joseph Bell
Director
SBDC
2440 Pearl St.
Boulder, CO 80302
30-344-2145; Fax:

Sonny Lastrella
Deputy State Director
SBDC
State of Colorado OBD
Denver, CO 80202
303-892-3840; Fax: 303-892-3848

Dennis O'Connor
Director
SBDC
136 W. Main St.
Trinidad, CO 81082
719-846-5644; Fax: 719-846-4550

Frank Pryor
Director
SBDC
2627 Redwing Rd., Suite 105
Ft. Collins, CO 80526
970-226-0881; Fax: 970-204-0385

Selma Kristel
Dir., Bus. Growth
South Metro Denver Chamber
7901 South Park Plaza
Littleton, CO 80120
303-795-0142; Fax: 303-795-7520

Julie Morey
SBDC Director
Western County Bus. Dev. Corp.
304 W. Main St.
Grand Junction, CO 81505
970-243-5242; Fax: 970-241-0771
mesastate@attmail.com

Connecticut

Jay Savery, CEO
Problem Solvers
48 Purnell Pl.
Manchester, CT 06040-5412
860-645-6980; Fax: 860-646-5301

Julie Rader
Director
Connecticut Innovations, Inc.
Tech. Assistance Center
40 Cold Spring Rd.
Rocky Hill, CT 06419
860-563-5851; Fax: 860-563-4877

Dennis Gruell
Regional Dir.
CT SBDC
1800 Asylum Ave., Univ. of
    Connecticut
West Hartford, CT 06117
860-241-4986; Fax: 860-241-4907
dennis@ct.sbdc.uconn.edu

Ilene G. Oppenheim
Director
Connecticut Small Business Dev./
    Outreach Center
101 South Main St.
Waterbury, CT 06706
203-757-8937; Fax: 203-756-9077

Innovators Network of Greater
    Danbury
52 Bank St., Suite A
New Milford, CT 06776-2706
860-350-2709; Fax: 860-355-8752

John A. Ruckes
Lead Planning Analyst
State of Connecticut/OPM
PO Box 341441 MS# 52ENR
Hartford, CT 06134-1441
860-418-6384; Fax: 860-418-6495

Delaware

David J. Freschman
President
Delaware Innovation Fund
3828 Kennett Pike, #100
Wilmington, DE 19807
302-777-1616; Fax: 302-777-1620

Clinton Tymes
Director
Delaware SBDC Network
005 Purnell Hall
Newark, DE 19716
302-831-1555; Fax: 302-831-1423

District of Columbia

John Curtin, Esquire
Assn. of Trial Lawyers of America
1050 31st St.
Washington, DC 20007
202-965-3500; Fax: 202-625-7312

Woodrow McCutchen
Exec. Dir.
Howard Univ.
SBDC
2600 6th St. NW
Washington, DC 20059
202-806-1550; Fax: 202-806-1777
husbdc@cldc.howard.edu

Fred Hart, Director
US Dept. of Energy
ERIP
1000 Independence Ave., EE 521,
   5E052
Washington, DC 20585
202-586-1478; Fax: 202-586-1605

Florida

Doug L. Davis
Director
Bay County Incubator
2500 Minnesota Ave.
Lynn Haven, FL 32444
904-271-1108; Fax: 904-271-1109

Victoria H. Peake
Coordinator
Brevard Community College
SBDC
3865 N. Wickham Rd.
Melbourne, FL 32935-2399
407-242-9416; Fax: 407-634-3721
peake.v@al.brevard.cc.fl.us

Marcela E. Stanislaus
Central Florida Development
600 N. BRd.way Ave.
Bartow, FL 33830
941-534-4370; Fax: 941-533-1247

Edward A. Cobham Jr.
Community Assistance
   Consultant
Dept. of Comm. Affairs
Florida Energy Office
2740 Centerview Dr.
Tallahassee, FL 32399-2100
904-488-2475; Fax: 904-488-7688

Dr. Gary Nelson
President
Edison Inventors Association, Inc.
PO Box 07398
Ft. Myers, FL 33919
941-275-4332; Fax: 941-267-9746

Earnie DeVille
President
Emerald Coast Inventors Society
c/o Univ. of West Florida SBDC
11000 University
Pensacola, FL 32514-5752
904-474-2908; Fax: 904-474-2126
urnmani@aol.com

Scott Faris
President
Enterprise Corporation
1111 NW Shore Blvd., Suite 200-B
Tampa, FL 33607
813-288-0445; Fax: 813-554-2356

William Healy
Regional Dir.
Florida Intl. Univ. SBDC
46 SW 1st Ave.
Dania, FL 33004
954-987-0100; Fax: 954-987-0106

Director
Florida Atlantic Univ.
SBDC
777 Glades Rd.
Boca Raton, FL 33431
561-362-5620; Fax: 561-362-5623

Royland Jarrett
Regional Mgr.
Florida Intl. Univ.
SBDC
HM112A N. Miami Campus
North Miami, FL 33181
305-940-5790; Fax: 305-940-5792

Doug L. Davis
Director
GCCC SBDC
2500 Minnesota Ave.
Lynn Haven, FL 32444
904-271-1108; Fax: 904-271-1109

Richard J. Carreno
Master Instructor
Indian River Comm. College
3209 Virginia Ave.
Fort Pierce, FL 34981
407-462-4756; Fax: 407-462-4830

Pamela H. Riddle
CEO
Innovative Product Technologies
4131 NW 13th St., Suite 220
Gainesville, FL 32609
352-373-1007; Fax: 352-337-0750

Frederic Bonneau
Director
Miami-Dade Comm. College
Entrepreneurial Education Center,
   SBDC
6300 NW 7th Ave.
Miami, FL 33150-4322
305-237-1900; Fax: 305-237-1908

Radcliffe S. Weaver
President
Naples Entrepreneurial Enterprise
   Development
40 9th Ave. South
Naples, FL 33940-6844
941-649-4094; Fax: 941-435-1718

Jerome Zajic
Tech. Specialist
PSPI, Inc.
15 Dahoon Court South
Homosassa, FL 34446-8922
352-382-1535

Philip R. Geist
Program Mgr.
SBDC
110 E. Silver Springs
Ocala, FL 34470-6613
352-622-8763; Fax: 352-351-1031
sbdcoca@mercury.net

Patricia N. McGowan
Exec. Dir.
SBDC
1157 E. Tennessee St.
Tallahassee, FL 32308
904-599-3407; Fax: 904-561-2409

Daniel V. Regelski
Certified Business Analyst
SBDC
8099 College Parkway SW
Fort Myers, FL 33919
941-489-9201; Fax: 941-489-9051

Raymond V. Purdy
Director
Tampa Bay Inventors Council
13543 Periwinkle Ave.
Seminole, FL 34646
813-391-0315

Walter B. Craft
Manager
Univ. of West Florida SBDC
1170 Martin Luther King, Jr. Blvd.
 2/250
Fort Walton Beach, FL 32547
904-863-6543; Fax: 904-863-6564

Martha J. Cobb
Area Mgr.
Univ. of West Florida SBDC
11000 University Blvd., 8
Pensacola, FL 32514-5752
904-474-2908; Fax: 904-474-2126

Georgia

Mary-Frances Panettiere
Head, Tech Resources
Georgia Inst. of Technology
Library & Information Center
Atlanta, GA 30244-0900
404-894-4508; Fax: 404-894-8190

Elizabeth S. Robertson
Program Mgr.
Governor's Office of Energy
 Resources
100 P St. NW, Suite 2090
Atlanta, GA 30303-1911
404-656-3887; Fax: 404-656-7970

Alexander T. Marinaccio
Chairman
Inventors Clubs of America, Inc.
PO Box 450261
Atlanta, GA 31145-0261
404-355-1692; Fax: 404-355-8889

Ronald L. Henderson
US Department of Energy
Atlanta Support Office
730 Peachtree St. NE, Suite 876
Atlanta, GA 30308
404-347-7139; Fax: 404-347-3098

Jeffrey R. Sanford
Area Director
Univ. of Georgia
SBDC
1061 Katherine St.
Augusta, GA 30904-6105
706-737-1790; Fax: 706-731-7937
sbdcaug@uga.cc.uga.edu

Ron E. Simmons
Area Director
Univ. of Georgia BOS
500 Jesse Jewell Pkwy., Suite 304
Gainesville, GA 30501-3773
770-531-5681; Fax: 770-531-5684

Lynn H. Vos
Savannah Area Dir.
Univ. of Georgia
Business Outreach Services
450 Mall Blvd., Suite H
Savannah, GA 31406-4824
912-356-2755; Fax: 912-353-3033

Thomas Snyder
Univ. of Georgia BOS
928 45th St., Rm. 523
Columbus, GA 31904-6572
706-649-7433; Fax: 706-562-9645

John R. Miquelon
Business Consultant
Univ. of Georgia BOS
PO Box 13212
Macon, GA 31208
912-751-6592; Fax: 912-751-6607
sbdcmac@uga.cc.uga.edu

Hawaii

Janice Kato
Business Development Mgr.
High Tech. Development Corp.
2800 Woodlawn Dr., #100
Honolulu, HI 96822
808-539-3814; Fax: 808-539-3611

Randy Gingras
Center Director
UHH SBDCN
3-1901 Kaumualii Hwy.
Lihue, HI 96766-9591
808-246-1748; Fax: 808-245-5102
randy@aloha.net

Darryl Mleynek
State Director
Univ. of Hawaii at Hilo
SBDC
200 W. Kawili St.
Hilo, HI 96720-4091
808-933-3515; Fax: 808-933-3683
darrylm@interpac.net

Idaho

John Wordin
President
East Idaho Inventors Forum
PO Box 452
Shelley, ID 83274-0452
208-346-6763; Fax: 208-346-6763

Bob Shepard
Regional Director
ID SBDC
1910 University Dr.
Boise, ID 83725
208-385-3875; Fax: 208-385-3877
bshepard@bsu.ldbsu.edu

Gerald Fleischman
Bioenergy Specialist
Idaho Dept. of Water Resources
PO Box 83720
Boise, ID 83702-0098
208-327-7959; Fax: 208-327-7866

Rick R. Ritter
Business Development Specialist
Idaho Innovation Center
2300 N. Yellowstone
Idaho Falls, ID 83401
208-523-1026; Fax: 208-523-1049

James R. Suiteinfort
Exec. Dir.
Idaho Manufacturing Alliance
1021 Manitou Ave.
Boise, ID 83706
208-385-3689; Fax: 208-385-3877

Laurence C. Bonar
Director, Technical Licensure
Idaho Research Foundation, Inc.
121 Sweet Ave.
Moscow, ID 83843-2309
208-885-3548; Fax: 208-882-0105

James E. Hogge
State Director
Idaho SBDC
State Office—Boise State Univ.
1910 Univ. Dr.
Boise, ID 83725
208-385-1640; Fax: 208-385-3877

Burt Knudson
Tech. Services Consultant
Idaho SBDC
1910 University Dr.
Boise, ID 83725-1655
208-385-3870; Fax: 208-385-3877
bknudson@bsu.idbsu.edu

Helen M. LeBoef-Binninger
Regional Director
Idaho SBDC
Lewis-Clark State College
500 8th Ave.
Lewiston, ID 83501
208-799-2465; Fax: 208-799-2878

Mary Capps
Regional Dir.
Idaho State Univ.
SBDC
2300 North Yellowstone, Suite 121
Idaho Falls, ID 83401
208-523-1087; Fax: 208-523-1049
cappmary@fs.isu.edu

Paul Cox
Regional Dir.
SBDC
1651 Alvin Ricken Dr.
Pocatello, ID 83201
208-232-4921; Fax: 208-233-0268

John Lynn
Regional Dir.
SDBC
505 W. Clearwater Loop
Post Falls, ID 83854
208-769-3444; Fax: 208-769-3223
jlynn@nidc.edu

Illinois

Andrew Fox
Portfolio Mgr.
ARCH Development Corp.
1101 East 58th St.
Chicago, IL 60637
312-702-1692; Fax: 312-702-0741

David K. Gay
Manager
College of DuPage
SBDC
22nd St. & Lambert
Glen Ellyn, IL 60137-6599
630-942-2771; Fax: 630-942-3789

Camilla McKinney
Decatur Industry & Tech Center
2121 S. Imboden Court
Decatur, IL 62521
217-423-2832; Fax: 217-423-7214

Kriss Knowles
Small Business Specialist
Elgin Comm. College
SBDC
1700 Spartan Dr.
Elgin, IL 60123-7193
847-888-7675; Fax: 847-931-3911

Thomas E. Parkinson
Evanston Business Investment Co.
1840 Oak Ave.
Evanston, IL 60202
847-866-1817; Fax: 847-866-1808

Paul Peterson
Deputy Dir.
Greater North Pulaski
    Development
4054 W. North Ave.
Chicago, IL 60639-5220
773-384-2262; Fax: 773-384-3850

Mindy B. Solomon
Exec. Dir.
Illinois Recycling Assn.
9400 Bormet Dr., Suite 5
Mokena, IL 60448
708-479-3800; Fax: 708-479-4592

Jeffrey J. Mitchell, Sr.
Director
Illinois SBDC
620 E. Adams St.
Springfield, IL 62701
217-524-5700; Fax: 217-524-0171
jeff.mitchell@accessil.com

Jim Charney
Director
Illinois SBIR Center
7500 S. Pulaski Rd., #200
Chicago, IL 60652
773-838-0319; Fax: 773-838-0303

Bruce R. Baumeister
CEO
Innovation Development
    Corporation
PO Box 1185
Calumet, IL 60409
708-891-0316; Fax: 708-891-0316

Don Moyer
Patent Agent
Inventors Council
431 S. Dearborn, #705
Chicago, IL 60605
312-939-3329; Fax: 312-922-7706

Boyd Palmer
Director
IVCC SBDC
815 N. Orlando Smith Rd.
Oglesby, IL 61348
815-223-1740; Fax: 815-224-3033
bpalmer@rs6000.ivcc.edu

Denise F. Mikulski
Joliet Junior College
SBDC
214 N. Ottawa
Joliet, IL 60432
815-727-6544, ext. 140; Fax: 815-722-1895
dmikulsk@jjc.cc.il.us

Bob Duane
Manager
Lewis & Clark Comm. College
SBDC
5800 Godfrey Rd.
Godfrey, IL 62035
618-467-2370; Fax: 618-466-0810

Carson A. Gallagher
Director
Loop SBDC
100 W. Randolph St., S3-400
Chicago, IL 60601-3218
312-814-6111; Fax: 312-814-5247
carson.gallagher@accessil.com

Joseph R. McLennan
President
Management Assn. of Illinois
2809 S. 25th Ave.
BRd.view, IL 60153
708-344-6400; Fax: 708-344-6989

Susan R. Whitfield
Director, SBDC
McHenry County College
8900 US Hwy. 14
Crystal Lake, IL 60012-2761
815-455-6098; Fax: 815-455-9319
sue.whitfield@accessil.com

Lisa N. Payne
Director
Rend Lake College
SBDC
Rt. 1
Ina, IL 62895
618-437-5321; Fax: 618-437-5353
payne@rendlake.rlc.cc.il.us

Richard C. Holbrook
Director
SBDC
1840 Oak Ave.
Evanston, IL 60201
847-866-1817; Fax: 847-866-1808

Alan Hauff
Director
SIU—E SBDC
Campus Box 1107
Edwardsville, IL 62026-1107
618-692-2929; Fax: 618-692-2647

Becky Williams
Director
Southeastern Illinois College
SBDC
303 S. Commercial
Harrisburg, IL 62946-2125
618-252-5001; Fax: 618-252-0210

Lynn Lindberg
Coordinator
Southern IL Mfg. Ext. Service
150 E. Pleasant Hill
Carbondale, IL 62901-6891
618-536-4451; Fax: 618-453-5040
lindberg@siu.edu

Raymond C. Lenzi
Exec. Dir.
Southern Illinois Univ.
Office of Econ. & Reg. Dev.
Carbondale, IL 62901-6891
618-536-4451; Fax: 618-453-5040
lenzi@siu.edu

Sheree Kirby
Manager
Technology Commercial
    Laboratory
2004 S. Wright St.
Urbana, IL 61801
217-244-7742; Fax: 217-244-7757
kirby@uxl.cso.uiuc.edu

Thomas V. Thornton
President
The Illinois Coalition
100 W. Randolph St., 11-600
Chicago, IL 60601
312-814-3482; Fax: 312-814-4942

Melvin J. Degeeter
Director
Univ. of Illinois
Res. & Tech. Mgmt.
417 Swanlund, 601 E. John
Champaign, IL 61820
217-333-7862; Fax: 217-244-3716

Iowa

Lori Harmening
Exec. Dir.
Circle West/SBDC
PO Box 204
Audubon, IA 50025
712-563-2623; Fax: 712-563-2301

William R. Berkland
Industrial Specialist—Community
    Cntr. for Industrial Research
    Services
500 ISU Research Park
2501 N. Loop Dr.
Ames, IA 50010-8286
515-294-3420

Ben C. Swartz
Director
Drake Univ., SBDC
Inventure Program
2507 University Ave.
Des Moines, IA 50311
515-271-2655; Fax: 515-271-1899

Sharon Tahtinen
Executive Officer
Iowa Dept. of Natural Resources
Wallace State Office Bldg.
Des Moines, IA 50319-0001
515-281-7066; Fax: 515-821-6794

Suiteven T. Carter
Director
ISU BDC
2501 No. Loop Dr., Bldg. #1,
    Suite 615
Ames, IA 50010-8283
515-296-7828; Fax: 515-296-6714
stc@iastate.edu

Charles Tonn
Director
Northeast Iowa SBDC
770 Town Clock Plaza
Dubuque, IA 52001-6837
319-588-3350; Fax: 319-557-1591

Paul D. Heath
Director
SBDC
5160 PBAB
Iowa City, IA 52242
319-335-3742; Fax: 319-353-2445
paul-heath@uiowa.edu

Richard Petersen
Director
SBDC
500 College Dr.
Mason City, IA 50401
515-422-4341; Fax: 515-422-4129

Mark Laurenzo
Bureau Chief
SBRO
Dept. of Economic Development
200 E. Grand Ave.
Des Moines, IA 50309
515-242-4740; Fax: 515-242-4809

Robin Travis
Director
Southwestern SBDC
1501 West Townline Rd.
Creston, IA 50801
515-782-4161; Fax: 515-782-3312

Indiana

Adele Purlee
Exec. Dir.
Bedford Chamber of Commerce
1116 16th St.
Bedford, IN 47421
812-275-4493; Fax: 812-279-5998
bedford@tima.com

Davida E. Parks
Asst. Dir.
BIDC—Purdue Univ.
1220 Potter Dr.
West Lafayette, IN 47906-1383
800-787-2432; Fax: 317-474-1352

Randall N. Redelman
Treasurer
Indiana Inventors Assn.
PO Box 2388
Indianapolis, IN 46206-2388
317-745-5597; Fax:

Robert Humbert
President
Indiana Inventors Assn.
5514 South Adams
Marion, IN 46953-6141
317-674-2845; Fax:

W. Sidney Johnson
Director
Industrial Research Liaison
    Program
One City Centre, Suite 200
Bloomington, IN 47404-3929
800-624-8315; Fax: 812-855-8570

Robert P. Quadrozzi
Exec. Dir.
Jay County Dev. Corp.
121 West Main St., Suite A
Portland, IN 47371
219-726-9311; Fax: 219-726-4477

Vivian G. Sallie
Exec. Dir.
Minority Business Dev.
401 E. Colfax Ave., Suite 30
South Bend, IN 46634
219-234-0051; Fax: 219-289-0358

James W. Byrd
Exec. Dir.
Randolph County Comm. & Econ.
    Dev.
PO Box 529
Winchester, IN 47394
317-584-3266; Fax: 317-584-3622

John D. Weber
Director
Regional Mfg. Ext. Center
33 South 7th St.
Richmond, IN 47374
317-966-3909; Fax: 317-966-0882

Julie A Hogsett
Exec. Dir.
Rush County Industrial
    Dev. Corp.
PO Box 156
Rushville, IN 46173-0156
317-932-5610; Fax: 317-932-4191

Carolyn J. Anderson
Regional Dir.
SBDC
300 Michigan St.
South Bend, IN 46601
219-282-4350; Fax: 219-236-1056

Cliff Fry
Director
SBDC
33 S. 7th St., Suite 3
Richmond, IN 47374
317-962-2887; Fax: 317-966-0882

David Miller
Director
SBDC
PO Box 248
Bloomington, IN 47402-0248
812-339-8937; Fax: 812-335-7352

Patricia A. Stroud
Director
Southern Indiana SBDC
1613 E. Eighth St., PO 1567
Jeffersonville, IN 47131
812-288-6451, ext. 160; Fax: 812-284-8327

Beth A. Clark
Coordinator
Sullivan County Chamber of
    Commerce
PO Box 325
Sullivan, IN 47882
812-268-4836; Fax: 812-268-4836

Ray E. Dickerson
Exec. Dir.
Union County Dev. Corp.
27 West Union
Liberty, IN 47353-1349
317-458-5976; Fax: 317-458-5976

Bruce A. Storm
President
Wabash Area Chamber of
    Commerce
111 South Wabash St., PO Box 371
Wabash, IN 46992-0371
219-563-1168; Fax: 219-563-6920

William E. Bradley Jr.
Exec. Dir.
Wabash Economic Dev. Corp.
111 S. Wabash St., PO Box 795
Wabash, IN 46992-0795
219-563-5258; Fax: 219-563-6920

Kansas

Bill Sander
Regional Dir.
Garden City Comm. College
SBDC
801 Campus Dr.
Garden City, KS 67846
316-276-9632; Fax: 316-276-9630
sbdc@gcnet.com

Brenda I. Gallo
Senior Secretary
Johnson County Comm. College
SBDC
12345 College Blvd.
Overland Park, KS 66210-1299
913-469-3878; Fax: 913-469-4415

Michael F. Renk
Director
Kansas State Univ.
2409 Scanlan
Salina, KS 67401
913-826-2616; Fax: 913-826-2630
mfr@mail.sal.ksu.edu

Clayton Williamson
President
Kansas Assn. of Inventors
1300 Kansas Ave.
Great Bend, KS 67530
316-793-1950; Fax: 316-793-1952

State Director
Kansas SBDC
700 SW Harrison St., Suite 1300
Topeka, KS 66603-3712
913-296-5298; Fax: 913-296-3490

Clyde C. Engert
Vice President Research
Kansas Tech. Enterprise
214 SW 6th, First Floor
Topeka, KS 66603
913-296-3686; Fax: 913-296-1160

Fredrick H. Rice
Director
KSU SBDC
2323 Anderson, Suite 100
Manhattan, KS 66502-2912
913-532-5529; Fax: 913-532-5827

Kathryn S. Richard
Regional Dir.
SBDC
Pittsburg State Univ.
Pittsburg. KS 66762-7560
316-235-4920; Fax: 316-232-6440
krichard@pittstate.edu

Tom Cornelius, Director
Seward County Comm. College
Business & Industry Services
1801 N. Kansas, Box 1137
Liberal, KS 67905-1137
316-629-2650; Fax: 316-629-2725

Wayne Glass, Director
Washburn Univ.
SBDC
1700 College
Topeka, KS 66621
913-231-1010, ext. 130;
    Fax: 913-231-1063
zzsbdc@acc.wuacc.edu

Joann Ard
Acting Regional Dir.
Wichita State Univ.
SBDC
1845 Fairmount
Wichita, KS 67260-0148
316-689-3193; Fax: 316-689-3647

Kentucky

William R. Keelen
Program Mgr.
Center for Mfg.
Univ. of Kentucky
Lexington, KY 40506-0108
606-257-6262; Fax: 606-257-1071

Mohamed H. Nasser
Coordinator
Central Kentucky Inventors &
    Entrepreneurs Council
117 Carolyn Dr.
Nicholasville, KY 40356
606-885-9593; Fax: 606-887-9856

Kimberly A. Jenkins
General Mgmt. Consultant
Morehead/Ashland SBDC
SBDC
1401 Winchester Ave., Suite 305
Ashland, KY 41101
606-329-8011; Fax: 606-324-4570
k.jenkins@morehead-st.edu

LouAnn Allen
Director
SBDC
238 West Dixie
Elizabethtown, KY 42701
502-765-6737; Fax: 502-769-5095

Richard Horn
Director
SBDC
2355 Nashville Rd.
Bowling Green, KY 42101-4144
502-745-1905; Fax: 502-745-1931
rshorn@wku.edu

Ken Blandford
Mgmt. Consultant
Univ. of Louisville
SBDC
Shelby Campus
Louisville, KY 40292
502-852-7854; Fax: 502-852-8573
klblan01@ulkyvm.louisville.edu

Louisiana

Charles D'Agostino
Exec. Dir.
Louisiana Business Tech. Center
South Stadium Dr.
LSU
Baton Rouge, LA 70803
504-334-5555; Fax: 504-388-3975

Ronald H. Schroeder
Director
Loyola Univ. New Orleans SBDC
College of Business Admin.
6363 St. Charles Ave.
Campus Box 134
New Orleans, LA 70118-6195
504-865-3187; Fax: 504-865-3496

Peggy Connor
Director
LSUS SBDC
One Univ. Place
Shreveport, LA 71115-2399
318-797-5144; Fax: 318-797-5208
ameachum@pilot.lsus.edu

Windell Millicks
Business Resource Specialist
Macon Ridge Econ. Dev.
PO Drawer 746
Ferriday, LA 71373
318-757-3033; Fax: 318-757-4212

Paul Dunn
Director
NLU SBDC
700 Univ. Ave.
Monroe, LA 71209
318-342-1224; Fax: 318-342-1209

Thomas C. Arata
Assistant to Dir.
UNO SBDC
1600 Canal St., Suite 620
New Orleans, LA 70112
504-539-9292; Fax: 504-539-9295
unosbdc@www.gnofn.org

Maine

Maine SBDC
Univ. of South Maine
96 Falmouth St.
Portland, ME 04103
207-780-4420

Cheri Cooledge
MSBDC
AVCOG
125 Manley Rd.
Auburn, ME 04210
207-783-9186; Fax: 207-783-5211

James A. Burbank
Director Business Assistance
Costal Enterprises
Box 268
Wiscasset, ME 04578
207-882-4340; Fax: 207-882-4456

Richard Angotti, Jr.
President
Katahdin Regional Dev. Center
PO Box 449
East Millinocket, ME 04430
207-746-5338; Fax: 207-746-9535
krdc@agate.net

James A. Burbank
Director
SBDC
PO Box 268, Water St.
Wiscasset, ME 04578-0268
207-882-4340; Fax: 207-882-4456
jab@cei.maine.com

Brian Burwell
SBDC
96 Falmouth St., PO Box 9300
Portland, ME 04104-9300
207-780-4420; Fax: 207-780-4810

James S. Ward
Dir. Industrial Coordination
Univ. of Maine
5717 Corbett Hall
Orono, ME 04469-5717
207-581-1488; Fax: 207-581-1479

Maryland

Terry M. Levinson
TML Consulting Group
1506 Constance St.
Silver Spring, MD 20902
301-649-3403; Fax: 301-649-9764

Lanny Herron
Lab to Market Prin.
Merrick School of Business
1420 N. Charles St.
Baltimore, MD 21201
410-837-5069; Fax: 410-837-5675
lherron@ubmail.ubalt.edu

Jacob Rabinow
National Institute of Standards &
Tech. (NIST)
Gaithersburg, MD 20899
301-975-5502; Fax: 301-975-3839

Jack E. Pevenstein
Engineering/Outreach
Coordinator
Office of Tech. Innovation
National Institute of Standards &
Tech.
Gaithersburg, MD 20899-0001
301-975-5500; Fax: 301-975-3839

Robin B. Douglas
Exec. Dir.
SBDC
3 Commerce Dr.
Cumberland, MD 21502
301-724-6716; Fax: 301-777-7504
robindougl@metbiz.net

Mary Ann Garst
Director
SBDC
7932 Opossumtown Pike
Frederick, MD 21702
301-846-2683; Fax: 301-846-2689

Pam Schaller
Consultant
SBDC
Chesapeake College
Wye Mills, MD 21617
410-827-5286; Fax: 410-827-5286

Michael E. McCabe
Senior Evaluator
US Department of Commerce
National Institute of Standards &
Tech.
Building 820, Room 251
Gaithersburg, MD 20899
301-975-5517; Fax: 301-975-3839

Massachusetts

Inventors Digest
Joanne M. Hayes-Rines
Publisher
310 Franklin St., Suite 24
Boston, MA 02110
617-367-4540; Fax: 617-723-6988
InventorsD@aol.com

Suiteven Cressy
President
Cape Cod Inventors Assn.
1600 Falmouth Rd., Suite 123
Centerville, MA 02632
508-428-8792; Fax:

Donald Job
Innovative Products Research &
Services
393 Beacon St.
Lowell, MA 01850
508-934-0035; Fax: 508-459-8126

Donald L. Gammon
Inventors Assn. of New England
PO Box 335
Lexington, MA 02173
508-474-0488; Fax: 509-474-0488

Robert Lougher
Inventors Awareness Group, Inc.
1533 East Mountain Rd., Suite B
Westfield, MA 01085-1458
413-568-5561; Fax: 413-568-5325
iagbob@aol.com

Frederick H. Young
Director
Salem State College SBDC
PO Box 15
Salem, MA 01970-0001
508-741-6343; Fax: 508-741-6345

Robert Allen
Program Officer
US Dept. of Energy
One Congress St., Suite 1101
Boston, MA 02114
617-565-9715; Fax: 617-565-9723

Michigan

Ed Zimmer
President
The Entrepreneur Network
1683 Plymouth Rd.
Ann Arbor, MI 48105-1891
800-468-8871; Fax: 313-663-9657

Dennis K. Whitney
Counselor
Business Dev. Center
131 South Hyne
Brighton, MI 48116
810-227-3556; Fax: 810-227-3080

Janet E. Masi
Vice President
Chamber of Commerce
30500 Van Dyke, Suite 118
Warren, MI 48093
810-751-3939; Fax: 810-751-3995
janet-masi@chambercom.com

Ram Kesavan
Director
College of Business Admin.
Univ. of Detroit Mercy
4001 W. McNichols
PO Box 19900
Detroit, MI 48219-0950
313-993-1115; Fax: 313-993-1052
kesavar@udmercy.edu

Todd J. Brian
Exec. Dir.
Industrial Dev. Corp.
800 Military St.
Port Huron, MI 48060
810-982-9511; Fax: 810-982-9531

Carl R. Shook
Director
Kalamazoo College SBDC
1327 Academy St.
Kalamazoo, MI 49001
616-337-7350; Fax: 616-337-7415
sbdc@kzoo.edu

Dennis K. Whitney
Director
Livingston County SBDC
131 Hyne St.
Brighton, MI 48116
810-227-3556; Fax: 810-227-3080

Donald L. Morandini
Director
Macomb County Business
   Assistance Center
115 S. Groesbeck
Macomb, MI 48043
810-469-5118; Fax: 810-469-6787
bacmac@bizserve.com

Thomas Kubanek
Exec. Dir.
Manistee County Economic
Dev. Office
375 River St., Suite 205
Manistee, MI 49660
616-723-4325; Fax:

Dani Topolski
Manager
MCIDC Genesis Centre for
   Entrepreneurial Dev.
111 Conant Ave.
Monroe, MI 48161
313-243-5947; Fax: 313-242-0009

Christine M. Greve
Regional Dir.
Michigan SBDC at SVSU
7400 Bay Rd.
Univ. Center, MI 48710
517-790-4388; Fax: 517-790-4983
cmgreve@tarois.svsu.edu

Carol R. Lopucki
Director
Michigan SBDC
301 W. Fulton, 718 S
Grand Rapids, MI 49504-6495
616-771-6693; Fax: 616-458-3872
lopuckic@gvsu.edu

Sarah McCue
Dir. of Publications
Michigan SBDC
2727 Second Ave.
Detroit, MI 48201
313-964-1798; Fax: 313-964-3648

Chuck Persenaire
Exec. Dir.
Oceana County E.D.C.
PO Box 168
Hart, MI 49420-0168
616-873-7141; Fax: 616-873-5914

Ken Rizzio
Exec. Dir.
Ottawa County Econ. Dev. Office
6676 Lake Michigan Dr.
Allendale, MI 49401
616-892-4120; Fax: 616-895-6670

Charles S. Fitzpatrick
Director
SBDC
256 AB
CMU
Mt. Pleasant, MI 48859
517-774-3220; Fax: 517-774-7992
34ntjen@cmuvm.csu.cmich.edu

Richard J. Beldin
Exec. Dir.
Traverse Bay Enterprise Forum
PO Box 506
Traverse City, MI 49685-0506
616-929-5017; Fax: 616-929-5012

Matthew T. Meadors
Vice President
Traverse City Chamber
PO Box 387
Traverse City, MI 49685-0387
616-947-5075; Fax: 616-946-2565

Minnesota

Tom Trutna
Director
Dakota County Technical College
  SBDC
1300 145th St. E.
Rosemount, MN 55068-2999
612-423-8262; Fax: 612-322-1501

Jim Jordan
SBDC Business Counselor
Hennepin Technical College
1820 Xenium Lane
Plymouth, MN 55441
612-550-7156; Fax: 612-550-7272

Danelle J. Wolf
Director
Hennepin Technical College
  SBDC
1820 North Xenium Lane
Plymouth, MN 55441
612-550-7218; Fax: 612-550-7272
dwolf@henn.tec.mn.us

Frank W. Allen
Director
Icasca Dev. Corp.
19 NE Theid St.
Grand Rapids, MN 55744
218-326-9411; Fax: 218-327-2242
idcsbdc.uslink.nct

Randall D. Olson
Exec. Dir.
Minnesota Project Innovation, Inc.
111 3rd Ave. S., Suite 100
Minneapolis, MN 55401-2551
612-338-3280; Fax: 612-338-3483

David Hepenstal
Tech. Info. Specialist
Minnesota Tech., Inc.
111 Third Ave. S., Suite 400
Minneapolis, MN 55401
612-338-7722; Fax: 612-339-5214

Lisa V. McGinnes
Exec. Dir.
Owatonna Incubator
PO Box 505
560 Dunnell Dr., Suite 203
Owatonna, MN 55060-0505
507-451-0517; Fax: 507-455-2788

James L. Antilla
Director
SBDC
1515 E. 25th St.
Hibbing, MN 55746
218-262-6703; Fax: 218-262-6717
j.antilla.hi.cc.mn.us

Paul G. Paris
President
Society of Minnesota Inventors
20231 Basalt St.
Anoka, MN 55303
612-753-2766; Fax: 612-753-2766

Andrew J. Amoroso
Econ. Devlop. Specialist
U.S. Small Business Admin.
610-C Butler Square,
    100 N. Sixth St.
Minneapolis, MN 55403-1563
612-370-2324; Fax: 612-370-2303

Lee Jensen
Director
UMD Center for Econ. Dev.
150 SBE 10 Univ. Dr.
Duluth, MN 55812-2496
218-726-6192; Fax: 218-726-6338
ced@d.umn.edu

Fred Amram
Professor
Univ. of Minnesota
General College
240 Appleby Hall
Minneapolis, MN 55455
612-625-2531; Fax: 612-626-7848

Missouri

Mark Manley
Patent Agent
Center for Tech.
Central Missouri State Univ.
Warrensburg, MO 64093
816-543-4402; Fax: 816-543-8159

Ed Stout
Consultant to Board
Mid-America Inventors
    Association
2018 Baltimore
Kansas City, MO 64108
816-221-2442; Fax: 816-221-3995

Darrell R. Drammer
Tech. Coordinator
Missouri SBDC
CMSY Grinstead #8
Warrensburg, MO 64093-5037
816-543-4402; Fax: 816-543-8159

Morris R. Hudson
Program Mgr.
Missouri Procurement Assistance
    Center
300 University Pl.
Columbia, MO 65203
573-882-3597; Fax: 573-884-4297
mopcol@ext.missouri.edu

Glen E. Giboney
Director
SBDC
100 E. Normal
Kirksville, MO 63501
816-785-4307; Fax: 816-785-4357

Fred Goss
Director
Tech. Search SBDC
104 Nagogami Terrace UMR
Rolla, MO 65409
573-341-4559; Fax: 573-341-6495

Nick Arends
Business Counselor
Univ. of Missouri—Columbia
   SBDC
Mid-Missouri Inventor Assn.
1800 Univ. Place
Columbia, MO 65211
573-882-7096; Fax: 573-882-9931

Paul F. Cretin
Business Specialist
Univ. Extension
200 North Main
Rolla, MO 65401
573-364-3147; Fax: 573-364-0436

V. E. Lorton
Business Specialist
Univ. Extension
1012A Thompson Blvd.
Sedalia, MO 65301
816-827-0591; Fax: 816-827-4888

Ray Marshall
Business Industrial Specialist
Univ. Extension
417 E. Urbandale
Moberly, MO 65270
816-626-3534; Fax: 816-263-1874
marshallr@ext.missouri.edu

Rebecca L. How
Univ. of Missouri
Business/Industry
PO Box 71
Union, MO 63084

Gerald G. Udell
Wal-Mart Innovation Network
901 S. National
Springfield, MO 65804
417-836-5671; Fax: 417-836-7666

Mississippi

Robert D. Russ
Director
Copiah Lincoln Comm. College
SBDC
11 Coln Circle
Natchez, MS 39120
601-445-5254; Fax: 601-446-1221

Marguerite H. Wall
Director
Hinds Comm. College SBDC
PO Box 1170
Raymond, MS 39154
601-857-3536; Fax: 601-857-3535

Henry C. Thomas
Director
JSU SBDC
931 Highway 80 West, Box 43
Jackson, MS 39204
601-968-2795; Fax: 601-968-2796

Bobby Lantrip
Mgr., Tech Services
Mississippi SBDC
216 Old Chemistry Blg.
Univ., MS 38677
601-232-5001; Fax: 601-232-5650

Robert L. Palmer
Director
Mississippi State Univ.
Tech. Transfer
PO Box 6156
Mississippi State, MS 39762
601-325-3521; Fax: 601-325-3803

Chuck Herring
Director
Mississippi Delta Comm. College
   SBDC
PO Box 5607
Greenville, MS 38704-5607
601-378-8183; Fax: 601-378-5349

Lucy R. Betcher
Director
SBDC
136 Beach Park Pl.
Long Beach, MS 39560
601-865-4578; Fax: 601-865-4581

Dean P. Brown
Director
SBDC
PO Box 100
Gautier, MS 39553
601-497-7723; Fax: 601-497-7696

Heidi C. McDuffie
Director
SBDC
5448 US Highway 49 South
Hattiesburg, MS 39401
601-544-0030; Fax: 601-544-0032

Dr. William Blair
President
Society of Mississippi Inventors
PO Box 13004
Jackson, MS 39236-3004
601-982-6229; Fax: 601-982-6610

Montana

Randy O. Hanson
Director
Bear Paw Dev. Corp.
SBDC
306 3rd Ave., Box 170
Havre, MT 59501-0170
406-265-9226; Fax: 406-265-5602

Gene Marcille
Director
Commerce SBDC
1424 9th Ave.
Helena, MT 59620-0501
406-444-4780; Fax: 406-444-1872

Fred E. Davison
Creativity Innovation,
   Productivity, Inc.
RR #1, Box 37
Highwood, MT 59450
406-733-5031; Fax: 406-733-2039

Ann P. Keenan
Senior Regional Dir.
Montana Business Connections
Montana State Univ.
Reid Hall
Bozeman, MT 59717
406-994-2024; Fax: 406-994-4152

John Balsam
Regional Dir.
Montana Business Connections:
   The Entrepreneurship Center
   School of Business
Univ. of Montana
Missoula, MT 59812
406-243-4009; Fax: 406-243-4030

Howard E. Haines
Montana Dept. of Environmental
   Quality
PO Box 200901
Helena, MT 59620-0901
406-444-6773; Fax: 406-444-1804

David P. Desch
Sr. Investments Mgr.
Montana Science & Tech. Alliance
1424 9th Ave.
Helena, MT 59620
406-444-2778; Fax: 406-444-1585

Bruce A. Hofmann
Business Dev.
Montana Tradeport Authority
2720 3rd Ave. North
Billings, MT 59101-1931
406-256-6871; Fax: 406-256-6877

Thomas C. McKerlick
Business Dev. Mgr.
Montana Tradeport Authority
2722 3rd Ave. N., Suite 300
Billings, MT 59101
406-256-6873; Fax: 406-256-6877

Roxanne L. Bunker
Director
SBDC
123 W. Main
Sidney, MT 59270
406-482-5024; Fax: 406-482-5306

Bret George
SBDC Coordinator
WEDCO
127 N. Higgins
Missoula, MT 59802
406-543-3550; Fax: 406-721-4584

Warren T. George
Yellowstone Inventors
3 Carrie Lynn
Billings, MT 59102
406-259-9110; Fax:

Nebraska

Roger Reyda
President
Lincoln Inventors Assn.
92 Ideal Way
Brainard, NE 68626
402-545-2179; Fax: 402-545-2179

Kay Payne
Director
Nebraska Business Dev. Center
19th & University Dr.
Kearney, NE 68849
308-865-8344; Fax: 308-865-8153
paynek@platte.unk.edu

Mary Woita
Asst. State Dir.
Nebraska Business Dev. Center
1313 Farnam, Suite 132
Omaha, NE 68182-0248
402-595-2381; Fax: 402-595-2385

Melinda K. Cruz
Consultant
Nebraska Business Dev. Center
1313 Farnam, Suite 132
Omaha, NE 68182
402-595-2381; Fax: 402-595-2385

Jeanne P. Eibes
Director
Nebraska Business Dev. Center
Omaha Center
1313 Farnam, Suite 132
Omaha, NE 68182
402-595-2381; Fax: 402-595-2385
jeibes@unomaha.edu

Cliff N. Hanson
Director
Nebraska Business Dev. Center
1000 Main St.
Chadron, NE 69337
308-432-6286; Fax: 308-432-6430
chanson@csc1.csc.edu

Herbert Hoover
Info. Specialist
Univ. of Nebraska—Lincoln
Univ. of Nebraska Engineering
    Extension
W191 Nebraska Hall
Lincoln, NE 68588-0535
402-472-5611; Fax: 402-472-0015

New Hampshire

Jon Cavicchi
Intellectual Property Librarian/
    Lecturer
Franklin Pierce Law Center
Intellectual Property Library
2 White St.
Concord, NH 03301
603-228-1541; Fax: 603-228-0388
jcavicchi@fplc.edu

James O'Donnell
Business Counselor
MicroEnterprise Assistance Pgm.
PO Box 628, Room 325
Portsmouth, NH 03802-0628
603-431-2000; Fax:60034271526

Gary Cloutier
Regional Mgr.
New Hampshire SBDC
Blake House—Keene St.
Keene, NH 30435-2101
603-358-2602; Fax: 603-358-2612
gc@christa.unh.edu

Janice B. Kitchen
Regional Mgr.
New Hampshire SBDC
MSC 24A Plymouth State College
Plymouth, NH 03264
603-535-2523; Fax: 603-535-2850
j.kitchen@plymouth.edu

Elizabeth Lamoreux
State Dir.
New Hampshire SBDC
Univ. of New Hampshire
108 McConnell Hall
Durham, NH 03824
603-862-2200; Fax: 603-863-4876

Anka Verweij-Jacobs
New Hampshire SBDC ITRC
International Training
601 Spaulding Turnpike #29
Portsmouth, NH 03801
603-334-6074; Fax: 603-334-6110

Robert C. Wilburn
Regional Mgr.
SBDC
One Indian Head Plaza
Nashua, NH 03060
603-886-1233; Fax: 603-595-0188
sbdc-bw@mv.mv.com

New Jersey

Mira Kostak
Director
Kean College SBDC
215 North Ave.
Union, NJ 07083
908-527-2946; Fax: 908-527-2960

Harry Roman
Vice President Prog.
New Jersey Inventors Congress
   Hall of Fame
25 Laurel Ave.
East Orange, NJ 07017-2113
210-430-6646; Fax: 210-504-8414

LeRoy A. Johnson
Director
SBDC
180 Univ. Ave., 3rd Floor
Newark, NJ 07102-1895
201-648-5950; Fax: 201-648-1175

New Mexico

Terry R. Sullivan
Director
Dona Ana Comm. College
SBDC
Box 30001, Dept 3DA
Las Cruces, NM 88003
505-527-7601; Fax: 505-527-7515

Erich Strebe
Program Mgr.
Industry Network Corp.
1155 Universey SE
Albuquerque, NM 87106
505-843-4250; Fax: 505-843-4255

James M. Greenwood
Exec. Dir.
Los Alamos
Econ. Dev. Corp.
PO Box 715
Los Alamos, NM 87544
505-662-0001; Fax: 505-662-0099

Allan Gutjahr
Vice President
New Mexico Tech
Brown 200C New Mexico Tech
Socorro, NM 87801
505-835-5646; Fax: 505-835-5649

Lily F. Tercero
State Dir.
New Mexico SBDC
PO Box 4187
Santa Fe, NM 87502-4187
505-483-1362; Fax: 505-438-1237
ltercero@santa-fe.cc.nm.us

Michael McDiarmid
Engineer
New Mexico State Energy &
    Minerals
2040 South Pacheco St.
Santa Fe, NM 87505
505-827-5948; Fax: 505-827-5912

Susan Glenn-James
Director
SBDC
911 S. 10th Ave.
Tucumcari, NM 88401
505-461-4413; Fax: 505-461-1901

Clemente Sanchez
Director
SBDC
709 E. Roosevelt Ave.
Grants, NM 87020
505-287-8221; Fax: 505-287-2125

Cal Tingey
Director
SBDC
4601 College Blvd.
Farmington, NM 87402
505-599-0346; Fax: 505-599-0385

Dwight Harp
Director
SBDC at NMSUA
1000 Madison, Suite C
Alamagordo, NM 88310
505-434-5272; Fax: 505-434-5272
dharp@nmsua.nmsu.edu

Richard Reisinger
Dir. Product Dev.
Tech. Ventures Corp.
1155 Univ., SE
Albuquerque, NM 87106
505-843-4286; Fax: 505-246-2891

Ray A. Garcia
Dir., SBDC
UNM Valencia Campus SBDC
280 La Entrada
Los Lunas, NM 87031
505-925-8980; Fax: 505-925-8981
rayg@unm.edu

Nevada

Donald G. Costar
Editor/Spokesman
Nevada Inventors Assn.
PO Box 9905
Reno, NV 89507-0905
702-322-9636; Fax: 702-322-0147

Robert Holland
Business Devel. Specialist
Nevada SBDC
University of Nevada—Las Vegas
4504 Maryland Pkwy., Box 456011
Las Vegas, NV 89154-6011
702-895-0852; Fax: 702-895-4095
nsbdc@ccmail.nevada.edu

Sharolyn Craft
Director
Nevada SBDC
Univ. of Nevada—Las Vegas
4505 Maryland Pkwy., Box 456011
Las Vegas, NV 89154-6011
702-895-0852; Fax: 702-895-4095

Bryan Leipper
Staff Liaison
Nevada Tech. Council
4001 S. Virginia St.
Reno, NV 89502
702-829-9000; Fax: 702-829-9000

Nicole H. Maher
Mgmt. Consultant
SBDC
PO Box 820
Winnemucca, NV 89446-0820
702-623-1064; Fax: 702-623-5999

Thomas Gutherie
President/CEO
Southern Nevada CDC
2770 S. Maryland Pkwy.,
    Suite #212
Las Vegas, NV 89109
702-732-3998; Fax: 702-732-2705

Teri Williams
Exec. Dir.
Tri-County Dev.
PO Box 820
Winnemucca, NV 89446
702-623-5777; Fax: 702-623-5999

New York

Jeffrey A. Kohler
Dir. of Commercialization
Aztech, Inc.
1576 Sweet Home Rd.
Amherst, NY 14228
716-636-3626; Fax: 716-636-3630

Eugene Williams
Dir. SBDC
Bronx
Bronx Comm. College
McCracken Hall W.,
    181st Univ. Ave.
Bronx, NY 10453
718-563-3570; Fax: 718-563-3572

H. Walter Haeussler
President
Cornell Research Foundation, Inc.
Cornell Business & Tech.
20 Thornwood Dr., Suite 105
Ithaca, NY 14850
607-257-1081; Fax: 607-257-1015

Philip Knapp
New York Society of Proffesional
    Inventors
116 Stuart Ave.
Amityville, NY 11701
516-598-3228; Fax: 516-598-3241

Daniel Weiss
President
New York Society of Professional
    Inventors
Box 216
Farmingdale, NY 11735-9998
516-798-1490; Fax:

Maria A. Circosta
Coordinator
New York State SBDC
555 BRd.way
Dobbs Ferry, NY 10566
914-674-7485; Fax: 914-693-4996

Merry Gwynn
Coordinator
New York State SBDC
Clinton Comm. College
Plattsburgh, NY 12901
518-562-4260; Fax: 518-563-9759

Joanne Bauman
Reg. Dir.
SBDC
Binghampton Univ.
Binghampton, NY 13902-6000
607-777-4024; Fax: 607-777-4029
sbdcbu@spectra.net

Peter J. George
SBDC
135 Western Ave.
Albany, NY 12222
518-442-5577; Fax: 518-442-5581

Judith M. McEvoy
Director
SBDC
State Univ. of New York
Stony Brook, NY 11794-3775
516-632-9070; Fax: 516-632-7176

Joseph Schwatrz
Director
SBDC
State Univ. of Tech.
Campus Commons
Farmingdale, NY 11735
516-420-7930; Fax: 516-293-5243
schwarjf@snyfarva.farmingdale.e
du

Charles L. Van Arsdale
Exec. Dir.
SBDC SUNY Geneseo
111 South
Geneseo, NY 14451-1485
716-245-5429; Fax: 716-245-5430

Thomas Reynolds
Director
SBDC Mfg. Field Office
385 Jordan Rd.
Troy, NY 12180-7602
518-286-1014; Fax: 518-286-1006
mfo@wizvax.net

Sandra J. Bordeau
Dir. of Admin.
SUNY Brockport SBDC
74 N. Main St.
Brockport, NY 14428
716-637-6660; Fax: 716-637-2102

John Petersen
Deputy Director
The Research Foundation of
   SUNY
Tech. Transfer
SUNY at Stony Brook
Stony Brook, NY 11794-3368
516-632-6955; Fax: 516-632-9839

Carol Oldenburg
Admin. Coordinator
United Inventors Assn. of the USA
PO Box 23447
Rochester, NY 14692-3447
716-359-9310; Fax: 713-359-1132

North Carolina

John Hogan
Facilities Mgr.
First Flight Venture Center
PO Box 13169
Research Technical Park, NC
   27709-3169
919-990-8558; Fax: 919-588-8802

Michael R. Twiddy
Business Counselor
NC SBTDC
Wesleyan College
3400 N. Wesleyan Blvd.
Rocky Mount, NC 27804
919-985-5130; Fax: 919-977-3701

Wauna L. Dooms
Director
SBTDB
Elizabeth City State Univ.
Campus Box 874
Elizabeth City, NC 27909
919-335-3247; Fax: 919-335-3648

Counselor
SBTDC at Univ. of North
   Carolina—Charlotte
BCC at 8701 Mallard Creek Rd.
Charlotte, NC 28262
704-548-1090; Fax: 704-548-9050

North Dakota

Bruce Gjovig
Director
Center for Innovation
Box 8372, UND Station
Grand Forks, ND 58202
701-777-3132; Fax: 701-777-2339

Chuck Pineo
Consultant
Center for Innovation
Box 8372
Grand Forks, ND 58202-8372
701-777-3132; Fax: 701-777-2339

Jan M. Peterson
Regional Director
North Dakota SBDC
400 East BRd.way Ave., Suite 416
Bismarck, ND 58501-4071
701-223-8583; Fax: 701-255-7228
janpeter@prairie.nodak.edu

Wally Kearns
State Dir.
North Dakota SBDC
PO Box 7308
Grand Forks, ND 58202-7308
701-777-3700; Fax: 701-777-3225

Brian Argabright
Regional Dir.
SBDC
PO Box 940
Minot, ND 58702
701-852-8861; Fax: 701-838-2488
brian@minot.ndak.net

Beverly Fischer
Admin. Officer
Tech. Transfer, Inc.
1833 E. Bismarck Expy.
Bismarck, ND 58504
701-328-5329; Fax: 701-328-5320

Ohio

Michael Lehere
Director
Akron Industrial Incubator
526 S. Main St.
Akron, OH 44811
330-375-2173; Fax: 330-762-3657

David E. Guza
Principal Research Engineer
Battelle Memorial Institute
11-2-065
505 King Ave.
Columbus, OH 43201-2693
614-424-5516; Fax: 614-424-3228

Karen A. Patton
Exec. Dir.
Enterprise Dev.
900 E. State St., #101
Athens, OH 45701-2116
614-592-1188; Fax: 614-593-8283

Nicholas J. Cashier
Business Dev.
Great Lakes Industrial Tech.
Business Strategy Dev.
25000 Great Northern Corporate
  Center, Suite 260
Cleveland, OH 44070-5310
216-734-7553; Fax: 216-734-0686

Nicola Harmon
President
Innovation Alliance
2000 Henderson Rd., 140
Columbus, OH 43220
614-326-3822; Fax: 614-326-3824

Murray H. Henderson
President
Inventors Connection CLEY
PO Box 360804
Cleveland, OH 44136
216-226-9681; Fax:

Henry B. Ferguson
Secretary/Treasurer
Inventors Council Lorain
Inventors Council of Greater
  Lorain County
1101 Park Ave.
Elyria, OH 44035
216-322-1540; Fax:

Richard A. Hagle
President
Inventors Network, Inc.
1275 Kinnear Rd.
Columbus, OH 43212
614-470-0144; Fax:

Tom Farbizo
Director
Kent Tuscarawas SBDC
330 University Dr. NE
New Philadelphia, OH 44663
330-339-9070; Fax: 330-339-2637

Nancy J. Morcher
Exec. Dir.
London Area Chamber of
    Commerce
66 W. High St.
London, OH 43140
614-852-2250; Fax: 614-852-5133

Barbara A. Harmony
Director
Mid Ohio SBDC
PO Box 1208
Mansfield, OH 44901
919-525-1614; Fax: 919-522-6811
mosbdc@rich.net

Dinah Adkins
Exec. Dir.
National Business Incubation
    Assn.
20 E. Circle Dr., #190
Athens, OH 45701
614-593-4331; Fax: 614-593-1996

Joseph F. Wilson
Director
North Central SBDC
Terra Comm. College
2830 Napoleon Rd.
Fremont, OH 43420
419-334-8400; Fax: 419-334-9414
wilson_j@kwik.terra.cc.oh.us

Mary Ann Reis
Research Associate
Ohio Applied Tech. Transfer
1080 Carmack, Rm. 216
Columbus, OH 43210-1002
614-892-5485; Fax: 614-292-1893

Director
SBDC
200 Tower City Center
Cleveland, OH 44113
216-621-3300; Fax: 216-621-4617

Thomas M. Farbizo
Director
SBDC
124 Chestnut St.
Coshocton, OH 43812
614-622-5435; Fax: 614-622-9902

Linda S. Suiteward
Vice President
SBDC
37 High St.
Columbus, OH 43215
614-225-6910; Fax: 614-469-8250

Warren Holden
Acting Exec. Dir.
SBDC, Inc.
300 E. Auburn Ave.
Springfield, OH 45505
513-322-7821; Fax: 513-322-7874

Amber Wilson
Consultant
Southeast SBDC
PO Box 488
US Route 52 & Solida Rd.
South Point, OH 45680
614-894-3838; Fax:

Bill Floretti
Directpr
UC SBDC
1111 Edison Dr.
Cincinnati, OH 45216-2265
513-948-2081; Fax: 513-948-2007

Thomas A. Knapke
Director
Wright State Univ. SBDC
Lake Campus
7600 State Route 703
Celina, OH 45822
419-586-3055; Fax: 419-586-0358
sbdc@lady.lake.wright.edu

Oklahoma

Thomas E. Mosley, President
New Products Coalition
4617 S. Quincy Place
Tusla, OK 74105
918-743-4933; Fax: 918-743-7208
e-mail: tekscout@onpc.com
Web page: www.onpc.com

Bill Gregory, Coordinator
Inventors Resource Center
100 S. University Ave.
Enid, OK 73701
405-242-7989; Fax: 405-242-7989

Oklahoma Inventors Congress
PO Box 27850
Tulsa, OK 74149-0850
918-245-6465; Fax: 918-245-2947

Danielle Coursey
Business Devel. Specialist
Oklahoma SBDC
309 N. Muskogee Ave.
Tahlequah, OK 74464-2399
918-458-0802; Fax: 918-458-2105

Alan H. Simon
Business Devel. Specialist
Oklahoma SBDC
215 I St. NE
Miami, OK 74354
918-540-0575; Fax: 918-540-0575

Susan Urbach
Regional Dir.
SBDC
115 Park Ave.
Oklahoma City, OK 73102-9005
405-232-1968; Fax: 405-232-1967
sbdc@aix1.ucok.edu

Oregon

Robert L. Newhart II
Director
Central Oregon Community
  College
BDC
2600 NW College Way
Bend, OR 97701-5998
503-383-7290; Fax: 503-383-7503
newhart@metolius.cocc.edu

Phil Goodenough
Counselor
Chmeketa SBDC
365 Ferry St. SE
Salem, OR 97301-3622
503-399-5088; Fax: 503-581-6017
philg@chemek.cc.or.us

John Prosnik
Director
Eastern Oregon State College
  SBDC
1410 L Ave.
La Grande, OR 97850-2899
541-962-3895; Fax: 541-962-3668
prosnij@eosc.osshe.edu

Bill Nasset
Public Information Provider
Little Inventor Assn.
Web page:
  www.inventorworld.com
3923 Lancaster Dr. NE
Salem, OR 97305
503-391-4464; Fax: 503-391-4887
patwiz@inventorworld.com

Oregon Innovation Center
PO Box 1510
Redmond, OR 97756
541-383-7299; Fax: 541-317-0265
oic@cocc.edu

John A. Beaulieu
President
Oregon Resource & Tech.
Dev. Fund
4370 NE Halsey St.
Portland, OR 97213-1566
503-282-4462; Fax: 503-282-2976

Nancy Hudson
Counselor
SBDC
332 W. 6th St.
Medford, OR 97501
541-772-3478; Fax: 541-734-4813

Jan S. Suitennick
Director
SBDC
7616 SE Harmony
Milwaukie, OR 97222
503-656-4447; Fax: 503-652-0389

Gerald E. Wood
Director
SBDC
37 SE Dorion
Pendleton, OR 97801
541-276-6233; Fax: 541-276-6819

Nancy L. Hudson
SBDC Counselor
Southern OR Inventors Council
332 W. 6th
Medford, OR 97501
541-772-3478; Fax: 541-734-4813

Jon Richards
Director
Southwestern Oregon Comm.
College SBDC
340 Central
Coos Bay, OR 97420
541-269-0123; Fax: 541-269-0323
jrichards@oretel.org

Kathleen A. Simko
Director
TVCC SBDC
88 SW 3rd Ave.
Ontario, OR 97914
541-889-2617; Fax: 541-889-8331

Pennsylvania

Jay W. Cohen
President
American Society of Inventors
PO Box 58426
Philadelphia, PA 19102
215-546-6601; Fax:

Mary T. McKinney, PhD
Director
Duquesne Univ. SBDC
Rockwell Hall
600 Forbes
Pittsburgh, PA 15282
412-396-6233; Fax: 412-396-5884
duqsbdc@duq.edu

Bruce M. Smackey
Lehigh Univ.
Technology Commercialization
621 Taylor St.
Bethlehem, PA 18015-3117
610-758-3446; Fax: 610-758-5865

Charles W. Duryea, Sr.
Director
Pennsylvania Inventors Assn.
10819 Wales Rd.
Erie, PA 16510
814-739-2928; Fax: 814-489-3572

Gregory L. Higgins, Jr.
State Dir.
Pennsylvania SBDC
Vance Hall 4th Floor,
   3733 Spruce St.
Philadelphia, PA 19104-6374
215-898-1219; Fax: 215-573-2135
pasbdc@wharton.upcnn.edu

Elaine M. Tweedy
Director
SBDC
800 Linden St.
Scranton, PA 18510-4639
717-941-7588; Fax: 717-941-4053
tweedye1@uofs.edu

Geraldine A. Perkins
Director
Temple SBDC
Room 6 Speakman Hall
Philadelphia, PA 19122
215-204-7282; Fax: 215-204-4554
perkins@sbm.temple.edu

Robert S. Krutsick
Executive Vice President
Univ. City Science Center
3624 Market St.
Philadelphia, PA 19104-2614
215-387-2255; Fax: 215-382-0056

Ann Dugan
Director
Univ. of Pittsburgh SBDC
208 Bellefield Hall
Pittsburgh, PA 15213
412-648-1544; Fax: 412-648-1636

Ruth Hughes
Business Consultant
Wilkes Univ. SBDC
192 South Franklin St.
Wilkesbarr, PA 18766
717-831-4340; Fax: 717-824-2245
sbdc@wilkes.edu

Rhode Island

Claudia Terra
Exec. Dir.
Rhode Island Partnership for
    Science & Technology
One West Exchange St.
Providence, RI 02903
401-277-2601; Fax: 401-277-2102

Domenic Bucci
President
Rhode Island Solar Energy Assn.
42 Tremont St.
Cranston, RI 02920-2543
401-942-6691

Samuel F. Carr
Manager, East Bay Office
Rhode Island SBDC
45 Valley Rd.
Middletown, RI 02842
401-849-6900; Fax: 401-849-5848
samcarr@aol.com

Janice McClanaghan
Energy Program Mgr.
Rhode Island State Energy Office
275 Westminster St.
Providence, RI 02907
401-277-3370; Fax: 401-277-1260

South Carolina

Johnny Sheppard
President
Carolina Inventors Council
2960 Dacusville Hwy.
Easley, SC 29640
803-859-0066

George L. Long
Area Mgr.
Clemson Univ. SBDC
PO Box 1366
Greenwood, SC 29648-1366
864-941-8071; Fax: 864-941-8090
glong@sisn.com

Jackie W. Moore
Area Mgr.
SBDC
171 University Pkwy.
Aiken, SC 29801-6309
803-641-3646; Fax: 803-641-3647
jackiem@aiken.sc.edu

Matt L. Scarborough
Area Mgr.
SBDC
School of Business
Coastal Carolina Univ.
Conway, SC 29526
803-349-2169; Fax: 803-349-2455
matthew@coastal.edu

John W. Gadson Sr.
Director
South Carolina State Univ.
SBDC
PO Box Campus—7176
Orangeburg, SC 29117
803-536-8445; Fax: 803-536-8066

Judy Clements
Mgr.
Univ. of South Carolina/Aiken
Private Investor Network
171 Univ. Pkwy.
Aiken, SC 29801
803-641-3518; Fax: 803-641-3362

Merry S. Boone
Area Mgr.
USC SBDC
5900 Core Dr., #104
West Charleston, SC 29406
803-740-6160; Fax: 803-740-1607
sbdc1@infoave.net

South Dakota

Bryce K. Anderson
Regional Dir.
South Dakota SBDC
620 15th Ave. SE
Aberdeen, SD 57401-7610
605-626-2565; Fax: 605-626-2667
andersob@wolf.northern.edu

Valerie S. Simpson
Regional Dir.
SBDC
444 N. Mount Rushmore Rd., #208
Rapid City, SD 57701
605-394-5311; Fax: 605-394-6140

Robert J. Knecht
Chairman
SCORE
PO Box 747
Rapid City, SD 57709-0747
605-341-9007

Steven M. Wegman
South Dakota Public Utilities
    Commission
State Capitol Bldg.
Pierce, SD 57501
605-773-3201; Fax: 605-773-3809

Kent W. Rufer
Program Mgr.
South Dakota State Univ.
Box 2220 Harding Hall
Brookings, SD 57007-0199
605-688-4184; Fax: 605-688-5880

Tennessee

David G. Beall
President
Innovative Ventures Corp.
1055 Commerce Park Dr.
Oak Ridge, TN 37830
615-483-5060; Fax: 615-483-3938

Oak Ridge National Lab
Energy Related Inventions
    Program
PO Box 2008,
    4500 N. Mail Stop 6205
Oak Ridge, TN 37830-6205
423-576-7071; Fax: 423-574-8884

Joseph R. Schultz
Exec. Dir.
Rivervalley Partners, Inc.
835 Georgia Ave., Suite 800
Chattanooga, TN 37402
423-265-3700; Fax: 423-265-7924

Teri T. Brahams
Dir., SBDC
301 East Church Ave.
Knoxville, TN 37915
423-525-0277; Fax: 423-971-4439
tbrahams@pstcc.cc.tn.us

Robert Lytle
Business Counselor
SBDC
1501 University Blvd.
Kingsport, TN 37660
423-392-8017; Fax: 423-392-8017

Donna G. Marsh
Small Business Specialist
SBDC
100 Cherokee Blvd., Suite 202
Chattanooga, TN 37405
423-753-1774; Fax: 423-752-1925

John X. Volker
Director
SBDC
PO Box 4775 APSU
Clarksville, TN 37044
615-648-7764; Fax: 615-648-5985
volkerj@apsu0s.apsu.edu

Robert A. Justice
Director
Tennessee SBDC
East Tennessee State Univ.
PO Box 70698
Johnson City, TN 37614-0698
423-929-5630; Fax: 423-461-7080
justiceb@etsu-tn.edu

Sharon Taylor McKinney
Small Business Specialist
Tennessee SBDC
320 South Dudley St.
Memphis, TN 38104
901-527-1041; Fax: 901-527-1047

Dorothy A. Vaden
Business Specialist
Tenneessee SBDC
PO Box 63
Hartsville, TN 37074
615-374-9521; Fax: 615-374-4608

Janis Elsner
Associate Dir.
Vanderbilt Univ.
Office of Tech. Transfer
405 Kirkland Hall
Nashville, TN 37240
615-343-2430; Fax: 615-343-0488

Texas

Worth Hefley
President
Amarillo Inventors Assn.
PO Box 15023
Amarillo, TX 79105
806-376-8726; Fax: 806-376-7753

Thomas J. Suitephenson
Dir. of Education
Austin Tech. Incubator
3925 W. Braker Lane, Suite 400
Austin, TX 78759-5321
512-305-0000; Fax: 512-305-0009

Samuel A. Harwell
Director
Brazos Valley SBDC
4001 East 29th
Bryan, TX 77802
409-260-5222; Fax: 409-260-5229
sam@bvsbdc

Charles Mullen
Chairman
Houston Inventors Assn.
204 Yacht Club Lane
Seabrook, TX 77586
713-326-1795; Fax: 713-326-1795

Tim Bigham
Principal Researcher
Information Insights
906 Stillhouse Spring
Round Rock, TX 78681
512-246-7040; Fax: 512-451-1885

Beth S. Huddleston
Director
International SBDC
Box 580299
Dallas, TX 75258
214-747-1300; Fax: 214-748-5774

Timothy L. Thomas
Director
MSU SBDC
3410 Taft
Wichita Falls, TX 76308
817-689-4373; Fax: 817-689-4374

Jan Chisham
Exec. Dir.
Network of American Inventors &
    Entrepreneurs
11371 Walters Rd.
Houston, TX 77007-2615
713-537-8277; Fax: 713-537-1548

Ray Bell
Tech. Counselor
SBDC
1500 Houston St.
Fort Worth, TX 76102
817-871-6028; Fax: 817-336-5086

Pat Bell
Director
SBDC
2400 Clarksville St.
Paris, TX 75460
903-784-1802; Fax: 903-784-1801
pssbdc@stargate.istarnet.com

Donna Dulfer
Acting Dir.
SBDC
3110 Mustang Rd.
Alvin, TX 77511
713-388-4686; Fax: 713-388-4903

Chris Jones
Director
SBDC
4800 Preston Park Blvd., Box 15
Plano, TX 75243
214-985-3770; Fax: 214-985-3775

Catherine J. Keeler
Director
SBDC
1525 W. California
Gainesville, TX 76240
817-668-4220

Karl V. Painter
Director
SBDC
4901 E. University
Odessa, TX 79762
915-552-2455; Fax: 915-552-2433
evans_c@utpb.edu

Howard N. Sheward
Director
SBDC
250 N. Sam Houston Pkwy.
Houston, TX 77060
713-591-9373; Fax: 713-591-9324

Elizabeth Soliz
Director
SBDC
635 East King
Kingsville, TX 78863
512-595-5088; Fax: 512-592-0866

Frank X. Viso
Director
SBDC
1530 SSW Loop 323, Suite 100
Tyler, TX 75701
903-510-2975; Fax: 903-510-2978
fviso@tyler.net

Texas Inventors Assn.
4000 Rock Creek Dr., #100
Dallas, TX 75204-1626
817-265-1540; Fax: 214-526-6725

Daniel Altman
Field Engineer
Texas Mfg. Assistance Center,
    Gulf Coast
1100 Louisiana St.
Houston, TX 77002
713-752-8434; Fax: 713-756-1515

Al E. Sammann
Director
Texas Tech Univ. SBDC
2579 S. Loop 289
Lubbock, TX 79423
806-745-3973; Fax: 806-745-6207

David Gerhardt
Exec. Dir.
The Capital Network
3925 W. Braker Lane #406
Austin, TX 78759
512-305-0826; Fax: 512-305-0836

Jill Fabricant, Ph.D.
Director
The Enterprise Center
2200 Space Park Dr.
Houston, TX 77058
713-335-1250; Fax: 713-333-9285

Roy Serpa
Region Dir.
TMAC Gulf Coast
1100 Louisiana, #500
Houston, TX 77002
713-752-8440; Fax: 713-756-1515
royserpa@uh.edu

Mike Young
Dir. Lead Center
University of Houston SBDC
1100 Louisiana, Suite 500
Houston, TX 77502-5211
713-752-8400; Fax: 713-756-1515
fyoung@uh.edu

David I. Armstrong
Director
University of Texas, Pan American
   SBDC
1201 W. University
Edinburgh, TX 78540
210-381-3361; Fax: 210-381-2322
armstrong@panam.edu

Morrison Woods
Director
University of Texas—San Antonio
   SBDC
1222 N. Main, Suite 450
San Antonio, TX 78212
210-558-2460; Fax: 210-558-2464

Judith Ingalls
Director
University of Texas—San Antonio
   SBDC Tech. Center
1222 N. Main, Suite 450
San Antonio, TX 78212
210-558-2458; Fax: 210-558-2464

Utah

Karen Gudmundson
Marketing Dir.
CEDO
777 S. State St.
Orem, UT 84058
801-226-1521; Fax: 801-226-2678

David Morrison
Patent & Trademark Library
Documents Div., Marriott Library
University of Utah
Salt Lake City, UT 84112
801-581-8394; Fax: 801-585-3464

John Winder
President
Intermountain Society of
   Inventors & Designers
9888 Darin Dr.
Sandy, UT 84070
801-571-2617

Rod J. Linton
Director
Office of Tech. Dev.
324 S. State St., Suite 500
Salt Lake City, UT 84111
801-538-8770; Fax: 801-538-8773

Barry L. Bartlett
Director
SBDC
Salt Lake City Comm. College
8811 S. 700 East
Sandy, UT 84070
801-255-5878; Fax: 801-255-6393
bartleba@slcc.edu

Derek Snow
Director
SBDC
351 West Center
Cedar City, UT 84720
801-586-5400; Fax: 801-586-5493
snow@suu.edu

Denise E. Beaudoin
Info. Specialist
State of Utah
Office of Energy Services
324 S. State, Suite 230
Salt Lake City, UT 84111
801-538-8690; Fax: 801-538-8660

Josie Valdez
Asst. District Dir.
US Small Business Admin.
125 South State St.
Salt Lake City, UT 84101
801-524-3210; Fax: 801-524-5604

Peter R Genereaux
Utah Info. Tech. Assn.
6995 Union Park Center, Suite 490
Midvale, UT 84047
801-568-3500; Fax: 801-568-1072

Utah Technology Finance Corp.
177 East 100 South
Salt Lake City, UT 84111
801-364-4346; Fax: 801-364-4361

Bradley B. Berton
Wayne Brown Institute
PO Box 2135
Salt Lake City, UT 84110-2135
801-595-1141; Fax: 801-595-1181

Bruce Davis
Director
Weber State Univ. SBDC
3815 Univ. Circle
Ogden, UT 84408-3815
801-626-6070; Fax: 801-626-7423
brdavis@weber.edu

Virginia

Martha Morales
Associate Exec. Dir.
AIPLA
2001 Jefferson Davis Hwy.,
    Suite 203
Arlington, VA 22202
703-415-0780; Fax: 703-415-0786

Deirdre Le
Secretary
Association of SBDCs
1300 Chain Bridge Rd., Suite 201
McLean, VA 22101-3967
703-448-6124; Fax: 703-448-6125

Taylor K. Cousins
Exec. Dir.
Capital Area SBDC
One N. Fifth St.
Richmond, VA 23219
804-648-7838; Fax: 804-648-7849

Phillip Shaw
President
Capital Inventors Society
3212 Old Dominion Blvd.
Alexandria, VA 22305
703-739-0868; Fax:

Cathy Renault
Managing Dir.
Center for Innovative Tech.
2214 Rock Hill Rd.
Herndon, VA 22070
703-689-3000; Fax: 703-689-3041

Paul G. Hall
Director
Geo Mason Univ. SBDC
3401 N. Fairfax Dr.
Arlington, VA 22201
703-993-8129; Fax: 703-993-8130
phall@osfi.gmu.edu

Julie Janoski
Director
George Mason Univ. SBDC
4031 University Dr.
Farifax, VA 22030-3409
703-277-7700; Fax: 703-277-7722

Roger Crosen
Coordinator
Lord Fairfax SBDC
PO Box 47
Middletown, VA 22645
540-869-6649; Fax: 540-868-7002

Tim B. Blankenbecler
Director
Mountain Empire Comm. College
SBDC
PO Drawer 700, Rt. 23 S.
Big Stone, VA 24219
540-523-6529; Fax: 540-523-8139

Joy L. Bryant
President
NAPP
435-2 Oriana, Box 215
Newport News, VA 23608
800-216-9588; Fax: 804-874-6278

Sally Rood
Associate Dir.
National Tech. Transfer Center
Wheeling Jesuit College
2121 Eisenhower Ave., Suite 400
Alexandria, VA 22314
703-518-8800; Fax: 703-518-8986

David O. Shanks
Director
NRV SBDC
600 Norwood St.
Radford, VA 24141
540-831-6056; Fax: 540-831-6057
dshanks@runet.edu

Donald Kelly
Director
Patent & Trademark Office
US Dept. of Commerce
PO Box 2863
Arlington, VA 22202
703-308-0975; Fax: 703-305-3463

James B. Boyd
Director
SBDC
PO Box SVCC
Richlands, VA 24641
540-964-7345; Fax: 540-964-5788
jim_boyd@sw.cc.us

Robert A. Hamilton
Director
SBDC
918 Emmet St. North, Suite 200
Charlottesville, VA 22903-4878
804-295-8198; Fax: 804-295-7066
hamilton@sbdc.acs.virginia.edu

William J. Holloran, Jr.
Senior Vice President
SBDC
525 Butler Farm Rd.
Hampton, VA 29670
804-825-2957; Fax: 804-825-2960

Wanda Hylton
Conference Coordinator
Virginia Tech Graduate Center
2990 Telestar Court
Falls Church, VA 22042
703-698-6016; Fax: 703-698-6062

Rob Edwards
Director
Wytheville Comm. College SBDC
1000 East Rain St.
Wytheville, VA 24382
540-223-4798; Fax: 540-223-4716

Vermont

James B. Suitewart
Exec. Dir.
Addison County Econonomic
  Dev. Corp.
RR 4, Box 1309A
Middlebury, VT 05753-8626
802-388-7953; Fax: 802-388-0119

Samiko A. Cartin
SBDC
PO Box 455
Morrisville, VT 05661
802-888-5640; Fax: 802-888-7612

Vermont SBDC
256 N. Main St.
Rutland, VT 05701-2413
802-773-9147; Fax: 802-773-2772

Don Kelpinski
State Director
Vermont SBDC
PO Box 422
Randolph, VT 05060-0422
802-728-9101; Fax: 802-728-3026

Washington

Edmund F. Baroch
Business Specialist
Big Bend Comm. College
Business Dev. Center
7662 Chanute St.
Moses Lake, WA 98837
509-762-6289; Fax: 509-762-6329

Glynn Lamberson
Director
Columbia Basin College SBDC
901 N. Colorado
Kennewick, WA 99336
509-735-6222; Fax: 509-735-6609

Jack A. Wicks
Director
Edmonds Comm. College
SBDC
20000 68th Ave. West
Lynnwood, WA 98036
206-640-1435; Fax: 206-640-1532
jwicks@edcc.ctc.edu

Jeevan Rego
Innovation/Tech. Specialist
Innovation Assessment Center
Washington State Univ. SBDC
501 Johnson Tower
Pullman, WA 99164-4851
509-335-7869; Fax: 50-935-0949

Barbara Campbell
Director, Northwest Office
NASA—Far West RTTC
12318 NE 100th Pl.
Kirkland, WA 98033
206-827-5136; Fax: 206-827-5430

Ann Tamura
Export Dev. Specialist
North Seattle Comm. College
SBDC
2001 6th Ave., Suite 650,
   Westin Bldg.
Seattle, WA 98121
206-553-0052; Fax: 206-553-7253
atamura@doe.gov

Marvin Clement
Manager
Pacific Northwest National
   Laboratory
ORTA
PO Box 999 MSIN K9-87
Richland, WA 99352
509-375-2789; Fax: 509-375-6731

Janet A. Harte
Business Dev. Specialist
SBDC
Washington State Univ.—
   Vancouver
217 SE 136 Ave., Suite 105
Vancouver, WA 98684-6929
360-693-2555; Fax:
harte@vancouver.wsu.edu

Richard Monacelli
Business Dev. Specialist
SBDC
500 Tausick Way
Walla Walla, WA 99362
509-527-4681; Fax: 509-525-3101

Lynn Trzynka
Director
SBDC
Western Washington Univ.
College of Business & Economics
Bellingham, WA 98225-9073
360-650-3899; Fax: 360-650-4844
trzynka@cbe.wwu.edu

Terry Chambers
Group Coordinator
SIRTI
665 N. Riverpoint Blvd.
Spokane, WA 99202-1665
509-358-2042; Fax: 509-358-2019
terryc@sirti.org

John J. Ryan
Group Coordinator
Spokane Intercollegiate Research
 & Tech. Institute (SIRTI)
665 N. Riverpoint Blvd.
Spokane, WA 99202-1665
509-358-2023; Fax: 509-358-2019

Dr. Norman Brown
President
Tech. Targeting, Inc.
4579 144th Ave. SE
Bellevue, WA 98006
206-603-1940; Fax: 206-603-1972

Laura L. Dorsey
Marketing Mgr.
The Washington Tech. Center
Box 352140
Seattle, WA 98195-2140
206-685-1920; Fax: 206-543-3059

Ray K. Robinson
Chairman
Tri-Cities Commercialization
 Partnership
200 Hillview Dr., Suite 100
Richland, WA 99352
509-627-6135; Fax: 509-627-6141

Johan Curtiss
Technology Assistance Manager
Tri-Cities Enterprise Association
2000 Logston Blvd.
Richland, WA 99352
509-375-3268; Fax: 509-375-4838
jcurtiss@owt.com

Susan Sande
Resource Center Mgr.
Tri-Cities Enterprise Assn.
2000 Logston Blvd.
Richland, WA 99352
509-375-3268; Fax: 509-375-4838
erc@owt.com

Stuart R. Leidner
Coordinator, Innovation &
 Research
Washington SBDC
Washington State Univ.
501 Johnson Tower
Pullman, WA 99164-4851
509-335-1576; Fax: 509-335-0949

Neil Delisanti
Business Devel. Specialist
Washington State University
SBDC
950 Pacific Ave., Suite 300
Tacoma, WA 98402
206-272-7232; Fax: 206-597-7305

LoAnn Ayers
Manager, Admin. & Planning
Washington State Univ.—
 Tri-Cities
100 Sprout
Richland, WA 99352
509-372-7252; Fax: 509-372-7100
ayers@beta.tricity.wsu.edu

Suiteven Loyd
Chairman
Western Investment Network
411 University St., #1200
Seattle, WA 98101
206-441-3123; Fax: 206-463-6386

Corey Hansen
Business Devel. Specialist
Yakima Valley Comm. College
SBDC
PO Box 1647
Yakima, WA 98907-1647
509-575-2284; Fax: 509-454-4155
yvccsbdc@televar.com

West Virginia

Daniel Tryon
Manager
Discovery Lab
West Virginia Univ.
PO Box 6107
Morgantown, WV 26506-6101
304-293-3612; Fax: 304-293-3472

Dale Bradley
Program Dir.
Fairmont State College SBDC
1201 Locust Ave.
Fairmont, WV 26554
304-367-4125; Fax: 304-366-4870

Kenneth S. Peters
Program Mgr.
SBDC
PO Box AG
Beckley, WV 25802-2830
304-255-4022; Fax: 304-252-9584
sbdc@cwv.edu

James R. Martin
Business Analyst
SBDC/Elkins
10 Eleventh St., Suite 1
Elkins, WV 26241
304-637-7205; Fax: 304-637-4902
jrjm@access.mountain.net

James E. Epling
Program Dir.
West Virginia Institute of Tech.
SBDC
Engineering Bldg., Rm. 102
Montgomery, WV 25136
304-442-5501; Fax: 304-442-3307
jepling@olie.wvitcoe.wvnet.edu

Edward R. Huttenhower
Director
West Virginia Northern Comm.
  College
SBDC
1704 Market St.
Wheeling, WV 26003
304-233-5900; Fax: 304-232-0965
ehuttenhower@nccvax.wvnet.edu

Hazel K. Palmer
Director
West Virginia SBDC
950 Kanawha Ave. SE
Charleston, WV 25301
304-558-2960; Fax: 304-558-0127
palmerh@mail.wvnet.edu

Gregory A. Hill
Director
West Virginia Univ.—
  Parkersburg SBDC
Route 5, Box 167A
Parkersburg, WV 26101
304-424-8277; Fax: 304-424-8315

Wisconsin

Louie M. Rech
Technology Devel. Coordinator
Tech. Deployment Fund
Wisconsin Dept. of Development
PO Box 7970
Madison, WI 53707-7970
608-267-9382; Fax: 608-267-0436

Carla Lenk
Director
Univ. of Wisconsin—Whitewater
  SBDC
Room 2000 Carlson Hall
Whitewater, WI 53190-1790
414-472-3217; Fax: 414-472-5692
lenk@uwwvax.uww.edu

Debra Malewicki
Director
Wisconsin Innovation Service
  Center
Univ. of Wisconsin—Whitewater
402 McCutchan Hall
Whitewater, WI 53190
414-472-1365; Fax: 414-472-1600

Milissa E. Guenterberg
Research Mgr.
Wisconsin Innovation Service
  Center
402 McCutchan Hall
Whitewater, WI 53190
414-472-1365; Fax: 414-472-1600

Wyoming

Larry Stewart
Regional Dir.
Mid-America Mfg. Tech. Center
PO Box 3362, Univ. Station
Laramie, WY 82071-3362
307-766-4811; Fax: 307-766-4818
lstewart@uwyo.edu

Kay Stucker
US Small Business Administration
PO Box 2839
Casper, WY 82602-2839
307-261-6500; Fax: 301-261-6535

Leonard Holler
Director
Wyoming SBDC
111 West 2nd, Suite 502
Casper, WY 82601
307-234-6683; Fax: 307-577-7014

Bill Ellis
Region I Dir.
Wyoming SBDC
PO Box 1168
Rock Spring, WY 82902-116807-
352-6894; Fax: 307-352-6876
bellis@uwyo.edu

Dwayne Heintz
Regional Dir.
Wyoming SBDC
Box 852
Powell, WY 82435
307-754-2139; Fax: 307-754-0368
nwwsbdc@wave.park.wy.us

Arlene M. Soto
Region 4 Dir.
Wyoming SBDC
Region 4
1400 E. College Dr.
Cheyenne, WY 82007-3298
307-632-6141; Fax: 307-632-6061
sewsbdc@wyoming.com

Diane Wolverton
State Dir.
Wyoming SBDC
Box 3922
Laramie, WY 82071-3922
307-766-3505; Fax: 307-766-3406
ddw@uwyo.edi

BIBLIOGRAPHY

Achenbaum, Alvin. 1989. "How to Succeed in New Products." *Advertising Age*, June 26.

Adamo, Kenneth R. 1986. "Problems Connected with Acquisition, Licensing and Enforcement of Intellectual Property." *Albany Law Review*, 50: 475-494.

Allen, Oliver E. 1990. "The Power of Patents." *American Heritage*, September-October.

American Intellectual Property Law Association. "Fraudulent Invention Development Companies. How To Protect and Benefit From Your Ideas."

Andrews, Edmund L. 1989. "The New Minimalists." *Venture*, January.

Anonymous. 1990. "New Product Development to Be the Growth Strategy of the 1990s." *The Corporate Growth Report*, September.

Baker, Gregory A., and Jose de Souza Neto. 1988. "The Rapid Market Assessment (RMA) of New Products." *Agribusiness*, vol. 4,5: 467–473.

Bangs, David H. 1995. "*Business Planning Guide*, 7th edition. Chicago: Upstart Publishing Company."

———. *Smart Ways to Smart Choices. Testing Your Business Idea.* 1996. Chicago: Upstart Publishing Company.

———. The Market Planning Guide, 4th edition. 1995. Chicago: Upstart Publishing Company.

Bello, Daniel C., and Gloria J. Barczak. 1990. "Using Industrial Trade Shows to Improve New Product Development." *The Journal of Business and Industrial Marketing*, Summer/Fall.

Bernard, Dr. Martin J., Editor. 1991. "Royalties, How Small Are They?" *Inventor-Assistance Program News.* Argonne National Laboratory, January.

Bowman-Upton, Nancy, Samuel L. Seaman, and Donald L. Sexton. 1989. "Innovation Evaluation Programs: Do They Help the Inventors?" *Journal of Small Business Management*, July.

Bronikowski, Karen. 1990. "Speeding New Products to Market." *The Journal of Business Strategy,* September/October.

Buzzell, Robert D., and Bradley T. Gale. 1987. *The PIMS Principles.* New York: The Free Press.

Cagle, Dary. 1990. "Negotiating a Licensing Agreement . . . Part 2. What We Want Is Different Than What They Want." *Invent!* magazine, August.

Caltrider, James M. 1988. "A Simple Form for Evaluating New Product Investment." *Cost Engineering,* December.

Cooper, R. G. 1988. "Predevelopment Activities Determine New Product Success." *Industrial Marketing Management,* 17: 237–247.

Cooper, R. G. and E. J. Kleinschmidt. 1990. "New Product Success Factors: A Comparison of 'Kills' Versus Successes and Failures." *R&D Management,* Volume 20, Number 1.

―――. 1987. "New Products: What Separates Winners from Losers?" *The Journal of Product Innovation Management,* Volume 4.

―――. 1988. "Resource Allocation in the New Product Process." *Industrial Marketing Management,* 17: 249–262.

Cooper, Robert G. 1990. "Stage-Gate Systems: A New Tool for Managing New Products." *Business Horizons,* May–June.

―――. 1990. "New Products: What Distinguishes the Winners?" *Research Technology Management,* November/December.

Copulsky, William. 1989. "Ready, Fire, Aim: Explaining an Entrepreneurial Strategy for New Products." *The Journal of Consumer Marketing,* Spring.

Cozzolino, John M. 1981. "Joint Venture Risk? How to Determine Your Share." *Mergers & Acquisitions,* Fall.

Dorr, R. C. and C. Peterson. 1990. "Preparing and Filing Federal Intent to Use Tradmark Applications." *Colorado Lawyer,* December.

Cu-Uy-Gam, Miria. 1991. "Getting a Patent: Long, Complicated, But It Beats Losing Your Invention." *Financial Post,* June 15.

Dougherty, Deborah. 1990. "Understanding New Markets for New Products." *Strategic Management Journal,* Volume 11.

Drucker, Peter F. 1985. *Innovation and Entrepreneurship: Practice and Principles.* New York: Harper & Row.

Ebel, Jack E., and David J. Aston. 1980. "A Field Guide to Intellectual Property." *The Colorado Lawyer,* January.

Fox, Harold W. 1982. "Successful Strategies for Introducing New Products. S.A.M." *Advanced Management Journal,* Autumn.

Fried, Vance H., and Robert D. Hisrich. 1990. "The Role of the Venture Capitalist in the Management of Entrepreneurial Enterprises." Unpublished White Paper.

Friedrich, Jackie. 1981. "Putting a Price on Patents." *Venture,* February.

Fuld, Leonard M. 1985. *Competitor Intelligence: How to Get It; How to Use It*. New York: John Wiley & Sons.

Gasbarro, Ron. 1990. "Ideas; Profits Pending; The Long Road from Invention to Market Shelf." *The Washington Post*, September 14.

Gatty, Bob. 1987. "Mishaps that Mothered Invention." *Nation's Business*, February.

Gladstone, David. 1988. "Investigation & Analysis: The Due Diligence Process." Unpublished paper presented for use at the 14th Annual NASBIC Venture Capital Institute, September 6–9.

Gladstone, David J. 1983. *Venture Capital Handbook*. Englewood Cliffs, N.J.: Reston Publishing Company, Inc.

Goldratt, Eliyahu M., and Jeff Cox. 1986. *The Goal: A Process of Ongoing Improvement*. Croton-on-Hudson, N.Y.: North River Press.

Halvonik, John P. 1990. *The Inventor's Handbook*. Gaithersburg, Md.: John P. Halvonik.

Hastings, Hunter. 1990. "Mixing Markets: Introducing New Products Without Advertising." *Vital Speeches of the Day*, August 1, 1990.

Hayes, Joanne M., Editor. 1990. "Getting Your Foot in the Door." *Inventors Digest*, March/April.

———. Editor. 1990. "State Spotlight: Oklahoma." *Inventors Digest*, January/February.

———. Editor. 1990. "Will It Sell?" *Inventors Digest*, July/August.

Hise, Richard T., Larry O'Neal, A. Parasuraman, and James U. McNeal. 1989. "Marketing/R&D Interaction in New Product Development: Implications for New Product Success Rates." *The Journal of Product Innovation Management*, June.

Howley, Michael. 1990. "Criteria for Success in New Product Development for Consumer Goods: A Comparative Study." *European Journal of Marketing*, 24:6.

Huthwaite, Bart, and Glenn Spence. 1989. "The Power of Cost Measurement in New Product Development." *National Productivity Review*, Summer.

Javed, Naseem. 1991. "Trademarks—Around the World in 80 Words: Naming Companies Has Become Risky Business." *Pennsylvania Law Journal-Reporter*, May 27.

Kortge, G. Dean, and Patric A. Okonkwo. 1989. "Simultaneous New Product Development: Reducing the New Product Failure Rate." *Industrial Marketing Management*, November.

Kurtz, David L., and Louis E. Boone. 1984. *Marketing*. Orlando, Fl.: Dryden Press.

Langowitz, Nan S. 1989. "Mangaging New Product Design and Factory Fit." *Business Horizons*, May–June.

Levitt, Theodore. 1975. "Marketing Myopia." *Harvard Business Review*, September/October.

Licensing Executives Society, Inc. 1988. *The Basics of Licensing.* Norwalk, Conn.: Licensing Executives Society, Inc. (71 East Avenue, Suite S, Norwalk, CT 06851)

Livesay, Harold C. 1989. "Entrepreneurial Dominance in Businesses Large and Small, Past and Present." *Business History Review,* Spring.

Livesay, Harold C. 1979. *American Made: Men Who Shaped the American Economy.* Boston: Little, Brown and Company.

Livesay, Harold C., Marcia L. Rorke, and David S. Lux. 1989. "Technical Development and the Innovation Process." *The Journal of Product Innovation Management*, Volume 6.

MacMillan, Ian C., Robin Siegel, and P. M. Narasimha. *Criteria Used by Venture Capitalists to Evaluate New Venture Proposals.* Center for Entrepreneurial Studies, New York University.

Maturi, Richard J. 1989. "The Financial Manager's Role in New Product Development." *The Financial Manager,* September/October.

Mazumdar, Tridib, and Kent B. Monroe. 1990. "The Effects of Buyers' Intentions to Learn Price Information on Price Encoding." *Journal of Retailing,* Spring.

McCarthy, Robert. 1986. "Distribution: More Art Than Science." *High-Tech Marketing,* June.

Mehler, Mark. 1989. "Money: 39 Sources of Cash to Help Your Business Take Off." *Success,* December.

Minutes of the Subcommittee on Inventors' Assistance of Joint Interim Committee on State Agencies and Governmental Affairs. November 30, 1990. State Capitol, Little Rock, Arkansas.

Mohawk Research Corporation. 1989. "From Invention to Innovation: Commercialization of New Technology by Independent and Small Business Inventors." U.S. Department of Energy and Argonne National Laboratory.

Mulkins, Phil. 1991. "If You Have Bright Idea, Get a Patent, by George." *Tulsa World*, April 21.

———. 1990. "Necessity Mother of Invention Caution Plea." *Tulsa World*, June 20.

New Product Development Newsletter. 1985. Point Pleasant, N.J.: Point Publishing Co., Inc. Volume 5, November.

Nickolaus, Nicholas. 1990. "Marketing New Products with Industrial Distributors." *Industrial Marketing Management*, November.

Nugent, William M., Esq. 1986. "Making Your Mark." *Invent!*, August.

Office of Energy-Related Inventions. 1986. "Invention Review Guide for OERI Consultants. National Bureau of Standards." Washington, DC: U.S. Department of Commerce, February.

Oldenburg, Don. 1990. "Toying Around; A Professional Plays the Invention." *The Washington Post,* November 14.

Ollerenshaw, Kay. 1981. "How to Perform a Patent Search: A Step by Step Guide for the Inventor." *Law Library Journal,* Volume 73.

Paynter, Henry M. 1990. "The First U.S. Patent." *Invention & Technology,* Fall.

Peterson, Michael. 1991. "Thomas Edison, Failure." *Invention & Technology,* Winter.

Pooley, James. 1982. "Trade Secrets." *Computerworld,* March 22.

Porter, Glenn, and Harold C. Livesay. 1971. *Merchants and Manufacturers: Studies in the Changing Structure of Nineteenth-Century Marketing.* Baltimore, Md.: The Johns Hopkins Press.

Posch, Robert J., Jr., 1988. *The Complete Guide to Marketing and the Law.* New York: Prentice Hall.

Posner, Bruce G. 1985. "Strategic Alliances." *Inc.,* June.

Pressman, David. 1985. *Patent It Yourself.* Berkeley, Calif.: Nolo Press.

Ram, S. 1989. "Successful Innovation Using Strategies to Reduce Consumer Resistance." *Journal of Product Innovation Management,* March.

Reddy, N. Mohan, and Michael P. Marvin. 1986. "Developing a Manufacturer–Distributor Information Partnership." *Industrial Marketing Management,* 15:157–163.

Redmond, William H. 1989. "Effects of New Product Pricing on the Evolution of Market Structure." *The Journal of Product Innovation Management,* 6: 99–108.

Richman, Tom, and Susan Greco. 1991. "How to Keep the Ideas Flowing." *Inc.,* November.

Ries, Al, and Jack Trout. 1986. *Positioning: The Battle for Your Mind.* New York: McGraw-Hill, Inc.

Roberts, Edward B. 1988. "What We've Learned: Managing Invention and Innovation." *Research Technology Management,* January–February.

Romano, Richard E. 1987. "A Note on Market Structure and Innovation When Inventors Can Enter." *The Journal of Industrial Economics,* March.

Rorke, Marcia L., and David S. Lux. 1990. "World of Small-Firm Licensing." *les Nouvelles,* December.

Rosenau, Milton D., Jr. 1988. "Phased Approach Speeds Up New Product Development." *Research & Development,* November.

Rosendahl, Iris. 1990. "More Science, Less Art in Today's Buying Decisions." *Drug Topics,* July 23.

Salmen, Gerald G. 1989. "Protect Yourself Against Product Liability Claims." *Agency Sales,* December.

Sammon, William L., Mark A. Kurland, and Robert Spitalnic. 1984. *Business Competitor Intelligence: Methods for Collecting, Organizing, and Using Information.* New York: John Wiley & Sons.

Sarin, Sharad, and Gour M. Kapur. 1990. "Lessons from New Product Failures: Five Case Studies." *Industrial Marketing Management,* November.

Schroeder, Robert A. 1986. "Licensing of Rights to Intellectual Property." *Albany Law Review,* Volume 50.

Shapin, Alice Rindler. 1988. "Careers—Toy Testing: More Than Fun and Games." *The Washington Post,* September 16.

Smith, Geoffrey N., and Paul B. Brown. 1986. "Sweat Equity: What It Really Takes to Build America's Best Small Companies—By the Guys Who Did It." New York: Simon and Schuster.

Stanton, Thomas M. 1988. "Decision Analysis for Intellectual Property Licensing." *Licensing Law and Business Report,* March.

Toole, Roberta G., Editor. 1990. "What Do America's Independent Inventors Need?" White Paper. Inventors' Association of St. Louis. (PO Box 16544, St. Louis, MO 63105)

Udell, Gerald G. 1989. "Invention Evaluation Services: A Review of the State of the Art." *The Journal of Product Innovation Management,* Volume 6.

Wheelwright, Steven C., and Earl W. Sasser, Jr. 1989. "The New Product Development Map." *Harvard Business Review,* May–June.

White, Edward P. 1990. *Licensing—A Strategy for Profits.* Chapel Hill, NC: KEW Licensing Press. (907 Linden Road, Chapel Hill, NC 27514-9162.)

Zaretsky, Barry L. 1988. "Protection of Intellectual Property Licenses." *New York Law Journal,* December 16.

Zirger, Billie Jo, and Modesto A. Maidique. 1990. "A Model of New Product Development: An Empirical Test." *Management Science,* July.

INDEX